THE
Dyscalculia
Toolkit

Sara Miller McCune founded SAGE Publishing in 1965 to support the dissemination of usable knowledge and educate a global community. SAGE publishes more than 1000 journals and over 800 new books each year, spanning a wide range of subject areas. Our growing selection of library products includes archives, data, case studies and video. SAGE remains majority owned by our founder and after her lifetime will become owned by a charitable trust that secures the company's continued independence.

Los Angeles | London | New Delhi | Singapore | Washington DC | Melbourne

3rd Edition

THE Dyscalculia Toolkit

Ronit Bird

Supporting Learning Difficulties in Maths

$SAGE

Los Angeles | London | New Delhi
Singapore | Washington DC | Melbourne

Los Angeles | London | New Delhi
Singapore | Washington DC | Melbourne

SAGE Publications Ltd
1 Oliver's Yard
55 City Road
London EC1Y 1SP

SAGE Publications Inc.
2455 Teller Road
Thousand Oaks, California 91320

SAGE Publications India Pvt Ltd
B 1/I 1 Mohan Cooperative Industrial Area
Mathura Road
New Delhi 110 044

SAGE Publications Asia-Pacific Pte Ltd
3 Church Street
#10-04 Samsung Hub
Singapore 049483

Editor: Jude Bowen
Associate editor: George Knowles
Production editor: Nicola Carrier
Copyeditor: Elaine Leek
Proofreader: Sharon Cawood
Marketing manager: Dilhara Attygalle
Cover design: Wendy Scott
Typeset by: C&M Digitals (P) Ltd, Chennai, India
Printed in the UK

Library of Congress Control Number: 2016962273

British Library Cataloguing in Publication data

A catalogue record for this book is available from
the British Library

ISBN 978-1-47397-425-8
ISBN 978-1-47397-426-5 (pbk)

At SAGE we take sustainability seriously. Most of our products are printed in the UK using FSC papers and boards.
When we print overseas we ensure sustainable papers are used as measured by the PREPS grading system.
We undertake an annual audit to monitor our sustainability.

Contents

CONTENTS

CONTENTS

SECTION 3: PLACE VALUE   117

About the Author

Ronit Bird is a teacher whose interest in pupils with specific learning difficulties began with a focus on dyslexia. She qualified as a teacher at London University and subsequently gained a further qualification as a specialist teacher of learners with SpLD. While working with dyslexic pupils in a mainstream school, Ronit started to develop strategies and teaching activities to help support the learning of pupils who were experiencing difficulties in maths.

Ronit has taught in both primary and secondary settings, and has worked as a SENCO in both the independent and state sectors. As part of the Harrow Dyscalculia Project in 2006–2010, Ronit ran training courses on dyscalculia for subject leaders, teachers and teaching assistants, later working in an advisory capacity with participating schools across the Harrow LEA.

Ronit currently works as a teacher and continues to create and deliver professional development courses for teachers. Over the past few years Ronit has developed a growing interest in making demonstration videos for teachers and parents.

Ronit can be contacted through her website: www.ronitbird.com

About the Companion Website

With your purchase of the new edition of *The Dyscalculia Toolkit* you have been given access to the Companion Website, available at https://study.sagepub.com/birdtoolkit3e.

The website contains a large number of resources, allowing teachers to put together a tailor-made package of suitable activities from different sections of the book for particular pupils or groups.

The availability of resources on the website is highlighted in the text with the following symbol: ⟨

Resources on the Companion Website

Teaching resources to download and print off:

Summary of the main teaching points addressed by the games

Table of activities and games according to their numeracy topic or main teaching point

Tracking sheets

Leaflet: Some things you can do with your Cuisenaire rods

Dot pattern cards 1–10

Dot pattern cards 1–10 with box

Extra large (nugget-sized) dot pattern cards 1–10

Number track with Slavonic shading

Digit cards, 0–9 and 1–10

1 cm squared paper

Shallow trays: 2 cm × 10 cm and 10 cm × 10 cm

The Basic 8 cards

Place value mat

100-squares with horizontal or vertical numbering

Times tables squares, complete and blank

Activity sheets to download and print off:

Change one dot pattern into another

Sort and re-sort a set of dominoes

Compare the difference and equalise

Complements to 100

Complements to 100 tracking exercise

Money and change

Double and half

Reasoning from complements or doubles facts

Which strategy?

Add 10

Subtract 10

Area model of multiplication and division

Times tables on a number line

Game boards to download and print off:

Make 5

Collect 5s

Draw Your Race on a Number Line

Post-It Note Subtraction

Cover the Number / Shut the Box

Ten in a Bed

Regroup

It All Adds Up

Five and What's Left

Race Along a Number Line and Bridge

Race to the End of the Number Line

Four Throws to Reach 100

Race Through a 100-Square

Place Value Boxes

Don't Walk If You Can Take the Bus

Mouse Tables Multiplication

Mouse Tables Division

The Multiples Game

Factors

More Factors

Videos to help demonstrate practice:

Section 1: Using Concrete Materials to Learn Relationships Between Numbers Up to 10

Collect 5s Game

Key Components Guessing Game

Section 2: Extending Earlier Work on Addition and Subtraction to Numbers Above 10

Frame Games

Section 3: Place Value, Exploring Through Concrete Materials

Race to Cover 100 Game

The Six-Card Rounding Game

Section 4: Times Tables, Multiplication and Division

Areas on a Grid Game

Accessing the Companion Website

To access the Companion Website (CW), follow these four simple steps.

Step 1: Visit https://study.sagepub.com/birdtoolkit3e

Welcome to the companion website

Welcome to the companion website for *The Dyscalculia Toolkit*, Third Edition, by Ronit Bird. The resources on the site have been specifically designed to support your study.

On this website you will find:

- **Tables and Tracking Sheets** to download and print off
- **Teaching Resources** to download and print off
- **Activity Sheets** to download and print off
- **Game Boards** to download and print off
- **Videos** to help demonstrate practice

Just click on links to the left.

About the book:

The new edition of the bestselling *Dyscalculia Toolkit* continues to meet the needs of specialist and non-specialist teachers working with learners aged 6 to 14 years, who have difficulty with maths and number.

Now with **over 200 activities and 50 games**, new and improved illustrations, and an expanded list of recommended readings, useful websites & resources, the new edition also includes exclusive access to this a brand **new companion website** which features:

- 10 videos with over 45 minutes of material demonstrating a selection of games from every section

- Editable pupil tracking sheets organised by teaching point and section

- Over 70 pages of downloadable and printable teaching materials including activity sheets, game boards, teaching resources & summary tables.

Packed full of practical, creative and innovative ideas and strategies this is the complete toolkit to help teachers and parents support learners with dyscalculia or those struggling with mathematics.

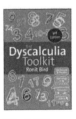

Author: Ronit Bird
Pub Date: December 2016

Buy the book

Order Review Copy

Step 2: Create or log in to your SAGE account

Step 3: Redeem your access code. This can be found on the inside front cover of the book

Step 4: Start using the additional resources

If you have any difficult redeeming your code, please contact: orders@sagepub.co.uk

For library and institutional access, please contact: ebooks@sagepub.co.uk

Introduction

This book is for teachers who are looking for practical ways to help pupils who struggle with numeracy. It is aimed mainly at primary teachers who do not have a specialist background in either maths or special needs.

I use the word 'teacher' loosely to mean anyone who supports children in their learning. Parents, for example, are ideally placed to use the practical activities and games in this book to promote maths as a practical subject full of patterns and puzzles, and therefore full of interest and fun. I hope the ideas in this book will be of interest to any adults who support pupils in junior school and in the early years of secondary school, no matter whether the adults in question are classroom teachers, teachers of numeracy, teaching assistants, parents or specialist staff in special needs departments. Because the suggestions presented here are designed to promote understanding and to help learners make mathematical connections, the ideas in this book can be used to teach the basic principles of numeracy to any learner.

What's new in this edition?

▶ Many more games. There are now 50 games in total, including twice as many games as previously provided in the section on basic calculation strategies (Section 2).

▶ Ten videos, with a total running time of 48 minutes, created specially for this new edition. On the CW ⏳ you can find separate videos with commentary for each of the four sections of the book, plus six short stop-motion silent movies demonstrating a selection of games from every section.

▶ New pupil tracking sheets, organised by teaching points and by section. The tracking sheets can be edited before being printed off.

▶ More downloadable teaching materials. There are now 70 pages of resources, ready to be printed off for immediate use. They comprise 18 pages of teaching resources, 18 pages of activity sheets, 20 game boards, 6 pupil tracking sheets and 10 pages of summary tables to help readers identify which activities and games are designed to target different numeracy topics. The new material available for the first time in this edition includes teaching resources, activity sheets and game boards as well as the tracking sheets mentioned above.

▶ Easier access to the teaching resources. All the extra material accompanying the book is now accessible from the CW ⏳.

▶ New and improved illustrations. Extra illustrations have been added and all the existing illustrations have been re-formatted to improve consistency and clarity.

▶ An expanded list of recommended reading that now includes useful websites and links to various resources and suppliers.

What does this book contain?

Inside this book you will find a collection of teaching activities and games. The activities have been developed over a number of years of teaching dyslexic, dyspraxic and dyscalculic learners, either on a one-to-one basis or in small groups of pupils who have been withdrawn from lessons for extra support. The activities are equally appropriate for children who have been diagnosed as dyscalculic as for those whose difficulties with number arise from other specific learning difficulties such as dyslexia or dyspraxia.

The book is organised into four sections:

▶ Section 1: Early Number Work with Numbers Under 10

▶ Section 2: Basic Calculations with Numbers Above 10

▶ Section 3: Place Value

▶ Section 4: Times Tables, Multiplication and Division.

Resources for all four sections can be found on the CW Ⓚ for the book.

The Appendix, which can be found on the CW, Ⓚ contains a summary of the more commonly used concrete materials, including an introduction to Cuisenaire rods. Because I use Cuisenaire rods so extensively in my teaching activities, and have found so many people unfamiliar with their use, I have also included on the CW Ⓚ a leaflet of practical ideas, written originally for parents.

The CW Ⓚ provides easy access to 70 pages of useful teaching resources, including masters for dot pattern cards and for digit cards, base-10 resources, number tracks with Slavonic shading, a variety of activity sheets, two summary tables to help you choose activities and games to target particular numeracy topics, new pupil tracking sheets, as well as 20 game boards for all the board games in this book.

The philosophy behind my teaching methods is to provide children with the kinds of practical experiences that will help them build sound cognitive models. Because the emphasis is on doing the maths rather than recording it on paper, you will find very few worksheets or ideas for written work in this book. What you will find instead is more than 200 teaching activities and 50 games. I have deliberately included activities that require only what can easily be found in a normal maths classroom or can easily be acquired by parents, such as counters, Cuisenaire rods, Dienes blocks, digit cards, dice, dominoes, paper and pencils. There is no need to buy special equipment, or commercial games and resources that tend to target only a single topic. My activities are simple to set up and most are ready for immediate use with individual pupils or small groups; others just require copies of the games boards or activity sheets from the CW Ⓚ.

Why is there such a strong emphasis on games?

I invariably use a lot of games in my teaching, and not simply because they are fun. Provided that the games are carefully chosen, or carefully designed, to target only a single mathematical idea at a time, games furnish pupils with the opportunity and the incentive to practise the specific techniques that we want them to acquire, allowing the ideas to become habitual and gradually more fluent. For example, having taught pupils the complement facts of 10 – the five number bonds 5 + 5, 4 + 6, 3 + 7, 2 + 8 and 1 + 9 – by allowing the pupils to manipulate concrete materials as they explore these numerical relationships in an active and practical way, pupils will still need plenty of practice using these five facts before they can become absolutely secure. That is why you will find four games, as well as several activities, that specifically target the complement facts of 10. Learners with specific learning difficulties tend to need much more repetition and rehearsal than their peers, spread over a longer period. But there are only so many times someone can recite the facts, or complete worksheets featuring them, without boredom setting in.

In parallel with work on key facts, I regularly and explicitly teach pupils reasoning strategies about how to derive an unknown fact from a known and practised fact, such as how to find various steps of a multiplication table from the three key facts for that table. A worksheet is likely to give only mechanical practice in producing the answer because it has been designed as a way of testing automatic recall, whereas a well-designed game will practise the necessary steps required to reach an answer through logic and deduction.

As a teacher, I am constantly aware of the need to contrive situations in which the facts and techniques that my pupils need to master can be rehearsed in as many different ways as possible. Games are extremely valuable in this context because children are naturally motivated to spend time playing games over and over again and rarely notice how much learning and reinforcing is taking place while they are actively and productively engaged in play. As well as being more enjoyable, games are more powerful than worksheets because each time a game is played different challenges might be presented, in a different sequence, leading to new considerations and different outcomes, all of which provides for a much more varied, stimulating and active learning experience.

Purposeful activities and targeted games are central to my approach to teaching learners who have difficulties with basic maths. The activities I specify in this book are never intended to simply back up paper-and-pencil techniques or abstract methods. Neither are my games ever intended as just a bit of fun to fill in the spare time at the end of a lesson. All the activities and games that I design are invented to provide the actual learning experience for a variety of very specific maths topics.

How to use this book

Please do not feel that you ought to start at the beginning of the book and work through to the end, or even to keep to the sequence in which the ideas are presented. You should feel free to pick and choose activities, depending on your pupils and your knowledge of their particular areas of difficulty. Some activities may need to be repeated often, or revisited at regular intervals; others may be valuable to try only once for particular pupils, or not at all. When activities naturally follow on from each other, the text clearly signals the fact. Some activities may need to be preceded by others from another section; for example, some understanding of place value (Section 3) is required before attempting some of the work on larger numbers (Section 2) and before some of the work on multiplication and division (Section 4). Once you begin working closely with pupils, you will find that you are the person best placed to uncover any misconceptions or sticking points that could usefully become the focus of subsequent lessons.

Each of the four sections starts with a short overview, putting the topic of that section into context. Following the overview, you will find a summary of the main problems associated with the topic leading to a list of ideas on how to help. These summaries are presented as bullet points for ease of reference. The remainder of each section is dedicated entirely to the teaching activities and games, set out as clearly and concisely as possible with a minimum of explanatory background or theory. Printable and photocopiable resources from all four sections are provided on the CW, ⃠ making the activities and games accessible and ready to use, with the minimum of preparation.

I have targeted what I know to be specific areas of difficulty and have deliberately broken down the teaching and learning into extremely small steps. Each section is loosely structured in order of difficulty, starting with concrete activities and progressing gradually through learning activities that are designed to help pupils move through the intermediate diagrammatic stage and right up to the abstract stage of calculation.

Most of the activities are designed to be teacher-led, rather than for children to work through on their own. It is important to ask lots of questions, to direct the discussion carefully, to point out any connections with previous activities and other maths topics and to encourage pupils to talk a lot about what they are doing, and why, while they are doing it. Naturally, pupils will do best in an atmosphere where mistakes are regarded as a normal, and even an instructive, part of the learning process.

Whether inside the classroom or at home, the best results will be achieved by frequent, regular, short but unhurried, sessions, each of which should include a variety of activities and topics and a sensitive balance between revision and new content. Daily sessions will soon improve pupils' attitude and will steadily boost their self-assurance, their sense of achievement and their maths performance.

The 200+ activities are each labelled according to the main teaching point they have been designed to address. A list of teaching points is also included in the instructions for each of the 50 games. The main numeracy topic addressed by each game is summarised in the first of the two tables at the end of this Introduction. The second summary table at the end of this Introduction links the activities and games in this book to a list of numeracy topics and teaching points so that you can easily find ideas to target a particular gap in a pupil's knowledge or to address a specific misconception or need. As well as appearing at the end of this chapter, both the summary tables can be found on the CW ⃠. Tracking sheets, accessible from the CW, ⃠ are provided for the first time in this latest edition of *The Dyscalculia Toolkit*. Closely linked to the summary tables, the tracking sheets are designed to help you plan work for individual students or groups of pupils, and to use for tracking and recording a learner's progress. The tracking sheets can be edited before being printed off.

What is dyscalculia?

Developmental dyscalculia was first recognised in the UK by the Department for Education and Science in 2001 and defined as: 'a condition that affects the ability to acquire arithmetical skills. Dyscalculic learners may have difficulty understanding simple number concepts, lack an intuitive grasp of numbers, and have problems learning number facts and procedures. Even if they produce a correct answer or use a correct method, they may do so mechanically and without confidence' (DfES 0512/2001, p. 2).

There is a debate about whether true dyscalculia differs from the maths difficulties experienced by some dyslexic and dyspraxic learners, a debate I am happy to leave to the academics. What matters to me is the fact that the same sorts of intervention seem to help many pupils who are underachieving in maths, whatever label they have been given. I believe that the coming years will see a growing recognition of the particular problems and educational needs of dyscalculic learners, in much the same way as the last three or four decades have seen an increasing acceptance of the existence of dyslexia and a developing consensus about the best teaching and learning approaches for these pupils.

Research into dyscalculia is still at an early stage, but it is estimated that dyscalculia affects roughly 4–6% of the population. This equates to at least one child in any average classroom.

What are the indicators for dyscalculia?

As a teacher, you might suspect that you have a dyscalculic pupil in your class if an otherwise competent student has a surprising level of difficulty with ordinary numeric operations and relies on finger-counting, often for all four arithmetic operations, well beyond the age at which most of the others in the class have progressed to more efficient strategies. A dyscalculic learner stands out as having no 'feel for numbers' at all, no ability to estimate even small quantities, and no idea whether an answer to an arithmetic problem is reasonable or not. Memory weaknesses, both long-term and short-term, are a great handicap and result in a pupil with dyscalculia being unable to remember facts and procedures accurately, or consistently, no matter how many times they try to learn them by heart. Pupils who have dyscalculia simply cannot remember their times tables reliably, and you may find they can recall some facts one day but not the next. They are also likely to lose track of what they are doing when attempting any procedure that requires more than two or three steps. Even basic counting can be a problem for pupils with dyscalculia, especially counting backwards.

Indicators for dyscalculia include:

▶ an inability to subitise (see without counting) even very small quantities

▶ an inability to estimate whether a numerical answer is reasonable

▶ weaknesses in both short-term and long-term memory

▶ an inability to count backwards reliably

▶ a weakness in visual and spatial orientation

▶ directional (left/right) confusion

▶ slow processing speeds when engaged in maths activities

- trouble with sequencing

- a tendency not to notice patterns

- a problem with all aspects of money

- a marked delay in learning to read a clock to tell the time

- an inability to manage time in daily life.

What about learners with other specific learning difficulties?

A dyslexic pupil might show many of the same indicators as those listed above, because it is thought that at least half of all dyslexics also have difficulties with maths. Outside the maths classroom, you might suspect that pupils are dyslexic if they read and write much less willingly and fluently than you would expect, if they read and re-read written material with little comprehension and if their spelling is particularly weak, inconsistent or bizarre. Dyslexic learners show much greater ability and understanding when speaking than you could ever guess from looking at the scrappy and minimal amount of written work they produce. Other indicators are memory weaknesses, problems with processing auditory information, and difficulties with planning and organisation.

A typical dyspraxic pupil does not seem to have the same long-term memory problems as a dyslexic and so might be able to remember times tables facts with ease. Dyspraxia, also known as DCD (developmental coordination disorder), mainly affects motor control, which results in pupils being clumsy and uncoordinated, poor at planning and organisation, and unsuccessful at subjects like PE and sports that require balance and coordination. Dyspraxic pupils cannot process sensory information properly and are therefore forever tripping and falling, dropping and breaking things, and mislaying their belongings. In the maths classroom, dyspraxic pupils have particular difficulty in handling equipment such as a ruler, a protractor or a set of compasses, and their written work is likely to be very messy and difficult to decipher.

A pupil with attention deficit hyperactivity disorder, may signal his (and it is usually a boy) presence by being unable to stop fidgeting or to sit still, being too easily distracted by outside stimuli, having a tendency to talk and interrupt excessively, and finding it extremely difficult to stay on task and see any undertaking through to the end. I mention the condition here only because nowadays pupils with ADHD or ADD tend to come under the umbrella term of 'learners with specific difficulties'. However, pupils with attention disorders may not have any specific problems with numeracy or maths once they have found a way to manage their impulsivity and concentration difficulties.

What kind of teaching do dyscalculic learners need?

All numeracy teaching should aim to help learners build up a sound mathematical understanding of numbers and their relationships. The basis of my own teaching approach with dyscalculic learners is to concentrate on numeracy and arithmetic, starting – crucially – with a variety of versatile concrete materials that provide practical experience and strongly visual models. Once a numerical concept has been understood at the concrete level, then, and only then, will I begin to lead the learner gradually but steadily towards some of the more abstract and symbolic methods associated with higher level mathematics.

My own view is that a set of Cuisenaire rods is indispensable for working with dyscalculic learners. I find it the best, most versatile and most powerful tool to offer learners who are struggling to build a coherent mental model of the number system. I supplement Cuisenaire rods at the lower end with discrete items, such as counters or nuggets, that can be arranged and re-arranged into dot patterns for the numbers up to 10, and at the upper end with Dienes blocks or other base-10 equipment that can combine with Cuisenaire rods for concrete modelling of 3-digit numbers. One of the great strengths of Cuisenaire is that numbers are not presented as a collection of ones, so that the learner's focus is directed away from counting and towards number relationships. See the Appendix for an introduction to Cuisenaire rods and other concrete materials.

Dyscalculic learners, just like other learners, need to be able to count properly. Counting is, after all, the foundation of all numeracy. But, as soon as counting is secure, children have to be taught calculation strategies that do not rely on counting in ones. For this reason, I recommend plenty of work on building numbers from smaller components, splitting quantities up again into smaller chunks, and recombining the component pieces once more in order to fully explore the composition of numbers and the connection between addition and subtraction. The component work that I describe in this book is less static than simply learning the number bonds because its emphasis is on performing operations on numbers and seeing quantities change as a result of whatever action is being performed.

Working with chunks, or components, rather than ones, is the only antidote to the immature – and damaging – dependence on counting that is so common in pupils who struggle with numeracy. When counting is the only strategy known to learners, they have fallen into the 'counting trap'. See the Overviews of Section 1 and Section 2 for more about this pervasive problem. The only way out of the vicious cycle is to explicitly teach learners calculation strategies based on components, i.e. chunks, and not on counting on, or counting back, in ones.

Similarly, the times tables work and the multiplication and division activities that I recommend in this book are very far removed from the all-too-common practice of giving children a list of tables facts to learn by heart, a situation that leaves many pupils without any idea about what multiplication or division mean or how to use or apply the facts they have been asked to memorise. My teaching approach to tables is based on the area model of multiplication and division, an interpretation that inherently connects multiplication with division from the very beginning and one that can be modelled with Cuisenaire rods to produce rectangular shapes that are easy to read, understand and visualise.

Problems with numeracy often go hand in hand with significant memory weaknesses. This is why simple repetition will never be a way forward for dyscalculic pupils, however hard or often they are drilled. The best way to work around learners' memory problems is to focus on only a few key facts, those that are more important or have the widest application: first allow learners to thoroughly explore and internalise the key facts; then teach them explicitly how to derive whatever other facts they might need by reasoning logically from the key facts they already know.

Visualisation is a strategy that should be explicitly taught to dyscalculic pupils as a route towards mental calculation strategies. Immediately after a session of concrete work, pupils can be asked to close their eyes and try to recreate some of the work in their mind's eye. Diagrammatic calculation methods, such as empty number lines for addition and subtraction or the area model for multiplication and division, can be introduced as a way of recording concrete work with Cuisenaire rods and later extended to support visualising techniques, thereby creating a bridge between concrete exploration with manipulative materials and the more abstract work that is the norm in mainstream schools. The transition between concrete and abstract work is an important stage that needs to be planned for and cannot be rushed.

My final observation about what kind of teaching approach works best for dyscalculic learners is a recommendation to break down every bit of teaching and learning into the tiniest of incremental steps and not to make any assumption about what pupils already know. For example, just because a child knows, say, that five counters can be arranged into the familiar dice pattern for 5, it does not follow that the same child will know that none of the other dice patterns can be created out of exactly five counters; or just because a child has discovered that adding 1 to each of the numbers up to 10 results in the next number in the counting sequence or that taking 1 away results in the previous number, it does not follow that the same child will know how to add 1 to a 2-digit number, let alone be able to work out how many to take away from a quantity in order to leave 1. Sound numerical understanding can only develop if it rests on secure foundations at every stage. The importance of tightly focused practical activities that address only a single new idea at a time cannot be overestimated.

What's next, after working through this book?

I have written two other books published by Sage that follow on from this one, although each book is complete in itself and can be used independently of the other two. *Overcoming Difficulties with Number* is aimed at learners who are working at a slightly higher level or who have, perhaps, already worked through many of the ideas in *The Dyscalculia Toolkit*. *Overcoming Difficulties with Number* analyses some key numeracy strategies – such as bridging through 10, or learning multiplication tables through the area model – in very great detail, setting out step-by-step instructions on how to teach the strategies to learners who find the concepts difficult. The focus is on teaching for understanding while at the same time helping learners make the transition from practical exploration to more abstract and canonical calculation methods.

The Dyscalculia Resource Book is a collection of ready-to-use and printable games and puzzles, all carefully targeted to practise the crucial foundation skills – such as adding and subtracting in component chunks rather than in ones, or deriving new numeracy facts from known key facts – that children who struggle with numeracy need to master before they can make any significant progress in maths. The games and puzzles in *The Dyscalculia Resource Book* are designed to reinforce what has previously been taught at a concrete level – for example through the activities and games in this *Dyscalculia Toolkit* book – and each is accompanied by clear instructions to the supervising adult on how to manage the activity so as to maximise the learning experience.

You are welcome to contact me through my website (www.ronitbird.com) with any feedback about how your children or pupils respond to the ideas in any of my books. On my website you will also find a list of Top Ten Tips for Parents, general information and online links to do with dyscalculia, a variety of free games and teaching resources, and details of my ebooks, all of which contain many demonstration videos.

SUMMARY OF THE MAIN TEACHING POINTS ADDRESSED
BY THE GAMES IN *THE DYSCALCULIA TOOLKIT*

This table is provided because the name of each game does not always reveal exactly what topic it was designed to target (unlike the main teaching points of the activities, which are spelled out by their titles).

A downloadable version of this table is available via the Companion Website

GAME	MAIN NUMERACY TOPIC/TEACHING POINT	LOCATION
Make 5	Split and recombine numbers up to 5	Section 1
Numbers Inside	Identify smaller components of larger numbers	Section 1
Collect 5s	Add numbers up to 4 + 4	Section 1
Key Components Guessing Game	The key component facts: doubles or near-doubles	Section 1
Odd and Even Collectors	Recognise odd or even up to 10	Section 1
Draw Your Race on a Number Line	Empty number line versus number track	Section 1
Race to Tell a Story	Build the same target number in different ways	Section 1
Post-It Note Subtraction	Focus on subtraction, as inverse of addition	Section 1
Cover the Numbers / Shut the Box	Split and recombine numbers up to 12	Section 1
Clear the Deck	Components of a target number up to 10	Section 1
How Many Beads? How Many Hidden?	Bridging through 5 and through 10	Section 1
Complements Number Search	Complements to 10 (i.e. components of 10)	Section 1
Complements Ping-Pong	Complements to 10 (i.e. components of 10)	Section 1
Ten in a Bed	Complements to 10 (i.e. components of 10)	Section 1
Who Has the Most Equations?	Add and subtract 1 or 2	Section 1
Polka Dots	Visualise and use reasoning for components of 12	Section 2
Regroup	Visualise and use reasoning for numbers up to 20	Section 2
It All Adds Up	Build 'teen' numbers out of smaller components	Section 2
5 and What's Left	Bridging through 5 and through 10	Section 2
Frame an Addition	Bridging through 10	Section 2
Race Along a Number Line and Bridge	Bridging through 10	Section 2
Race to the End of the Number Line	Recognise when bridging is not needed	Section 2
Frame a Subtraction	Bridging through 10 for subtraction	Section 2
Keep the Change!	Complements to 100 (i.e. components of 100)	Section 2
Double Take	Doubling and reasoning about near-doubles	Section 2
Magic 10s	Grouping tens for place value	Section 3
Race to Cover 100	Exchange and decomposition	Section 3
Four Throws to Reach 100	Place value decimal system up to 100 or 1000	Section 3
Dice and spinner games	Place value, explored actively	Section 3
Spot the Decomposition	Decomposition in subtraction	Section 3
Win Counters on a 100-Square	Place value structure of 2-digit numbers	Section 3
Race Through a 100-Square	Place value structure of numbers up to 100	Section 3
Steer the Number	Place value structure of 2-digit numbers	Section 3
Two-Digit Sequences	Sequencing 2-digit numbers	Section 3
Three-Digit Sequences (Focus on Tens)	Sequencing 3-digit numbers	Section 3
Place Value Boxes	Place value of large numbers (6 digits)	Section 3

(Continued)

(Continued)

GAME	MAIN NUMERACY TOPIC/TEACHING POINT	LOCATION
Calculator Skittles	Place value of large numbers (4 digits or more)	Section 3
Jump 10	Adding 10 to a number	Section 3
The Six-Card Rounding Game	Place value in 2-digit numbers	Section 3
The Rounding Challenge	Place value in 2-digit or 3-digit numbers	Section 3
Don't Walk if You Can Take the Bus	Derive multiplication facts from key tables facts	Section 4
Mouse Tables	Learn and practise a chosen times table	Section 4
Self-correcting tables cards Game 1	Learn and practise a chosen times table	Section 4
Self-correcting tables cards Game 2	Finding the questions and focusing on division	Section 4
Self-correcting tables cards Game 3	Matching questions to answers in a chosen table	Section 4
Self-correcting tables cards Game 4	Snap, matching multiplication to division	Section 4
Multiples from the 1–6 Times Tables	Practise tables facts up to 6×6	Section 4
Products in a Row	Connect pairs of related multiplication tables	Section 4
Factors	Division: find factors of given multiples	Section 4
Areas on a Grid	The area model of multiplication and division	Section 4

**ALL THE ACTIVITIES AND GAMES IN *THE DYSCALCULIA TOOLKIT*
LISTED ACCORDING TO THEIR NUMERACY TOPIC OR MAIN TEACHING POINTS**

Use this table to help you find activities and games to address a particular need or misconception. Tracking sheets, based on this table, are provided amongst the online resources available via the Companion Website ᗺ to help you make plans and programmes of work for individual pupils or groups and to record and track progress.

A downloadable version of this table is available via the Companion Website ᗺ

NUMERACY TOPIC/TEACHING POINT	ACTIVITY OR GAME	LOCATION
Visual patterns for numbers up to 10	Make dot patterns for the numbers 1 to 10	Section 1
Visual patterns for numbers up to 5	Make transparent dot pattern cards for the numbers 1 to 5	Section 1
Visual patterns for numbers up to 5	Make 5 Game	Section 1
Visual patterns for numbers up to 6	Explore smaller numbers inside larger numbers	Section 1
Visual patterns for numbers up to 10	Change one dot pattern into another	Section 1
Visual patterns for numbers up to 10	Use Cuisenaire rods to learn all components to 10	Section 1
Visual patterns for numbers up to 10	Make a 'Story' of a number	Section 1
Visual patterns for numbers up to 10	Change dot patterns by adding or subtracting	Section 1
Visual patterns for numbers up to 12	Sort and re-sort a set of dominoes	Section 1
Visual patterns for numbers up to 20	Connect 'teen' numbers to those below 10	Section 2
Visual patterns for numbers up to 20	Focus on the 'teen' numbers	Section 2
Visual patterns for numbers up to 20	Explore 'teen' numbers with Cuisenaire rods	Section 2
Key components up to 10	Make dot patterns for the numbers 1 to 10	Section 1
Key components up to 10	Use dot patterns to explore odd and even	Section 1
Key components up to 10	Key Components Guessing Game	Section 1
Key components up to 10	Connect subtraction to addition	Section 1
Key components up to 10	Regroup: Apply logic to find new component facts	Section 1
Key components up to 10	Post-It Note Subtraction Game	Section 1
Doubles and near doubles up to 5 + 5	Make dot patterns for the numbers 1 to 10	Section 1
Doubles and near doubles up to 5 + 5	Use dot patterns to explore odd and even	Section 1
Doubles and near doubles up to 5 + 5	Regroup: Apply logic to find new component facts	Section 1
Doubles and near doubles up to 5 + 5	Explore and learn the doubles up to 5 + 5	Section 1
Doubles and near doubles	Use reasoning to find near-doubles	Section 1
Odd and even numbers up to 10	Use dot patterns to explore odd and even	Section 1
Odd and even numbers up to 10	Explore with Cuisenaire rods and with money	Section 1
Odd and even numbers up to 10	Odd and Even Collectors Game	Section 1
Numbers in relation to each other	Explore smaller numbers inside larger numbers	Section 1
Numbers in relation to each other	Numbers Inside Game	Section 1

(Continued)

(Continued)

NUMERACY TOPIC/TEACHING POINT	ACTIVITY OR GAME	LOCATION
Numbers in relation to each other	Become familiar with Cuisenaire rods	Section 1
Numbers in relation to each other	Race to Tell a Story Game	Section 1
Numbers in relation to each other	Sort and re-sort a set of dominoes	Section 1
Components up to 5	Make 5 Game	Section 1
Components up to 5	Collect 5s Game	Section 1
Components up to 6	Explore smaller numbers inside larger numbers	Section 1
Components up to 6, 7, 8, 9 or 10	Clear the Deck Game	Section 1
Components up to 10	Sort and re-sort a set of dominoes	Section 1
Components up to 10	Regroup: Apply logic to find new component facts	Section 1
Components up to 10	Use Cuisenaire rods to learn all components to 10	Section 1
Components up to 10	Make a Story of a number	Section 1
Components up to 10	Find complements of 10 with Cuisenaire rods	Section 1
Components up to 10	Complementary addition	Section 1
Components up to 10	Use money for component work	Section 1
Components up to 12	Cover the Numbers / Shut the Box Game	Section 1
Complements to 10	Make a bead string	Section 1
Complements to 10	Learn complements of 10 on a bead string	Section 1
Complements to 10	How Many Beads? Game	Section 1
Complements to 10	Find complements of 10 with Cuisenaire rods	Section 1
Complements to 10	Ten in a Bed Game	Section 1
Complements to 10	Complements Number Search Game	Section 1
Complements to 10	Complements Ping-Pong Game	Section 1
Add/Subtract 1 or 2	Change dot patterns by adding or subtracting	Section 1
Add/Subtract 1 or 2	Focus on plus/minus 1 and plus/minus 2	Section 1
Add/Subtract 1 or 2	Who Has the Most Equations? Game	Section 1
Add 1, 2 or 3	Draw Your Race on a Number Line Game	Section 1
Add/Subtract small amounts	Collect 5s Game	Section 1
Add/Subtract small amounts	Numbers Inside Game	Section 1
Add/Subtract small amounts	Teach complementary addition	Section 1
Add/Subtract small amounts	Complementary addition on a number line	Section 1
Add/Subtract small amounts	Cover the Numbers / Shut the Box Game	Section 1
Missing numbers	Become familiar with Cuisenaire rods	Section 1
Missing numbers	Use Cuisenaire rods to learn all components to 10	Section 1
Missing numbers	Compare the difference and equalise	Section 1
Missing numbers	Hidden quantity subtraction	Section 1
Commutative property of addition	Make 5 Game	Section 1
Commutative property of addition	Collect 5s Game	Section 1
Commutative property of addition	Become familiar with Cuisenaire rods	Section 1

NUMERACY TOPIC/TEACHING POINT	ACTIVITY OR GAME	LOCATION
Commutative property of addition	Use Cuisenaire rods to learn all components to 10	Section 1
Commutative property of addition	Make and read equations with Cuisenaire rods	Section 1
Commutative property of addition	Cover the Numbers / Shut the Box Game	Section 1
Commutative property of addition	Learn complements to 10 with a bead string	Section 1
Commutative property of addition	Complements Number Search	Section 1
Commutative property of addition	Complements Ping-Pong Game	Section 1
Connect addition with subtraction	Change one dot pattern into another	Section 1
Connect addition with subtraction	Sort and re-sort a set of dominoes	Section 1
Connect addition with subtraction	Connect subtraction to addition	Section 1
Connect addition with subtraction	Regroup: Apply logic to find new component facts	Section 1
Connect addition with subtraction	Make and read equations with Cuisenaire rods	Section 1
Connect addition with subtraction	Draw and record equations in writing	Section 1
Connect addition with subtraction	Cover the Numbers / Shut the Box Game	Section 1
Connect addition with subtraction	Clear the Deck Game	Section 1
Connect addition with subtraction	Complements Number Search	Section 1
Connect addition with subtraction	Complements Ping-Pong Game	Section 1
Connect addition with subtraction	Ten in a Bed Game	Section 1
Connect addition with subtraction	Compare the difference and equalise	Section 1
Connect addition with subtraction	Post-It Note Subtraction Game	Section 1
Connect addition with subtraction	Hidden quantity subtraction	Section 1
Connect addition with subtraction	Teach complementary addition	Section 1
Connect addition with subtraction	Complementary addition on a number line	Section 1
Complementary addition below 10	Teach complementary addition	Section 1
Complementary addition below 10	Complementary addition on a number line	Section 1
Focus on the 'teen' numbers	Connect 'teen' numbers to those below 10	Section 2
Focus on the 'teen' numbers	Focus on the 'teen' numbers	Section 2
Focus on the 'teen' numbers	Explore 'teen' numbers with Cuisenaire rods	Section 2
Focus on the 'teen' numbers	Make a 20-step staircase	Section 3
Focus on the 'teen' numbers	It All Adds Up Game	Section 2
Focus on the 'teen' numbers	Locate 2-digit numbers	Section 2
Exchanging tens and units	Exchange units into tens	Section 3
Exchanging tens and units	Concrete counting on place value mats	Section 3
Exchanging tens and units	Magic 10s Game	Section 3
Complements to multiples of 10	Complements to 20	Section 2
Complements to multiples of 10	Cover 20 Game	Section 3
Complements to multiples of 10	Complements to larger multiples of 10	Section 2
Complements to multiples of 10	Complements on a number line	Section 2
Bridging through 5	How Many Beads? Game	Section 1
Bridging through 5	Five and What's Left Game	Section 2
Bridging through 10	Introduce bridging with Cuisenaire rods	Section 2

(Continued)

(Continued)

NUMERACY TOPIC/TEACHING POINT	ACTIVITY OR GAME	LOCATION
Bridging through 10	Bridge through 10 on a number line	Section 2
Bridging through 10	Practise bridging and reinforce commutativity	Section 2
Bridging through 10	Frame an Addition Game	Section 2
Bridging through multiples of 10	Bridge through multiples of 10	Section 2
Bridging through multiples of 10	Race Along a Number Line and Bridge Game	Section 2
Bridging is not always necessary	Polka Dots Game	Section 2
Bridging is not always necessary	Race to the End of the Number Line Game	Section 2
Complementary addition 2-digit nos.	Complementary addition for subtraction	Section 2
Complementary addition 2-digit nos.	Frame a Subtraction Game	Section 2
Complementary addition 2-digit nos.	Subtracting round numbers	Section 2
Complementary addition 2-digit nos.	Harder complementary addition	Section 2
Partitioning 2-digit numbers	A flexible approach to partitioning	Section 2
Partitioning 2-digit numbers	Explore partitioning methods	Section 2
Partitioning 2-digit numbers	Partition numbers into tens and units	Section 3
Partitioning 2-digit numbers	Split off the 'teen' numbers	Section 3
Partitioning 2-digit numbers	Calculator Skittles Game	Section 3
Decomposition in subtraction	A flexible approach to partitioning	Section 2
Decomposition in subtraction	Avoid decomposition	Section 2
Decomposition in subtraction	Practise subtraction and decomposition	Section 3
Decomposition in subtraction	Spot the Decomposition Game	Section 3
Complements to 100	Complements to 100	Section 2
Complements to 100	Keep the Change! Game	Section 2
Complements to 100	Race to Cover 100 Game	Section 3
Doubling	Learn the doubles up to 10 + 10	Section 2
Doubling	Key fact: Double means 'multiply by 2'	Section 4
Doubling	Practise and extend the doubles facts	Section 2
Doubling	Double Take Game	Section 2
Doubling and halving	Halving is the opposite of doubling	Section 2
Doubling and halving	Find half of round numbers	Section 2
Doubling and halving	Function machines	Section 2
Doubling and halving	Key facts: ×5 is half of ×10	Section 4
Mental arithmetic strategies	*All work on components, complements and numerous other activities*	Sections 1–4
Mental arithmetic strategies	Regroup Game	Section 2
Mental arithmetic strategies	The Basic 8 Strategies	Section 2
Mental arithmetic strategies	Identify the best strategy for different situations	Sections 1–2
Derive new number facts by reasoning	Make dot patterns for the numbers 1 to 10	Section 1
Derive new number facts by reasoning	Change one dot pattern into another	Section 1
Derive new number facts by reasoning	Use dot patterns to explore odd and even	Section 1
Derive new number facts by reasoning	Collect 5s Game	Section 1
Derive new number facts by reasoning	Sort and re-sort a set of dominoes	Section 1

NUMERACY TOPIC/TEACHING POINT	ACTIVITY OR GAME	LOCATION
Derive new number facts by reasoning	Regroup: Apply logic to find new component facts	Section 1
Derive new number facts by reasoning	Use Cuisenaire to learn all components to 10	Section 1
Derive new number facts by reasoning	How Many Beads? Game	Section 1
Derive new number facts by reasoning	Find complements of 10 with Cuisenaire rods	Section 1
Derive new number facts by reasoning	Estimate and measure using Cuisenaire rods	Section 1
Derive new number facts by reasoning	The Regroup Game	Section 2
Derive new number facts by reasoning	Polka Dots Game	Section 2
Derive new number facts by reasoning	It All Adds Up Game	Section 2
Derive new number facts by reasoning	Connect 'teen' numbers to those below 10	Section 2
Derive new number facts by reasoning	Focus on the 'teen' numbers	Section 2
Derive new number facts by reasoning	Explore 'teen' numbers with Cuisenaire rods	Section 2
Derive new number facts by reasoning	A flexible approach to partitioning	Section 2
Derive new number facts by reasoning	Explore partitioning methods	Section 2
Derive new number facts by reasoning	Avoid decomposition in subtraction	Section 2
Derive new number facts by reasoning	9 is almost 10	Section 2
Derive new number facts by reasoning	Find near-complements and near-doubles	Sections 1–2
ENL (empty number lines)	Draw Your Race on a Number Line Game	Section 1
ENL (empty number lines)	Complementary addition on a number line	Section 1
ENL (empty number lines)	Locate 2-digit numbers in context	Section 2
ENL (empty number lines)	Complements on a number line	Section 2
ENL (empty number lines)	Bridge through 10 on a number line	Section 2
ENL (empty number lines)	Practise bridging and reinforce commutativity	Section 2
ENL (empty number lines)	Frame an Addition Game	Section 2
ENL (empty number lines)	Bridge through multiples of 10	Section 2
ENL (empty number lines)	Race Along the Number Line and Bridge Game	Section 2
ENL (empty number lines)	Race to the End of the Number Line Game	Section 2
ENL (empty number lines)	Complementary addition for subtraction	Section 2
ENL (empty number lines)	Frame a Subtraction Game	Section 2
ENL (empty number lines)	Subtracting round numbers	Section 2
ENL (empty number lines)	Harder complementary addition	Section 2
ENL (empty number lines)	Complements to 100	Section 2
ENL (empty number lines)	Jump 10 Game	Section 3
ENL (empty number lines)	Locate any number on a number line	Section 3
ENL (empty number lines)	Practise mental step-counting from given tables facts	Section 4
ENL (empty number lines)	Make times tables patterns on number lines	Section 4
Place value: 2- and 3-digit numbers	Concrete counting on place value mats	Section 3
Place value structure of 'teen' numbers	Make a 20-step staircase	Section 3
Place value structure of 'teen' numbers	Cover 20 Game	Section 3
Place value: 2-digit numbers	Exchange units into tens	Section 3
Place value: 2-digit numbers	Magic 10s Game	Section 3
Place value: 2-digit numbers	Race to Cover 100 Game	Section 3

(Continued)

(Continued)

NUMERACY TOPIC/TEACHING POINT	ACTIVITY OR GAME	LOCATION
Place value: 2-digit numbers	Four Throws to Reach 100 Game	Section 3
Place value: 2-digit numbers	Win Counters on a 100-Square Game	Section 3
Place value: 2-digit numbers	Race Through a 100-Square Game	Section 3
Place value: 2-digit numbers	Steer the Number Game	Section 3
Place value: 2-digit numbers	Transform a 2-digit number in two steps	Section 3
Place value: 2-digit numbers	Two-Digit Sequences Game	Section 3
Place value: 2-digit numbers	Partition numbers into tens and units	Section 3
Place value: 2-digit numbers	Split off the 'teen' numbers	Section 3
Place value: 2-digit numbers	The Six-Card Rounding Game	Section 3
Place value: 2- or 3-digit numbers	Make and read numbers made of Cuisenaire rods or base-10	Section 3
Place value: 2- or 3-digit numbers	Dice and spinner games	Section 3
Place value: 2- or 3-digit numbers	Practise subtraction and decomposition	Section 3
Place value: 2- or 3-digit numbers	Spot the Decomposition Game	Section 3
Place value: 2- or 3-digit numbers	Practise adding / subtracting 10 and 100	Section 3
Place value: 2- or 3-digit numbers	Jump 10 Game	Section 3
Place value: 2- or 3-digit numbers	Locate any number on a number line	Section 3
Place value: 2- or 3-digit numbers	The Rounding Challenge Game	Section 3
Place value: 2- or 3-digit numbers	Teach × 10 and ÷ 10 as a shift between columns	Section 3
Place value: 2- or 3-digit numbers	Extend place value thinking to decimals	Section 3
Place value: 3-digit numbers	Build up large numbers, one column at a time	Section 3
Place value: 3-digit numbers	What is the value of …?	Section 3
Place value: 3-digit numbers	Three-Digit Sequences (Focus on Tens) Game	Section 3
Place value: decimal numbers	Teach ×10 and ÷10 as a shift between columns	Section 3
Place value: decimal numbers	Extend place value thinking to decimals	Section 3
Place value: decimal numbers	Connect decimal notation to money	Section 3
Place value: more than 3 digits	Use a spike abacus	Section 3
Place value: more than 3 digits	Teach the threefold repeating pattern	Section 3
Place value: more than 3 digits	Explore place value as a shorthand	Section 3
Place value: more than 3 digits	Read and write multi-digit numbers	Section 3
Place value: more than 3 digits	Place Value Boxes Game	Section 3
Place value: more than 3 digits	Calculator Skittles Game	Section 3
Place value: more than 3 digits	Teach ×10 and ÷10 as a shift between columns	Section 3
Place value: more than 3 digits	Extend place value thinking to decimals	Section 3
Place value: more than 3 digits	Connect decimal notation to money	Section 3
Multiplication as groups or arrays	Build small numbers out of equal-sized groups	Section 4
Multiplication as repeated addition	Connect step-counting with multiplication	Section 4
Multiplication as repeated addition	Step-count one or two steps from given facts	Section 4
Patterns created by tables facts	Make times tables patterns on a 100-square	Section 4

NUMERACY TOPIC/TEACHING POINT	ACTIVITY OR GAME	LOCATION
Patterns created by tables facts	Make times tables patterns on number lines	Section 4
Step-counting for multiplication facts	Build small numbers out of equal-sized groups	Section 4
Step-counting for multiplication facts	Connect step-counting with multiplication	Section 4
Step-counting for multiplication facts	Step-count one or two steps from given facts	Section 4
Step-counting for multiplication facts	Practise mental step-counting from given tables facts	Section 4
Area model of multiplication & division	Use Cuisenaire rods to show commutativity	Section 4
Area model of multiplication & division	Cuisenaire rods for multiplication and division	Section 4
Area model of multiplication & division	Key facts: ×5 is half of ×10	Section 4
Area model of multiplication & division	How many 10s? So, twice as many 5s	Section 4
Area model of multiplication & division	Find division facts by reasoning from key facts	Section 4
Area model of multiplication & division	×9 is almost ×10	Section 4
Area model of multiplication & division	Diagrammatic practice	Section 4
Area model of multiplication & division	Use rectangle sketches to derive new facts	Section 4
Area model of multiplication & division	Change the shape of the rectangle	Section 4
Area model of multiplication & division	Areas on a Grid Game	Section 4
Connect multiplication with division	Connect division to multiplication	Section 4
Connect multiplication with division	Diagrammatic practice	Section 4
Connect multiplication with division	Illustrate simple word problems	Section 4
Connect multiplication with division	Key facts: ×5 is half of ×10	Section 4
Connect multiplication with division	How many 10s? So, twice as many 5s	Section 4
Connect multiplication with division	Find division facts by reasoning from key facts	Section 4
Connect multiplication with division	Mouse Tables games	Section 4
Connect multiplication with division	Games using self-correcting cards	Section 4
Connect multiplication with division	Products in a Row Game	Section 4
Connect multiplication with division	Construct a multiplication grid	Section 4
Connect multiplication with division	Complete a partially-filled multiplication grid	Section 4
Connect multiplication with division	Multiples from the 1–6 Times Tables Game	Section 4
Connect multiplication with division	Factors Game	Section 4
Connect multiplication with division	Areas on a Grid Game	Section 4
Derive new tables facts by reasoning	Use Cuisenaire rods to show commutativity	Section 4
Derive new tables facts by reasoning	Step-count one or two steps from given facts	Section 4
Derive new tables facts by reasoning	Make times tables patterns on number lines	Section 4
Derive new tables facts by reasoning	How many 10s? So, twice as many 5s	Section 4
Derive new tables facts by reasoning	Find all the steps of any times table	Section 4
Derive new tables facts by reasoning	Find division facts by reasoning from key facts	Section 4
Derive new tables facts by reasoning	Practise all the steps of any times table	Section 4
Derive new tables facts by reasoning	Don't Walk If You Can Take the Bus Game	Section 4
Derive new tables facts by reasoning	Products in a Row Game	Section 4

(Continued)

(Continued)

NUMERACY TOPIC/TEACHING POINT	ACTIVITY OR GAME	LOCATION
Derive new tables facts by reasoning	Harder mixed tables practice	Section 4
Derive new tables facts by reasoning	Factors Game	Section 4
Derive new tables facts by reasoning	Change the shape of the rectangle	Section 4
Derive new tables facts by reasoning	Use rectangle sketches to derive new facts	Section 4
Derive new tables facts by reasoning	Areas on a Grid Game	Section 4
Prepare for more advanced work	Boxes for long multiplication	Section 4

SECTION 1

Early number work with numbers up to 10

Overview

This first section deals with very small numbers, but not necessarily with very small children. Older pupils often have difficulties that can be traced back to misconceptions at this very early stage.

Early number work depends on counting but some children have difficulty with counting. For example, dyspraxic children can find it very challenging to coordinate a one-to-one correspondence between the numbers they learn to recite and the objects they wish to count. Their counting is, therefore, often inaccurate. Some children learn to chant the string of numbers as if they were the words to a nursery rhyme, without really understanding what they mean.

Despite frequent inaccuracies, people with dyscalculia tend to rely on counting to an excessive degree. For example, most children do not need to count when quantities are extremely small: by the age of 2, many children are able to simply recognise when only 2 or 3 items are present in a group, without having to count them, and most can see up to 4 items at a glance by the time they are 4 years old. This ability, which is called 'subitising' and which someone with dyscalculia typically lacks, has an important role to play in early mathematical development.

Pupils who experience difficulties with number often believe that they are bad at all aspects of maths and feel that they cannot trust their own memory about even the most basic of number facts. This leads to an even greater reliance on counting on their fingers, in ones. The problem is that counting in ones is a very inefficient strategy. Every step provides another opportunity for mistakes to creep in. Furthermore, it puts an unnecessary strain on working memory, because calculating by counting involves a double-counting process: not only must children keep track of the running total, they must also keep a separate, parallel count of how much they are adding or subtracting so that they will know when to stop the reckoning. Another persistent problem for dyscalculic pupils is an uncertainty about where to start any count, because they are not sure whether they are supposed to be counting actual numbers or the intervals between numbers. Any new fact that is arrived at only after so much effort, anxiety and time is unlikely to be stored in long-term memory, and so a vicious cycle begins.

One of the best ways to help pupils with specific maths difficulties is to use the right kinds of apparatus to provide mathematical models that can be explored, understood and internalised.

Concrete, manipulative materials can help children develop a stronger number sense and can teach pupils how to see numbers and numerical quantities in relation to each other. See the Appendix for an introduction to concrete materials, and in particular to Cuisenaire rods, which are used extensively in the activities in this book.

You can find a video about this section of *The Dyscalculia Toolkit* on the CW.

What are the main problems?

▶ Reciting the string of numbers without understanding what counting really means.

▶ Not appreciating the concept of cardinality, i.e. that the final number of the count *is* the quantity of the set.

▶ Having very little sense of quantity and numerical magnitude, i.e. how many items are in a visible set or are represented symbolically by numerals.

▶ Being unaware of patterns, e.g. the fact that larger numbers contain smaller numbers.

▶ Being unable to subitise (see at a glance) even very small quantities.

▶ Being unable to recall simple number facts and number bonds reliably.

▶ Feeling constantly muddled about whether adding involves counting numbers, or the steps (intervals) between numbers.

▶ Falling into the 'counting trap', by relying far too much on counting in ones, with each unnecessary step putting more pressure on working memory and providing more opportunities to make mistakes.

▶ Using such inefficient calculation methods that number facts cannot lodge in long-term memory.

How to help

▶ Give pupils plenty of time at the early stages before moving on. Revisit basic activities often.

▶ Use appropriate concrete materials that will help build cognitive models.

▶ Let the pupils manipulate the concrete materials. Do not monopolise them yourself or use them only for demonstrations.

▶ Start by doing something concretely, before recording the maths in writing. Too often the reverse occurs, when manipulatives are used only to illustrate what a written calculation means.

▶ Bear in mind that work with concrete materials should come before diagrams, and that pictures and diagrams are invaluable during the important transitional stage between concrete and abstract work.

▶ Be explicit about what is happening at every step. Ask questions and encourage a lot of talk.

▶ Set up lots of opportunities to count, beginning at different starting points. Use actual objects for counting, especially for counting backwards, before progressing to more abstract counting.

▶ Give plenty of experience in exploring the individual numbers up to 10. Use both discrete and continuous concrete materials: counters, bead strings and Cuisenaire rods.

▶ Teach one 'key' fact about each of the numbers up to 10, a fact that the learner can get to know so well that it will provide a secure foundation from which to derive any other fact about that number through logic and reasoning.

▶ Play games that actually teach the points you want the pupils to learn. Send games home for homework sometimes instead of worksheets.

▶ Teach component work in a way that reinforces the connection between addition and subtraction.

▶ Explain to pupils that learning about components is what will help them overcome the need to rely on inefficient counting methods.

▶ Break topics down into the smallest of steps, e.g. teach plus or minus 1 before plus or minus 2.

▶ Minimise the number of facts that have to be known by heart.

▶ Minimise the number of strategies that a pupil must know. Even if you demonstrate or explain several different strategies, allow each pupil to choose only one or two to practise.

▶ Teach explicitly how to reason from known or given facts.

▶ Vary the mathematical vocabulary, e.g. use 'subtract', 'less than', 'decrease' or 'minus', as well as 'take away'.

▶ Show pupils how to identify what kinds of problems can be solved by each new strategy.

▶ Locate number problems in real situations that have meaning for the pupil, e.g. 'two more toys' rather than the abstract 'two more', or the unimaginable 'two more metres per second'.

▶ Allow informal jottings before teaching standard written notation.

▶ Have pupils make up their own number problems and their own word problems.

Activity

Make dot patterns for the numbers 1 to 10

Give pupils a pile of chunky, attractive and easy to handle objects such as glass nuggets, plastic counters or buttons. The objects should be of roughly the same size and colour as each other. Let pupils practise making and reading dot patterns for all the numbers from 1 to 10. This activity, together with the subsequent activities that encourage children to create, name, alter and rearrange dot patterns concretely (and to explore Cuisenaire rods in later activities and games) is designed to help children develop a better idea of numerical magnitude and a stronger sense of the numerical quantity represented by each of the numerals up to 10.

The patterns for the first six numbers are those found on dice, with which most children are already familiar. Children who do not recognise these patterns should be encouraged to play board games with dice at home. The numbers 7 to 10 are not standardised in the same way. I like to use the patterns proposed by Dorian Yeo in her book *Dyslexia, Dyspraxia & Mathematics*. Unlike most of the patterns found on playing cards and dominoes, Yeo's patterns are based on doubles and near-doubles and therefore illustrate a key fact about each number, from which other facts can be derived.

Traditional dice patterns for the numbers 1 to 6 and patterns showing the doubles and near-doubles facts for the numbers 7 to 10.

An early activity might be to transfer a given number of items from a number track onto an extra large dot pattern card (see CW) ⇱ and back again. The number track should be made of ten distinct areas all of the same size (squares are traditional, but you might like to draw circles that match the size of your nuggets or counters) arranged side by side in a single line. Instead of using a numbered track, I recommend using a blank track with the first five areas shaded a slightly different colour to the next five, so that the groups of five make a clear visual impact (see CW) ⇱. I borrowed this idea from the colour changes on a Slavonic abacus and find that it significantly helps to minimise the need for counting.

On a number track with Slavonic shading,
we can see there are 7 items, without any need to count them.

After inviting a child to make the dot pattern for a particular number, e.g. the number 9, ask as varied a set of questions as you can about the key components. Start with more descriptive language before making your question purely abstract. For example: *What must you add to the pattern of 5 if you want to make 9? If we take away the pattern of 5 from the pattern of 9, what is left? If I have a pattern of 5 and you have a pattern of 9, how many more dots do you have than I have? I have 5 and you have 9, so how much more than me do you have? Four and 5 more is what? Four and what number makes 9? Four add what is 9?* etc.

Next, hide the pattern and ask the same kinds of questions about the key fact.

I regularly remind my pupils that the doubles and near-doubles patterns show a key fact about the numbers up to 10. Frequent use of the label 'key fact' emphasises to pupils that they only need to be absolutely certain about one fact for each number. From this single key fact, all the other facts that might be needed can be derived by logical processes.

The aim is that, with enough practical experience followed by enough practice in visualising the dot pattern, any number up to 10 will automatically trigger a clear and visual pattern in the learner's mind that can be comprehended as a whole, rather than as a collection of ones that have to be counted. Once this stage has been achieved, children can begin to use logic and reasoning to derive new facts. For example, a child who 'sees' the number 8 as two groups of 4 can readily 'calculate' that $4 + 5$ must be 9 or that $8 - 4$ must be 4.

At later sessions, give pupils squared paper on which to make the dot patterns using small round stickers. Keep these activities going, using both concrete and diagrammatic representations, until pupils can answer any kind of question about the key facts, i.e. the double or near-double combination of components, for all the numbers up to 10 without hesitation and without having to make or look at the number patterns first.

Dot patterns for making cards are provided on the CW ⌖, including a set of extra large cards on which pupils can work concretely with nuggets or counters. Some activities to help children learn the doubles and near-doubles dot patterns can be found in Yeo's book *Dyslexia, Dyspraxia & Mathematics*, and three of her ideas for games are summarised on the back of the cut-out card box that is provided on the CW ⌖. A whole book full of activities and games (a few of which are presented below) together with numerous demonstration videos can be found in my ebook *Exploring Numbers Through Dot Patterns*. Activities based on dot patterns can either precede an introduction to Cuisenaire rods, or be carried out alongside work with Cuisenaire rods, depending on the needs and preferences of the individual learner.

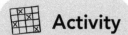 **Activity**

Make transparent dot pattern cards for the numbers 1 to 5

Cut out card-shaped rectangles from stiff transparent plastic. Good sources are the sheets used with overhead projectors or laminating pouches with nothing enclosed before being heated in a laminator. Provide small circular stickers. Depending on the child in question, you may choose to provide stickers all of one colour, or of six different colours so that the six number patterns can be more easily distinguished. Provide a template of the dot pattern for the number 5 to slip behind each transparent card while it is being made, so that the child can space the stickers evenly and consistently while making cards for the numbers up to 5.

Please note that, although it does not usually matter whether the numbers 2 and 3 are portrayed in a straight or a diagonal line, for this activity it is essential to make both patterns lie along diagonal lines and for the diagonals for each number to be in opposite directions. This is so that superimposing a card for the number 3 on top of a card for the number 2 makes the pattern of 5 appear, as if by magic. In just the same way, superimposing cards for 1 and 4 show the other way of creating 5 and superimposing cards for 1 and 2 create the linear pattern for 3.

This activity directs children's attention to the relationship between 5 and the whole numbers up to 5, reinforcing the fact that 5 can be built of, or split into, two components in only two ways (2 and 3, 4 and 1) and the fact that there is only one way to create or split the number 3 (2 and 1). Separating the pairs of superimposed cards is a good way of seeing subtraction in action and one way of reinforcing the connection between addition and subtraction.

If you have access to a laminator, you can make a more permanent set of transparent cards by arranging small round stickers into dot patterns inside the pouches before heating them. Depending on their size, several cards can be made from a single laminated sheet. A set of four small cards of each of the numbers 1 to 4 and one card for the number 5 will create a pack of transparent playing cards for the game 'Make 5' below.

Game

Make 5

A game for two players.

Teaching points:

▶ The game teaches children to split and recombine small numbers up to 5.

▶ It teaches that larger numbers contain smaller numbers within them.

▶ It teaches that there are only two different ways to build 5 from whole numbers: 1 + 4 or 2 + 3.

▶ It teaches the commutative property of addition, i.e. that 1 + 4 is equal to 4 + 1.

Equipment needed:

▶ A game board for each player (see CW, or sketch your own boards).

▶ A pack of 17 cards, made up of four cards each of the numbers 1–4 and one card of the number 5. Use dot pattern cards for younger players (the transparent cards from the preceding activity are ideal for the first few games) and digit cards with more experienced players.

Make 5

RULES **Make 5** is a game for two players, each with their own game board. The game needs a pack of 17 cards (made up of four each of the numbers 1 – 4 and one card for 5).

Each player puts three cards, face up, on the empty boxes on the board. The rest of the pack is put face down in the middle of the table.

On your turn, try to 'make 5' out of two of your three cards. If you have the card for 5, or if two cards add up to 5, put them on the **Make 5** box, before filling up the spaces on your board so that three cards are ready for your next turn. If you can't **make 5**, pick up a card from the top of the pile and pair it with one of your three cards to make 5 if you can, or put it back at the bottom of the pile if you can't use it. When the pack is used up, count the cards on each player's **Make 5** box to find the winner.

Make 5

© Ronit Bird

Rules:

Each player puts three cards, face up, on the empty boxes on the board. The rest of the pack is put face down in the middle of the table. On your turn try to 'make 5' out of two of your three cards.

(Continued)

(Continued)

If you have the card showing 5, or have two cards that add up to 5, put them on the Make 5 box. Then fill up the spaces on your board so that there are three cards face up, ready for your next turn. If you can't make 5, use your turn to pick up a card from the top of the pile and pair it with one of your three cards, or put it back at the bottom of the pile if you can't use it. When the cards are used up, count the cards on each player's Make 5 box to find the winner.

Tips:

Allow pupils to use their fingers, or counters, or a bead string of five large beads (all of the same colour) until they realise there are only two ways of making 5. If they do not realise on their own after playing the game more than once, tell them and then challenge them to play the game without fingers or other counting aids. The single card for 5 is introduced into the pack because otherwise the game would too often end in a draw. Alternatively, use a pack made of the numbers 1–4 but with an odd number of cards.

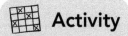 **Activity**

Explore smaller numbers inside larger numbers

Use large dot pattern cards for the numbers 1 to 6, and at a later stage for the numbers up to 10, so that the circles representing the dots are the same size as counters or nuggets (see CW). Have the child throw a die and explore how many different places that exact pattern can be recreated by placing nuggets onto the cards. For example, a throw of 1 can be copied in any position on any card, a throw of 2 can be matched on any card except the 1, whilst a pattern of 5 can be found only in the pattern for 5 and by extension the two larger numbers that contain a pattern of 5, namely 9 and 10. You can also encourage children to reverse their point of view by analysing one card at a time to see what smaller number patterns they can find. For example, inside the pattern for 6 one can find two 3s, three 2s, or a 4 and a 2.

You can follow up this activity by playing a game that targets the same teaching points, one version of which is provided below. (A slightly different version of the same game, together with a demonstration video, can be found in my ebook *Exploring Numbers Through Dot Patterns*.)

Game

Numbers Inside

A game for two players.

Teaching points:

▶ Playing the game forces players to notice the individual characteristics of the number patterns up to 6, and to distinguish between quantity and pattern (e.g. three dots or nuggets arranged in any configuration can represent the number 3, but they must be arranged in a straight line in order to represent the dice pattern for 3).

▶ The game gives practice in seeing how larger numbers can be built from the smaller components 1, 2 or 3 (a whole-to-parts approach).

▶ The game gives practice in looking for the smaller numbers 1, 2 or 3 and their patterns, within a larger quantity (a part-to-whole approach).

▶ The game helps make a connection between addition and subtraction.

Equipment needed:

▶ A set of extra large dot pattern cards for the numbers 1 to 6 for each player (see CW).

▶ Nuggets or counters to match the size of the circles on the cards.

▶ A 1–2–3 die. (Or, cover the three larger numbers on an ordinary die with stickers for 1, 2 and 3.)

Rules:

Each player shuffles their six cards before discarding two at random and turning over the remaining four cards to create a game board.

Take turns to throw the die and take the same number of nuggets. You may use the nuggets to cover a pattern that exactly matches the dice pattern, on any one card. For example, if you throw a 3, you can cover all the circles on the card for 3, or half the circles on the card for 6, or the diagonal line in the pattern for 5, but nothing else. This is because the rules of this game require players to match the dice pattern of 3, namely three dots in a row, an arrangement of dots that can be seen in 3, 5 and 6, but not 4 (and obviously not in 1 or 2). By contrast, if you throw a 1, you can put the single nugget anywhere at all; however, if you were to put it on a pattern of 4, for example, you would only be able to complete the pattern by throwing 2 and 1, or by throwing 1 three times, on subsequent turns.

Continue taking turns. Pass on your turn if you are unable to find a matching pattern of empty circles. The winner is the first player to completely cover any three of their four cards.

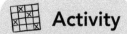 **Activity**

Change one dot pattern into another

Like the activity and game above, focusing on changing one dot pattern into another is primarily about learning to notice smaller numbers inside larger numbers. It is true that this activity is also about adding and subtracting the small quantities 1 and 2, but at this early stage I would avoid the words 'plus' or 'minus' or any suggestion that this is an activity that requires any calculation.

Hand the pupil one nugget at a time and explain that the challenge is to create the dot patterns – the same patterns that show the key facts and that have already been explored and learned in earlier activities – whilst moving as few nuggets as possible. In other words, when the pattern of 2 is on the table, and the pupil is given a new nugget and told to create a new pattern, the third nugget should be placed so as to create a single line of three without any rearranging of the nuggets comprising the previous pattern. The fact that the same two items contribute both to a quantity of 2 and to a quantity of 3 demonstrates the fixed relationship between the two amounts and highlights the general fact that every quantity contains lesser quantities within it. This is an important realisation for a pupil who may know that 'three' is the number word to use after 'two' while counting, but who still feels the need to count all the items from scratch when combining two small quantities, even when both quantities have already been counted in separate groups.

The activity of adding one nugget at a time, without starting to create a number pattern from scratch each time, forces pupils to notice that, for example, 4 is contained within all the larger numbers because the square pattern of 4 remains unchanged on the table through all the changes in the patterns for the numbers between 4 and 10. Make sure that there is no counting in ones during the whole of this activity and encourage plenty of talk, including the naming of each new pattern that is created.

Once 10 is reached, ask the pupil to remove one nugget at a time from each pattern, creating all the numbers from 10 down to 1 in turn, again focusing on minimising the amount of reorganisation necessary and talking about what is happening at every stage.

During a later session, ask the pupil to alter the dot patterns by first adding, then taking away, two nuggets at a time, starting sometimes from the pattern for 2 and sometimes from the pattern for 1, working up to 10 or 9, and then back down again. This helps pupils to see how regular and logical the patterns for all the even numbers are, how distinctive and unusual is the pattern for 7 (which is what makes it so popular and easy to memorise) and how there is a difference of two between every successive even number and between every successive odd number.

This activity also helps pupils to realise that the concrete, and visually memorable, dot patterns are immutable facts about each number between 1 and 10. In other words, pupils may need to discover for themselves that not only is the distinctive pattern for, say, 5 always made of exactly 5 items, but that it is impossible to create one of the other distinctive patterns for the numbers up to 10 out of exactly 5 items.

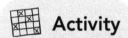 **Activity**

Change dot patterns by adding or subtracting

The activity detailed above can be revisited at a later stage when the pupil is ready to think about adding and subtracting 1 or 2. As a warm-up, pupils can simply repeat the same activity while adapting the accompanying talk. For example, whereas previously they might have said, *I had a 4 and now I am creating a 5 by putting one nugget in the middle*, at this stage pupils can be encouraged to say, *4 plus 1 more makes 5.*

The activity is made more challenging by taking numbers out of order as well as focusing on the operations of addition and subtraction. Using a die to generate random numbers up to 6, or digit cards to generate numbers up to 10, have pupils take a matching number of nuggets and create the dot pattern for that number. The teacher now directs the pupil to change the pattern into the pattern for a number that is only 1 or 2 more or less, for example to change an 8 into a 6. The pupil must say in advance what has to change, e.g. *I will have to take 2 away from the 8 to make 6*, before actually carrying out the operation to check that what was said is correct. As in the earlier activity, insist that the pupil maintains the discipline of minimising the physical rearrangement of the nuggets between one pattern and the next.

To extend this activity even further, begin to work towards a pictorial way of thinking about and recording the dot patterns for the numbers up to 10, with a view to moving towards an understanding of abstract calculation and standard notation. A useful exercise that can contribute to the transition between concrete and abstract work at this level is supported by an activity sheet about changing one dot pattern into another (see CW).

Activity

Use dot patterns to explore the idea of odd and even

The dot patterns for the numbers 1 to 10 that show the key component facts, based on the doubles and near-doubles facts about each number, are ideal for exploring what the terms 'odd' and 'even' actually mean. Pupils can make any of the dot patterns out of nuggets or counters and physically rearrange the items into pairs in order to discover whether there will be an 'odd one out' at the end. Another useful exercise is to move counters in pairs on and off a number track, preferably a track with Slavonic shading to minimise the need to count (see CW). A more sophisticated understanding of symmetrical patterns would be to recognise that in any pattern created by doubling a discrete number of items, each item can be paired with its own reflection, and that therefore the total quantity must be an even number. Focusing on the key facts of the numbers up to 10 provides a two-way reinforcement: the numbers 2, 4, 6, 8 and 10 can be represented by doubles patterns because they are even, and are even because their key fact is a doubles fact; the numbers 1, 3, 5, 7 and 9 cannot be created out of a doubles pattern but instead must be created out of a near-double pattern, because they are odd numbers, and vice versa.

Game

Collect 5s

A game for two players that is slightly more demanding than the related board game 'Make 5' above. You can find a short demonstration video of this game on the CW.

Teaching points:

▶ The game gives practice in adding numbers up to 4 + 4.

▶ It teaches the commutative property of addition, i.e. that 1 + 4 is equal to 4 + 1.

▶ It gives practice in using logic, rather than counting in ones, to find totals up to 8.

▶ It teaches that there are only two different ways to build 5 from two whole numbers: 1 + 4 or 2 + 3.

Equipment needed:

▶ A game board for each player on which five dot patterns of 5 are drawn so that each circular dot can accommodate a counter or nugget (see CW, or sketch your own boards).

▶ Counters or nuggets in two colours, matching the size of the circles on the game board.

▶ Two dice, altered (using stickers) so that the 5 and 6 on both dice are replaced by a 1 and a 4 on one die and by a 2 and a 3 on the other die.

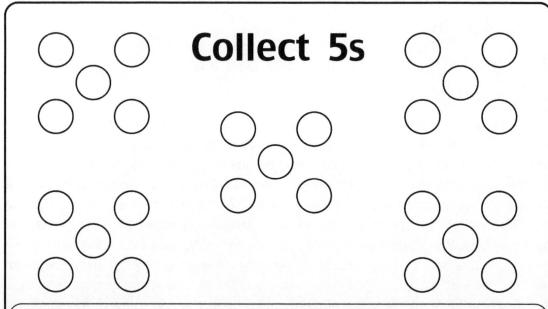

RULES **Collect 5s** is a game for two players, each with their own game board. You will need nuggets in two colours and two 6-sided dice on which the 5s and 6s have been replaced with a 1 and a 4 on one die, and a 2 and a 3 on the other die.

Take turns to throw both dice and announce the total. If the total is 5, take one colour of nuggets to match one die throw and the other colour to match the other die throw. Cover one of your spot patterns as follows: if one component is 3 the three nuggets must be arranged as a diagonal; if one component is 4 they are arranged as a square. The winner is the first to cover all five patterns.

Rules:

Take turns to throw both dice and announce the total. This total must be found without any counting in ones: having tried the activities detailed earlier in this chapter, pupils should now know what is 1 more or 2 more than a number, and they should also know 3 + 3, 3 + 4 and 4 + 4 because these are the key facts about 6, 7 and 8 respectively. If the total of both dice is any number other than 5, play passes to the next player. If your total is 5, take nuggets of one colour to match one die throw and nuggets of the other colour to match the other die throw, and arrange all 5 nuggets on top of one of the patterns of 5 on your game board, as follows: if one component is 3 arrange the three nuggets in a diagonal line and if one component is 4 arrange the nuggets as a square. In other words, the arrangement of colours on the board should be consistent with the dot patterns that have been learned for the numbers 1, 2, 3, 4 and 5 and that are seen on the dice. At the end of the game, each player's game board clearly shows whether each 5 was built of 2 + 3 or 4 + 1. The winner is the first player to cover all five patterns of 5 with nuggets.

Game

Key Components Guessing Game

A game for two players. You can find a short demonstration video of this game on the CW.

Teaching points:

▶ The game gives practice in the key component facts, namely the doubles and near-doubles facts for the numbers up to 10.

▶ The game helps players connect missing number situations to both addition and subtraction.

▶ There is a small element of memory training in this game.

Equipment needed:

▶ A set of dominoes.

▶ 10 counters in two colours, 5 of each colour.

Rules:

From a set of dominoes, players must identify and pick out the nine stones that show the key component facts from 2 to 10. [These are: 1–1, 1–2, 2–2, 2–3, 3–3, 3–4, 4–4, 4–5, 5–5, but do not show this list to the players, and do not be tempted to use prepared domino cards instead: identifying the required combinations is an important part of the learning experience.]

Turn the nine dominoes face down and mix them thoroughly. On your turn, take a single domino at random without letting your opponent see its face. On the table, in full view, arrange counters to recreate the dot pattern you can see on one side of the domino tile. Your opponent must guess which domino you have and complete the dot pattern accordingly, using counters in the other colour, while announcing both the total value of the domino and the two separate component parts. Your opponent wins the domino if the guess is correct; otherwise, you win the domino.

(Continued)

(Continued)

Dominoes that have been won are placed face down in separate winning piles and may not be looked at again by either player. This means that in the later stages of the game, you have more chance of guessing correctly if you can remember which tiles have already been played.

Continue playing until only one domino remains. If there is a clear winner at this stage, this is the end of the game. If there is a draw at this point, carry on playing for one more turn.

Tip:

Because the dominoes revealed at every turn help to inform later guesses, the older or stronger player should take the first turn.

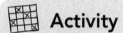 **Activity**

Sort and re-sort a set of dominoes

A standard set of European dominoes has 28 tiles or stones, from double-zero (double-blank) to double-six, with all the numbers up to 6 shown as dot patterns identical to dice patterns. This makes dominoes ideal for reinforcing various dot pattern activities that focus on components and on relationships between numbers.

This activity gives a child useful practice in switching focus between components that combine to make a larger number, and the total value resulting from two components having been combined. This shift in focus, sometimes looking at the relationship of the parts to the whole and sometimes from the whole to component parts, is very similar to the kind of thinking required to connect the concept of addition with the concept of subtraction.

Remove the double-zero (double-blank) and the two dominoes with a value of more than 10 (6–5 and 6–6). Have the pupil arrange the remaining dominoes in order, so that there is one row containing all the dominoes that feature a pattern of 1 on one side, another row containing all the dominoes that feature a pattern of 2 (this row will be one domino shorter, since the 1–2 has already been used), etc. Within each row, the dominoes should be arranged in order, with the same logic used for ordering the tiles in each row (i.e. all rows increasing from left to right, or from bottom to top).

Once all the dominoes are in ordered rows, have the pupil rearrange them into ten piles by picking out all the dominoes with a total value of 1, then of 2, and so on up to 10.

The final challenge is to take one of the piles at random and ask the child to use logic to work out what the domino faces show. For example, seeing that there are three dominoes in the pile with a total value of 7, the child must work out that the only ways of making 7 out of the numbers 1 to 6 are 1 + 6, 2 + 5 and 3 + 4. Children may not count on their fingers in response to this challenge. If they are inclined to do so, try the next activity before returning to this one on another occasion. Repeat the challenge with the other domino piles.

An activity sheet to support this sorting and re-sorting activity is provided on the CW.

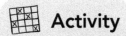 **Activity**

Connect subtraction to addition

Although many of the earlier activities have made connections between addition and subtraction, this activity has no function other than to make children notice the relationship between the operations. This is particularly important for the many children who have been told that addition and subtraction are related, but who have never really understood how, because they have never made the connection at the concrete level. Such children often arrange the trio of numbers belonging to 'a family of facts' randomly and might easily say that, for example, *Three minus six is three* without realising that there is anything wrong with such a statement.

Start by picking an even number, no greater than 10, and have the child make the dot pattern using nuggets or counters. The child has to say the key fact, aloud, expressed as addition. Next, the child removes one of the components and explains what is happening in terms of subtraction. For example, if the chosen number is 6, the child takes 6 nuggets and arranges them into the dice pattern of 6, saying, *Six is built of 3 and 3*, or *Six is made of two 3s*, or *Double 3 is 6*, or *The key fact about 6 is 3 plus 3*. Then, putting a hand over one side of the pattern so that 3 nuggets can be slowly removed in a single motion, the child must say *Six, take away 3, leaves 3*, or *Six minus 3 is 3*.

Repeat the activity with odd numbers, for which there will be two possible subtractions to perform and to describe in words. You can ask the child to model both, or to take away the larger component first to leave the smaller answer, or vice versa, or to subtract what is needed to create whichever answer the teacher requests.

The activity should be repeated as often as necessary, until the child internalises the fact that, if a quantity is built of two components, when one is removed the other remains. There will be more practice of this concept when the child begins to use Cuisenaire rods (later in this section).

This activity can be repeated at the pictorial or diagrammatic level by using a pack of dot pattern cards (see CW). The child reads each card by announcing its total value and the key fact for that number, before using one hand to cover up one of the two components and expressing the key fact as subtraction.

The game 'Post-It Note Subtraction' provides further practice of expressing the key facts as subtraction.

For practice at the pictorial level that is not restricted to the key facts, repeat the activity using a set of dominoes, from which any tiles featuring blanks have been removed, instead of dot pattern cards.

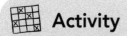 **Activity**

Regroup: Apply logic to find new component facts from given facts

From a set of dominoes, take the stones that show the key components, i.e. the doubles and near-doubles facts, for the numbers up to 10. Provide pupils with nuggets or large counters and a piece of paper on which is drawn a large rectangle split into two squares, to represent a large blank domino. Each of the two squares must be big enough to accommodate nuggets arranged in the dot patterns of the numbers 1 to 6.

Have the child place nuggets on the paper rectangle to copy one domino at a time. The child should read out the two components, and the combined value of both components, before moving one nugget from one side of the rectangle to the other, rearranging the nuggets into the recognised dot patterns if necessary. The child now reads the new arrangement of nuggets as a new way of building the same number out of two components.

This regrouping activity is the basis for a powerful reasoning strategy that allows children to derive new facts from known facts. It is therefore worth practising often, at the concrete stage, as described in this activity. For more about regrouping see the chapter called 'Regrouping: step-by-step' and watch the demonstration videos embedded into Chapter 10 in my ebook *Exploring Numbers Through Dot Patterns*. After enough practical exploration, remove the nuggets and paper and ask the child to imagine one dot moving from one side of a domino to the other, to produce a new pair of components with the same total value as the original domino.

Repeat the exercise with dominoes that do not necessarily show the key component facts. Start at the concrete level again if the child needs to do so, but make sure the focus of the activity is not on finding an answer mechanically but on giving the pupil enough practice in visualising the dot patterns and visualising movement between successive patterns. In the next section of this book you will find a game called 'Regroup' in which players practise the regrouping reasoning strategy by visualising dots moving from one pattern to another. (The game is located in Section 2 because it extends to numbers greater than 10.)

⊞ Activities

Become familiar with Cuisenaire rods

Cuisenaire rods provide an excellent concrete continuous resource for exploring the numbers up to 10. Their great advantage is that their physical size can be seen, or found – by measuring against other rods – without counting. They are deliberately designed to be identified by length, with the individual colours contributing to easy recognition. Do not be tempted to label them with numbers or to divide their lengths visibly into 'ones'.

Pupils must be given time to become familiar with the rods and their colours and relative sizes before using them as mathematical models. Many useful activities can be found in Professor Sharma's *Cuisenaire Rods and Mathematics Teaching* and a whole book full of ideas for activities and games, together with demonstration videos embedded into every chapter, can be found in my ebook *Exploring Numbers Through Cuisenaire Rods*.

Some of my favourite activities are summarised here. See also my leaflet, *Some things you can do with your Cuisenaire rods* which can be downloaded from the CW. ⌖

Encourage a lot of talk during all these activities.

1. Build a staircase, flat on the table or in the lid of the rods' box. Practise building it quickly, sometimes starting with the longest rod (orange) and sometimes with the shortest rod (white).

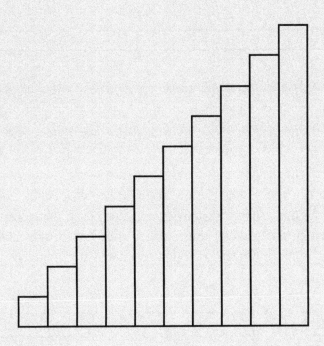

2. Match the numbers to the colours. Learn to recite the colours: white, red, light green, purple (or pink), yellow, dark green, black, brown, blue, orange. Pick out a rod at random and say its number, first with the help of the staircase and later with the staircase hidden. Say the colour and the number of the rod that is one bigger, or one smaller, than a rod picked at random.

(Continued)

(Continued)

3. Make flat patterns. Later, record the patterns with coloured pencils on 1 cm squared paper (see CW). Challenge pupils to recreate patterns that you or other pupils have made or have recorded on paper.

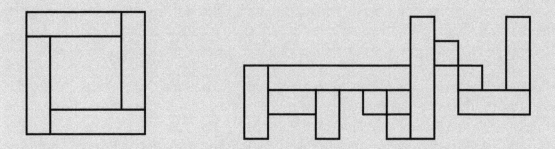

4. Make sequences. Challenge pupils to say which rod comes next in the sequence. Take one rod from a sequence while a pupil is not looking and close the gap. You can do this also for the staircase sequence. Challenge the pupil to name the missing rod and show its position in the sequence.

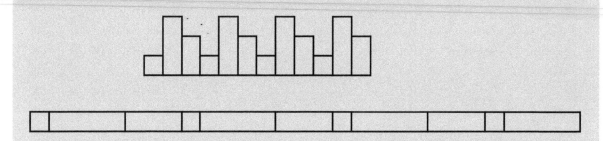

5. Explore relative sizes. Pick up a rod at random and ask the child to find a rod that is larger. Encourage pupils to notice that there is (usually) more than one right answer to this question. Next, ask for the rod that is only just, or one step, larger. This time there is only one right answer. Sometimes ask for a rod that is smaller than a chosen rod, or for a rod that is smaller by one.

6. Find one rod that is equal in length to two others, and vice versa. Put any two rods end to end and have the pupil first guess or estimate, and then measure, which single rod is equal in length. Next, put any two rods side by side, sometimes aligned at the left and sometimes at the right, and have the pupil estimate, then measure, which rod exactly fills the gap.

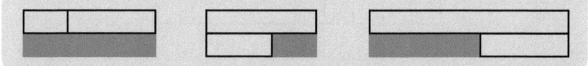

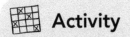 **Activity**

Explore odd and even with Cuisenaire rods and with money

Give pupils the task of measuring every rod against white rods (ones) and discussing what they find. They will, of course, find that every length of rod can be measured in ones, and that the number of units each rod is worth is also its position in the counting sequence.

Next, have pupils experiment to find which rods can be measured exactly using red rods (2s) only.

Provide heaps of 1p and 2p coins (or 1 cent and 2 cent coins). Have pupils make different amounts, up to 10, in different ways, as in the example above. Next, challenge pupils to make as many of these amounts as is possible using 2p (or 2 cent) coins only.

Get children to articulate what they now understand about the words 'odd' and 'even'.

By focusing on the fact that 10 is – and always will be – even, you can extend this activity by using the rods and the coins to explain how to determine which larger numbers are odd and which are even.

Game

Odd and Even Collectors

A game for two players.

Teaching points:

▶ The game teaches children to recognise odd and even numbers up to 10.

▶ It teaches that a fair die is as likely to produce an even throw as an odd throw.

▶ At the scoring stage, it gives practice in exchanging and counting up small numbers.

Equipment needed:

▶ Cuisenaire rods.

▶ A 1–10 die or spinner.

Rules:

At the start of the game, determine which player will collect the even numbers, and which the odd numbers. The player collecting the odd numbers starts by getting an orange 10-rod (to compensate for the fact that the even numbers on a die are worth more than the odd numbers). Players then take turns to throw the die and to pick up a Cuisenaire rod to match the throw. The rod is then either kept by that player or awarded to the opponent, depending on who is collecting the odd/even numbers. After three rounds (a total of six throws), players find who is the winner by exchanging their smaller rods for orange rods wherever possible, and then counting up the total amount in their collections.

Tips:

The exchange at the end of the game is harder for the player collecting odd numbers, so make sure this is not always the same person. Confusion can often result at the exchange and counting-up stage. Until pupils have had plenty of practice, it is therefore best if the teacher takes the role of banker and supervises each exchange, amidst lots of talk about what is happening.

Variation 1:

Use money instead of rods, allowing the children to collect 1p and 2p coins (or 1 cent and 2 cent coins), and to exchange them for 10p coins (or 10 cent coins) at the counting-up stage. The odd collector should get a 10p (or a 10 cent) coin to start the game. Real money, rather than plastic or cardboard, makes the game more exciting.

Variation 2:

Keep the rods or coins only if you are the collector of odd numbers and throw an odd number, or are the collector of even numbers when you throw an even number on your turn. In this variation the odd collector gets an extra turn, instead of being given the 10-rod or a 10p (or a 10 cent) coin at the start, by being both first and last to throw the die. A game in this variation consists of seven throws.

Game

Draw Your Race on a Number Line

A game for two or more players.

Teaching points:

▶ The game teaches children the relationship between a number track (where each number is represented by a physical area and where progress is made by counting whole numbers) and the more abstract number line (where each number is represented by a position on a line and where progress is made by counting the steps between whole numbers).

▶ The game teaches how to use an empty number line, and to understand what a number line represents.

▶ It gives practice in adding small quantities: +1, +2 and +3.

Equipment needed:

▶ A paper copy of the board for each player (see CW).

▶ A pencil and a token for each player.

▶ A 1–3 die (or, cover the three larger numbers on an ordinary die with stickers showing 1, 2 and 3).

Rules:

Take turns to throw the die and move your token along the track. Then draw the whole jump on your number line. Write how big the jump is (above the jump) and what number you

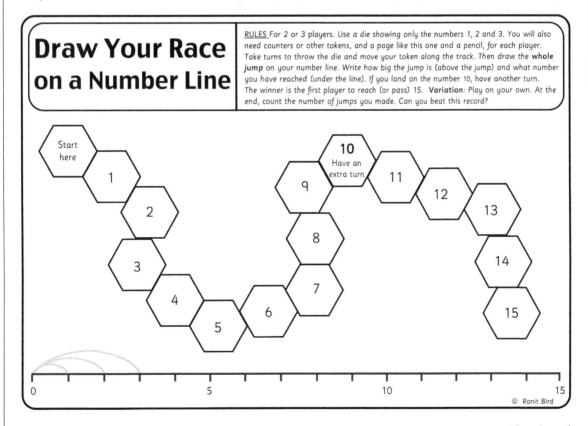

Draw Your Race on a Number Line

RULES For 2 or 3 players. Use a die showing only the numbers 1, 2 and 3. You will also need counters or other tokens, and a page like this one and a pencil, for each player. Take turns to throw the die and move your token along the track. Then draw the **whole jump** on your number line. Write how big the jump is (above the jump) and what number you have reached (under the line). If you land on the number 10, have another turn. The winner is the first player to reach (or pass) 15. **Variation:** Play on your own. At the end, count the number of jumps you made. Can you beat this record?

© Ronit Bird

(Continued)

(Continued)

have reached (under the line). If you land on the round number 10, have another turn. The winner is the first player to reach (or pass) 15.

Tips:

Use this game to teach the conventions of number lines: that the movements along the line are shown as jumps drawn above the line and are labelled with the size of the jump, while the position on the number line is shown by a small perpendicular mark on the line together with a number below the line. A very useful activity at the end of the game is for each child to recreate their moves by looking at their drawn jumps. For example: *First I threw a two and landed on 2, then I threw a one and got to 3,* etc.

Variation:

This can be played as a solitaire game, aiming for the fewest throws of the die.

 Activities

Use Cuisenaire rods to learn all components of the numbers 1–10

1. Start with the key facts of a number, which are the double or near-double components. Pupils should already be familiar with these from their earlier work with dot patterns. For example, the key components of 8 are 4 and 4; the key components of 9 are 4 and 5 (or 5 and 4). Remind pupils that they know these facts and challenge them to use the rods to demonstrate that the facts are true.

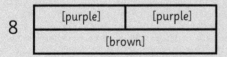
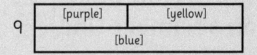

2. Take two rods of the same colour and sandwich a smaller rod between them, aligning them sometimes at the left and sometimes at the right. Have the pupil first guess, and then measure, which single rod exactly fills the gap.

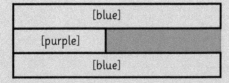
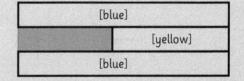

3. Explore each number in turn, finding all the components and asking lots of questions, varying the vocabulary you use. If you challenge pupils to find as many ways of making 7 as they can, you might find one pupil offering a combination such as red, red and light green, while another offers the same combination in a different order, such as red, light green and red. This is an opportunity to discuss with pupils whether these solutions are the same, and to explore with them how combinations that are not identical may still have equal values.

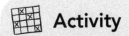 **Activity**

Make a 'Story' of a number

Have pupils set out, in a logical sequence, all the ways of making a number out of two components, for example the 'Story of 7' as shown below.

Start with the key fact (i.e. the double or near-double fact) and ask the child to add one complete row, namely two Cuisenaire rods, at a time. Make sure the arrangement of the rods is consistent from row to row (i.e. insist that the child keeps to the same decision about positioning the rods that increase in size either at the left or at the right) so that a zig-zag pattern is created along one diagonal of the rectangle of rods. This distinctive zig-zag makes visible the important fact that, as soon as the size of one of the components gets bigger by one, the other component must become one smaller to compensate, and vice versa. This is the same logic that we used during the regrouping activity with dot patterns.

The reasoning process depends on an understanding of the conservation of number and also on understanding that addition is commutative. Both these important concepts are strengthened by children carrying out this activity often, focusing on different numbers on different occasions.

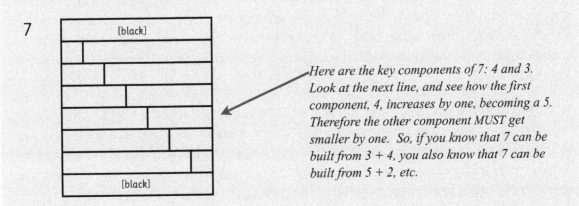

7

Here are the key components of 7: 4 and 3. Look at the next line, and see how the first component, 4, increases by one, becoming a 5. Therefore the other component MUST get smaller by one. So, if you know that 7 can be built from 3 + 4, you also know that 7 can be built from 5 + 2, etc.

Once the Story has been built, the rods can be pulled apart so that there is a visible gap between each pair of components. This reinforces the fact that if we know how to build a number out of two components, for addition, we also know how to split the number into two components, for subtraction.

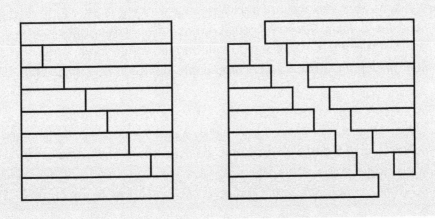

Game

Race to Tell a Story

A game for two or three players.

Teaching points:

▶ The game gives practice in building numbers out of pairs of components, in all possible ways.

▶ Each game explores two adjacent numbers in the counting sequence, in relation to each other.

▶ The game reinforces the connection between addition, subtraction, and missing numbers.

Equipment needed:

▶ A paper game board of rod outlines for two numbers, drawn by each player (see CW for 1 cm squared paper).

▶ Cuisenaire rods.

▶ A 1–6 die, for target numbers up to 7. A spinner for larger target numbers (see variations).

Rules:

Start by deciding which two consecutive counting numbers to target: e.g. 5 and 6, or 6 and 7 (or see variations). Players prepare their own game board by drawing outlines of the Story of both target numbers. In the illustration, you can see a game set up to target the numbers 6 and 7.

Take turns to throw the die, or spin the spinner. Take a single rod to match and put it on your board on top of an outline of the same size. (Try not to count the squares: instead, use the rod in your hand to measure the size.) Once a rod has been placed, it cannot be moved. As soon as you have covered all the outlines of a particular length, you will have to miss any turn on which you throw or spin the same number again.

The winner is the player with four consecutive rows of rods, on either one of the Story outlines. The single rod at the top or bottom of a Story may count as one of the four rows (but remember that the largest available rod is 6 if you are playing with an ordinary die). No row may be covered by more than two rods.

The winner 'tells the Story' by reading aloud the four winning facts, e.g. *1 and 6 is 7, 2 plus 5 makes 7, 3 add 4 is 7, 4 plus 3 equals 7*. Read the rods from left to right so that if your winning rows include the same fact twice, you will be reading the components in a different order. The other player(s) read aloud any completed rows they have made on their board(s).

Variations:

Choose two larger adjacent numbers, i.e. 7 and 8, 8 and 9, or 9 and 10, as target numbers. Use a spinner, instead of a die, with a spinner base split into eight equal sections showing numbers adapted to your chosen targets as follows: for targets of 7 and 8 or 8 and 9 write the numbers 1–8 on the spinner base; for targets of 9 and 10 write the numbers 2–9 on the spinner base.

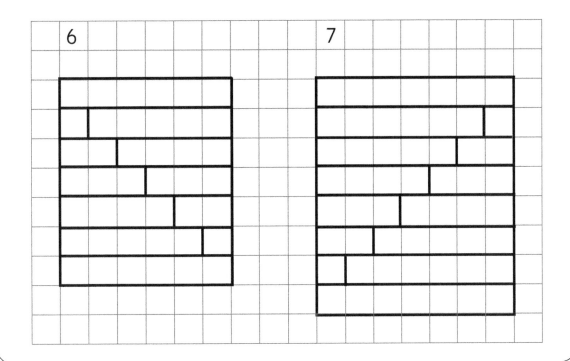

Game

Post-It Note Subtraction

A game for two or three players.

Teaching points:

▶ The game highlights the connection between addition and subtraction.

▶ It focuses on expressing familiar number relationships as subtraction.

▶ The game provides practice in the key component facts (the doubles and near-doubles facts).

Equipment needed:

▶ A game board for each player on which there is room for three subtractions, one for each of the target answers 1, 2 and 3, with space for a small Post-It note on either side of the minus sign (see CW, or sketch your own game boards).

▶ A pack of dot pattern cards (see CW) for the numbers 2–10.

▶ Small Post-It notes (or pieces of card or paper) and a pencil.

Rules:

Take turns to pick up a card from the shuffled pack. On your turn, announce the key component fact about the number on the card, and express it aloud as a subtraction, before writing the answer on a Post-It note. For example, on picking up a card showing 7, say: *The*

(Continued)

43

(Continued)

key components of 7 are 3 and 4, so 7 minus 3 is 4, and write the answer 4 on a Post-It note (or say: *The key components of 7 are 3 and 4, so 7 minus 4 is 3*, and write the answer 3 on a Post-It note). Cover one side of the dot pattern with your hand, to model what you are taking away, as you read the subtraction aloud. Keep the Post-It note anywhere on your board. Return the card to the bottom of the pack.

Whenever you have two numbers with a difference that matches one of the target numbers, 1, 2 or 3, arrange the numbers as a subtraction problem on your game board. You may arrange and rearrange your own Post-It notes as often as you like.

The winner is the first player to use six Post-It notes arranged so as to complete all three subtractions on the board, creating all three target numbers.

Variation:

Use digit cards instead of dot pattern cards, as soon as players know the key components well enough and are able to express the facts in terms of subtraction, without any visual prompts.

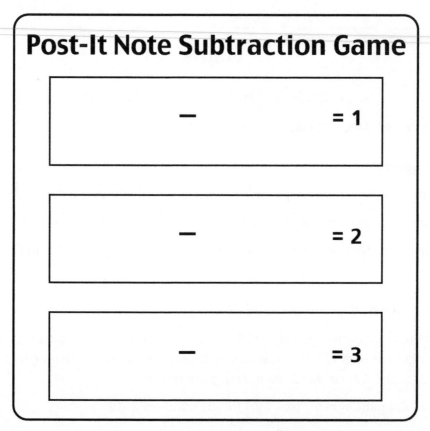

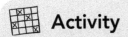 **Activity**

Make and read equations with Cuisenaire rods

This is one of the activities suggested by Professor Sharma in his *Cuisenaire Rods and Mathematics Teaching* booklet.

Put any two rods end to end and have the pupil find a single rod that is the same length. Tell pupils that they have just made an equation. Children love to hear that they have made something so complex. The rods should sometimes be arranged horizontally, sometimes vertically and sometimes diagonally, so that children are clear that it is the equality in terms of length and size that creates an equation, and that the orientation is irrelevant.

The equation can now be read in different ways, both as additions and as subtractions. Model the different ways, pointing to the relevant rod as you say each number, before asking the pupil to do the same. For example:

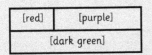   or   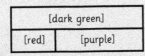   or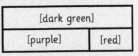

Two and four is six. (Alternate the words 'add', or 'plus' or 'and … more' instead of always using the word 'and'.)

Four and two is six. (Alternate the use of 'is', with 'is the same as', 'equals' or 'makes'.)

Six is equal to two and four.

Six is equal to four add two.

Six minus two is four. (Alternate the use of 'minus' with 'take away' or 'subtract'.)

Six minus four is two.

Activities

Draw and record equations in writing

1. Get the pupils to record the equations they have made in the activity above by drawing on 1 cm squared paper (see CW) ↘ with coloured pencils that match the Cuisenaire rod colours.

2. At later sessions, the original equations can be recreated by putting the rods on top of the coloured drawings. The equations can now be read in the same way as they were in the activity above. The equations can also be read, in the same variety of ways, from the pictures alone.

3. Record the same facts using an informal triad notation, as shown here. The notation reflects what we can see on the rods equation, with one quantity being visibly built out of two smaller quantities. I generally encourage children to insert a plus sign between the two smaller components, but this is only to make sure that the two numbers are separated and cannot be misread as a single 2-digit number. The triad notation has the advantage of showing a whole family of facts at a glance and can be read, just like the rods equations, as both addition and subtraction.

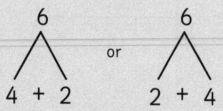

4. Record the equations in the more conventional way, using digits and symbols. Make sure that equations are recorded both as additions and as subtractions, in any order, so as to reinforce the relationship between addition and subtraction. Do not always put the equals sign at the end of the number sentence, otherwise pupils believe that the equals sign means 'now find the answer' instead of actually meaning 'everything on the left of this sign is equal in value to everything on the right of this sign'.

That is, not only:

$$2 + 4 = 6 \qquad 6 - 2 = 4 \qquad 4 + 2 = 6 \qquad 6 - 4 = 2$$

but also:

$$6 = 2 + 4 \qquad 2 = 6 - 4 \qquad 6 = 4 + 2 \qquad 4 = 6 - 2$$

5. Get pupils to turn the equations above into written number problems for other pupils to solve. That means leaving a gap in place of one of the three numbers in the equation. Show pupils how the gap can be left in any position, so long as two numbers are given from which the third can be found.

For example, the first equation above, $2 + 4 = 6$, can be turned into written questions in three different ways: $2 + 4 = \square$, $2 + \square = 6$, or $\square + 4 = 6$. The last two show the missing-addend notation and should be read as *Two and what makes six?* and *What and four makes six?* Missing-addend work is much more difficult than a straightforward sum, because pupils must simultaneously hold two ideas in their head: the concept of addition and the concept of equality. The activity described here helps to minimise that difficulty. Note that each of the eight equations above can be rendered as three different written questions.

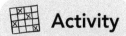 **Activity**

Make up word problems to match a given number fact

Children understand arithmetic questions much more readily when a problem is situated in a context that has some meaning for them. It is much better to ask about 'two more toys' than about the abstract '+ 2'. Similarly, although a teacher sees immediately that 'two million pounds and three million pounds' is essentially the same problem as 'two balloons and three balloons', children who do not really know what a million is will not be able to solve the first problem even when they can easily solve the second.

Pupils who have only been given word problems in order to test their understanding of abstract calculation procedures they have just been taught, will often panic when faced with mixed word problems. Their typical strategy is to pick out all the numbers, ignore the words, and guess what operation to perform on those numbers. To counter this kind of response, Sharma advocates getting children to make up problems themselves for a given number fact. He also persuades the children to insert some irrelevant number details into the problem, e.g. the age of a child, or a date, so that pupils learn to be more discerning about whether all the numbers provided are needed for a solution.

This is a good activity to do with a group, because the variety of answers will provide lots of opportunity for useful discussion. Some children may need a scribe for this exercise.

Game

Cover the Numbers, or Shut the Box

A game for one, two or more players.

Teaching points:

▶ The game teaches splitting all the numbers up to 12, in many different ways.

▶ It gives practice in adding and recombining small numbers to make the numbers up to 12.

Equipment needed:

▶ Either a manufactured version of this game (several, called Shut the Box, are widely available) or my paper version (see CW) called Cover the Number, for which you will also need pencils.

▶ Two 1–6 dice.

Rules:

Each player controls one set of the numbers 1–9. On your turn, throw two dice and announce the total. Choose one or more numbers from your set that add up to the same total, and remove them from play. Continue like this until you throw a total that cannot be matched, or created, from the numbers that remain available. Record your score as the number of numbers left uncovered. Now it is the next player's turn. The winner has the lowest score after three rounds.

Cover the Numbers (or Shut the Box)

RULES Throw two dice and announce the total. Choose a number, or a combination of numbers, that add up to the same total and remove it/ them from play by shading the square(s). Continue to throw the dice and remove numbers from the same 1–9 set, until you throw a total that cannot be created from the numbers that remain. Your score is the number of numbers left uncovered in the 1–9 set. (Variation: Score by adding the numbers left uncovered.) It is now your opponent's turn to keep throwing both dice and removing numbers from play, until a dice throw cannot be matched by using, or combining, any of the remaining numbers in the 1–9 set. The winner has the lowest score after 3 rounds.

First Player

1	2	3	4	5	6	7	8	9

1	2	3	4	5	6	7	8	9

1	2	3	4	5	6	7	8	9

Second Player

1	2	3	4	5	6	7	8	9

1	2	3	4	5	6	7	8	9

1	2	3	4	5	6	7	8	9

There are enough sets of numbers on this page for 2 players to play 3 rounds.

Variation 1:

This can be played as a solitaire game, in which a perfect score is achieved if you can use all the numbers in the set.

Variation 2:

For older pupils, the score at the end of the round is calculated by adding the numbers still uncovered, with the total counting against the player. This calls for a different strategy during the game, i.e. making use of the larger numbers as components wherever possible.

Game

Clear the Deck

A solitaire game for one player.

Teaching points:

▶ The game reinforces all the number bonds of the target number. The target can be any number between 6 and 10, inclusive.

Equipment needed:

▶ A pack of cards with four cards of each digit, doctored according to the target number.

Rules:

Decide on the target and discard from the pack any digits that are equal to or greater than the target number. Shuffle the pack well. Lay out an array of cards face up, so that the number of cards on show is one less than the target number. For example, if the target is 6, keep only the numbers 1–5 in the pack and lay out five cards face up; if the target is 10, construct the pack out of the numbers 1–9 and lay out nine cards face up. Play by clearing away any two cards that add up to the target number and immediately filling the two spaces with new cards. The aim is to clear the whole pack of cards.

Tip:

Encourage the player to talk aloud as the pairs are cleared away, e.g. *Two and four are six, One plus five is six,* etc.

Card array if the target number is 6

Card array if the target number is 10

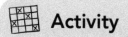 **Activity**

Make a bead string, in two colours, of 10 beads

You will need to find beads of the size, colour and shape to suit the age and sex of your pupils. Younger children need large unbreakable beads. Fancy shapes, such as stars, are fine as long as they are chunky enough to be easily distinguished, while fiddly shapes like clowns or crescents, should be avoided. Pupils who feel they are too old for brightly coloured plastic beads enjoy using strings made of slim wooden ovals in natural colours.

It is important to use beads of the same size, in only two colours, arranged in two groups of five. The two colours should not be too close in tone. The idea of the bead strings is that children can learn to 'see' most of the numbers up to 10 without counting in ones.

When the bead string is completed, you should be able to slide beads along it and have them stay in place. Therefore, depending on the size of the holes, some beads can be threaded on a thick cord like a shoelace, while others may need double-threading with the kind of strong nylon yarn sold for threading necklaces. Follow the instructions in the diagram below.

Children can be given a bead string as a personal calculator for the numbers up to 10, for example when learning to play a game such as 'Ten in a Bed' (see below). At first, children will need to physically move the beads for any calculation; after a while it should be enough just to look at the bead string. Finally, children should be encouraged to visualise the string and do the calculation mentally.

SINGLE THREADING
Large round beads threaded on a shoelace knotted at both ends.

Chunky fancy beads on a shoelace.

DOUBLE THREADING
Start by threading the yarn through the first bead twice in the same direction.

Both free ends of the yarn are now threaded into each bead, in opposite directions.

A bead string suitable for older pupils can be made of small oval wooden beads.

▦ Activities

Learn complements of 10 with the bead string

The word 'complement' comes from the word 'complete'. The *complements of 10* or *complements to 10* are the pairs of numbers that add up to 10. These five number bonds are key facts that pupils must learn by heart. The following activities and games help teach these key facts.

1. Give children practice in 'subitising', i.e. seeing a quantity without counting. Most people can subitise very small numbers, such as 2 or 3, easily. Show a small number of beads on the string, keeping the rest hidden in your hand, and pass the other hand repeatedly back and forth in front of the beads, so that they cannot be counted. Practise first with numbers up to 3, then include 4.

2. Explain to children how they can also 'see' the numbers 6, 7 and 8, and maybe 9, because they can see numbers up to 4 and because they know that there is a colour change at 5. Give lots of practice.

3. Slide the beads apart so that they form two groups. Ask children to match your pattern on their own bead strings as quickly as they can. It is obviously quicker to do this if they do not count either group first.

4. Show on the bead string how 10 can be built, or split, by sliding one bead at a time from left to right. Have the pupils copy you 'reading' the complements aloud: *1 and 9, 2 and 8*, etc.

Game

How Many Beads? How Many Are Hidden?

A game for two players.

Teaching points:

▶ The game gives practice in subitising small numbers.

▶ It teaches bridging through 5 (building the larger numbers, mentally, from '5 and some more').

▶ It teaches the complements to 10.

Equipment needed:

▶ A bead string for each child.

Rules:

While one child looks away, the other hides some of the beads from one end of the string in their hand, leaving the rest dangling and visible. The first child now looks and must say how many beads are showing and how many are hidden, without counting.

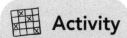 **Activity**

Find complements of 10 with Cuisenaire rods

Have the pupils build a staircase, from 10 down to 1, with Cuisenaire rods. Now get them to transform the staircase into a wall, by adding 'the complement' to the top of each rod, i.e. making each column add up to 10. It can be a moment of revelation for some children, when they discover that in the process of following these instructions they are actually building another staircase, upside down.

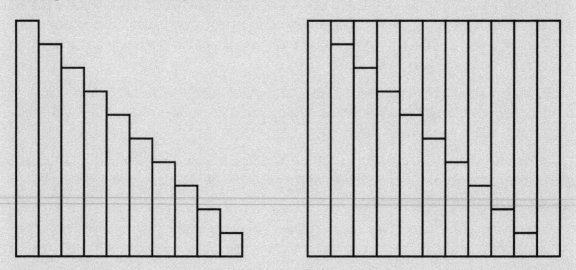

Use the wall to talk about complements to 10, to read equations, to pose addition and subtraction questions, and to write number problems, including missing-number problems, just as you did for the component work detailed earlier in this section. The only difference here is that the paired components of 10 are so important for the pupils to know that these five or six facts need more attention, and more time spent on exploring and learning them, than other number bonds.

The five (or six) complement facts are: $(0 + 10)$

$$1 + 9$$
$$2 + 8$$
$$3 + 7$$
$$4 + 6$$
$$5 + 5$$

Game

Complements Number Search

This is a solitaire activity, or can be turned into a competitive game by seeing which member of the group can find the most complement pairs in a limited time period.

Number searches are very easy to make. They are just as easy, and instructive, for pupils to make for each other.

Teaching points:

▶ Complements to 10 (i.e. the pairs of numbers that add up to 10).

Equipment needed:

▶ Pre-prepared 8 × 8 or 10 × 10 grids, with a single digit in each square.

Rules:

Circle any neighbouring or diagonally adjacent pairs of numbers that are complements to 10. A digit may contribute to more than one pair of complements.

Search for complements to 10

Find two numbers next to each other that add up to 10. Circle them.

1	8	2	0	5	4	6	9
9	3	6	4	5	5	3	2
7	5	1	9	3	2	8	8
1	3	7	1	7	1	5	1
9	5	4	4	6	9	0	8
1	5	0	8	2	9	1	9
6	3	5	5	2	4	5	5
5	7	4	2	8	6	0	6

Game

Complements Ping-Pong

A game for a group of pupils.

Teaching points:

▶ The game gives practice in fast recall of the five complement facts.

Equipment needed:

None, although it would be useful to have a way of generating random numbers from 0 to 10, e.g. a die or a pack of number cards.

Rules:

The teacher calls out a number from 0 to 10 and each pupil must immediately 'bounce back' its complement to 10. Any pupil who is too slow is deemed to have dropped the ball and is out, until the next round.

Tip:

This is a quick game that makes a good warm-up activity for the start of a lesson.

Game

Ten in a Bed

'Ten in a Bed' was once a commercially produced game that is, sadly, no longer available. What I provide on the CW, ⬚ therefore, are the rules, which can be photocopied on A5 paper or card to become the reverse of a game board. The pupils should draw a bed, with people or animals lying in bed, on the other side of their own game board.

This is a game for two or three players.

Teaching points:

▶ The game reinforces the complements of 10 facts.

Equipment needed:

▶ A board for each player (see CW). ⬚

▶ A pack of 36 dot cards (for younger players) or digit cards, the packs being made of four cards of each of the digits 1–9.

Rules:

Each player gets four cards to start. Take turns to pick up a card from the shuffled pack until all the cards are gone. As soon as you have two cards that add up to 10, put the pair of cards to bed (i.e. collect them in a pile on your board) and take another card from the pack, which may help you to make a new pair that can be put to bed immediately, and so on. The winner is the player with most cards put to bed.

Tips:

Add an extra card showing the number 10 to the pack, or use a pack with an odd number of cards, to prevent the game ending too often in a draw. Tell the players they are not allowed to count while playing this game, but that they may use a bead string as a personal calculator, until they know the complements to 10 by heart.

Variation:

When playing with digit cards, a more challenging way to find the score at the end of the game is for each player to find the total value of the cards put to bed. This is not as hard as it sounds (providing the cards are kept in a tidy pile as they are won) because every other card will bring the running total to a multiple of 10.

Activities

Explore and learn the doubles up to 5 + 5

1. Use nuggets or bricks, and use a mirror to see what happens when the pattern is doubled. Then have the pupils make the doubled pattern without a mirror. Pupils should practise reading the doubles patterns in several ways, e.g. *Double 2 is 4*, or *When 2 is doubled we get 4*, or *2 and another 2 makes 4*, or *Twice 2 is 4*, or *2 times 2 is 4*. If the pupils only use the formulation *2 and 2 is 4* they will get into the habit of thinking that doubling is all about adding, whereas it is really about multiplication.

Hold a mirror perpendicular to the desk top, to illuminate the meaning of 'double'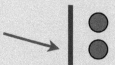

2. Have children make the dot patterns for the numbers 1–10 out of nuggets or other discrete concrete materials and remind them that they are built from doubles or near-doubles patterns. Pupils must say what half of each of the even numbers is, and be able to explain in their own words what the problem is with finding half of the odd numbers.

3. Give pupils one of each of the five smallest rods out of the Cuisenaire box. They must take a second rod of each colour, lay it end to end next to its matching pair, and then find the single rod that measures the same. Pupils should now read the equation they have made: as well as all the different ways they have already learned from earlier activities, they can now practise using the words *twice, double, times 2, 2 times, half, halve, half of, divided by 2, split equally into two parts, divided into two equal parts*, etc., as they read the equations. They can also record the equations on paper as additions and subtractions, as in earlier activities, and now also as multiplications (× 2) and divisions (÷ 2).

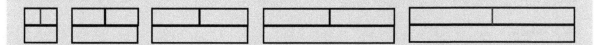

4. On 1 cm squared paper (see CW), fold along a straight line and draw over the fold. Have children colour in squares, or stick small round stickers in squares, so that all the even numbers in turn are shown with half of the amount on either side of the fold line. The fold line can sometimes be horizontal, at other times vertical on the page. Pupils should read these representations both as double and half facts, and can also record the double and half facts using words and all four operations signs, as illustrated here.

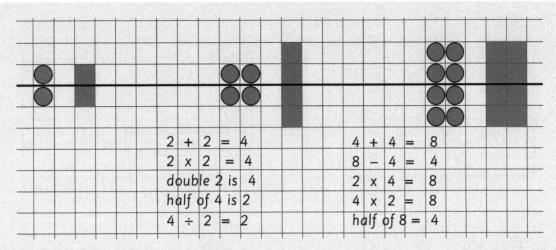

5. Depending on the age and conceptual understanding of the pupils, this may be a good opportunity to discuss what happens when halving odd numbers. Pupils can cut out the relevant number of squares from paper with large squares and fold it in half to show that half of, say, 7 is 3½.

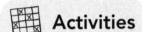 **Activities**

Estimate and measure using Cuisenaire rods

Many mathematical educationalists recommend estimating exercises as a way of building number sense. Indeed, consistently giving wildly inaccurate estimates of small numbers can, like the inability to count backwards, be a quick way to identify children who may have dyscalculia. As already mentioned, an inability to subitise is an indicator for dyscalculia, and both subitising and estimating depend upon a sensitivity to quantity.

Estimating can be achieved in the brain by assessing numerical quantity or by assessing spatial coverage, or a combination of both. Therefore, when pupils are engaged in estimating activities, it is very important to vary the size and shape of your single unit on different occasions.

Here are some activities using Cuisenaire rods. The advantage of using them is that the pupils can check their estimates by measuring instead of counting.

1. Out of a pile of no more than 20 white rods, or other 1 cm cubes, take a small handful and drop the cubes onto the lid of a Cuisenaire rods box, letting the cubes remain in the random pattern in which they fall. Pass your hand, or a sheet of paper, back and forth over the cubes, so that the pupil is forced to estimate, or guess, the quantity without counting. After making a guess, children can shake the cubes into a straight line against a side of the box lid and should then use the larger rods to measure the length of the row of cubes and thus check the accuracy of their guess.

(Continued)

(Continued)

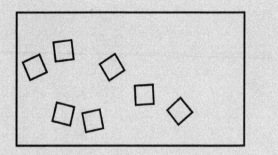 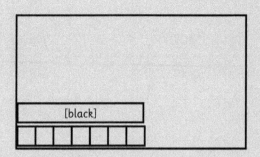

2. Pupils throw a 1–3 die and take one rod to match each throw. They collect the rods by putting them in a row, end-to-end, on top of an orange 10-rod, or on a row of 10 squares outlined on 1 cm squared paper (see CW). In this way, pupils can see how the smaller amounts build up to 10. After every turn, pupils must say how many they have so far, not by counting, but by guessing and then measuring against a single coloured rod. Pupils can race against each other to be the one to cover their 10 in the fewest throws. Conduct this activity with the rods sometimes set out horizontally and sometimes vertically.

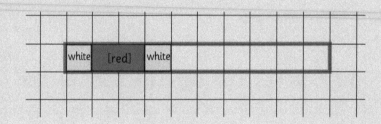

3. Identify objects for the pupils to measure, e.g. a book or a chair. Pupils must first guess, and then measure, how many whole orange rods they can fit along the length or the height of each object. As only the 10-unit rods are being used, you can choose objects that are up to 10 rods in length or height, i.e. up to a metre.

4. Provide pupils with a page full of drawn straight lines, each measuring a whole number of centimetres less than or equal to 10 cm and drawn at various angles to each other, i.e. not all horizontal or vertical on the page. Pupils must estimate the length of each line. Pupils check their estimates by measuring the line against a single Cuisenaire rod.

Pupils can prepare this activity for each other. Drawing straight lines accurately to whole centimetres is a skill that needs practice. Dyspraxic pupils should be given a ruler with a handle.

5. Pupils throw a die and, starting from a line drawn on the floor, take as many steps forward as matches the throw. Depending on the length of their stride, different pupils will cover a different amount of ground for the same throw of the die. Pupils mark where they have reached and estimate or guess how far they have moved. Pupils then use a metre rule to verify their estimate. If possible (as we are still working with numbers up to 10 at this stage), have them use one of those metre sticks with a channel running along the centre, into which Cuisenaire rods or Dienes longs can be fitted, so that they are thinking in 10 cm lengths as the units of measurement that build up to 1 metre.

⊞ Activities

Focus on plus/minus 1 and plus/minus 2

Remind pupils that adding and subtracting the small quantities 1 and 2 have already formed part of their earlier work, for example the Cuisenaire rods activities on making and reading equations and also their investigations into the components of all the numbers up to 10.

Be explicit about the fact that when 1 is added the result is the next number in the counting sequence, and that when 1 is subtracted the result is the previous number in the counting sequence. Plus 2 and minus 2 are achieved by following the same procedure twice, i.e. + 2 is not the next number but the one after, and − 2 is not the previous number but the one before. Children who have experienced the earlier activity in which dot patterns are altered, two by two, should also be able to appreciate that adding or subtracting 2 to an even number results in the next even number, while adding or subtracting 2 to an odd number results in the next odd number.

1. Have the child make a Cuisenaire rod staircase before picking out alternate rods to create two separate staircases, one of even numbers and one of odd numbers. Take a red rod, i.e. a 2, and 'walk' it up and down the staircases. Many children already know that there is a gap of 2 between every successive even number, but far fewer realise – until trying out this activity – that there is exactly the same difference, i.e. 2, between every successive odd number.

2. Take a small number of counters or nuggets. The pupil can arrange them into the familiar dot patterns, or may count them into a straight line. Use a piece of card to screen the counters. Slide one (and later, two) counters from under the screen, showing the pupil how many have been extracted. The pupil must say how many are left under the screen, without using fingers or other aids. Repeat the exercise by displaying and then adding one, or two, items to a group that were seen but are now hidden under a screen.

   A slightly harder activity is to screen a small number of counted items, as before, but now ask pupils to tell you how many must be taken out so as to leave only one (and later, two) under the screen. It is this kind of activity that helps pupils realise that a problem such as 8 – 7 can be solved by the plus/minus 1 strategy, even though the number 1 does not appear in the question.

3. Give pupils a paper number track, which is built out of 10 large squares or rectangles. At first, allow pupils to write the numbers in digits in the spaces on the track; at a later stage do the same activity on empty, unlabelled, tracks that have Slavonic shading or any other kind of visible division separating the two groups of five. Call out a number and instructions for adding or subtracting 1 or 2 to the number, instructions that pupils follow by putting a token on the track as quickly as possible. Use as varied a vocabulary as you can manage when calling out instructions. For example, for the number 5 and the instruction plus 1: *One more than 5, The number that is 5 and 1 more, The amount that is 1 greater than 5, The sum of 5 and 1, The sum total of 1 and 5, The total of 5 and 1, One plus 5, One add 5, One added to 5, Five and 1 together, Five increased by 1, An increase of 1 from 5.*

(Continued)

(Continued)

4. Pupils pick a Cuisenaire rod at random and are instructed first to show the rod for that number plus 1, and then the rod for that number minus 1 (or vice versa). Pupils should notice that this activity results in them showing adjacent rods from the rods staircase, a sequence with which they are already familiar.

5. Have pupils make and read equations involving plus or minus 1 or 2 with Cuisenaire rods, which they then record on paper. Encourage pupils to turn the rods upside down or back to front every so often, to help them understand that the equation is produced by the relationship between the numbers, not the order in which the numbers are presented. Pay special attention to those equations where 1, or 2, is the answer to a subtraction problem, e.g. not only $7 - 2 = 5$, but also $7 - 5 = 2$ and $2 = 7 - 5$.

Game

Who Has the Most Equations?

This game is for two or three players.

Teaching points:

▶ The game gives practice in adding and subtracting 1 or 2.

▶ It teaches pupils to recognise on which occasions they can use the plus/minus 1 or 2 strategies.

▶ It shows that the plus/minus 1 or 2 strategies can be used even when the numbers 1 or 2 do not appear on the left of the equal sign.

▶ It gives practice in making and writing simple equations.

Equipment needed:

▶ Two 1–6 dice.

▶ Paper and pencil for each player.

Rules:

Take turns to throw both dice and to write down any number problems for which you can use the plus/minus 1 or 2 strategies. Complete the equation with the correct answer.

For example, if you were to throw two 2s, you could write two equations, each of which would earn a point: $2 + 2 = 4$ and $2 - 2 = 0$. If you were to throw a 4 and a 3, you could write three equations: $4 - 3 = 1$, $4 - 1 = 3$ and $3 + 1 = 4$ (or $1 + 3 = 4$), which could earn three points in total. However, if you were to throw two 5s, there are no possible equations for which these strategies could be used. The winner, at the end of a certain number of turns, or a certain length of time, is the one with the most correct equations.

Tip:

Tell pupils that they will get points for each equation, and remind them to look out for both additions and subtractions, but let them find out for themselves when they can win more than one or two points. (Of the 36 possible combinations of two dice, only 21 produce different combinations, and of these only 5 combinations will produce a situation where no points can be scored.)

Variation:

Play with one 6-sided and one 10-sided die, which will extend the possible combinations, but will also produce a few more situations where no points can be scored.

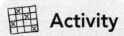 **Activity**

Compare the difference and equalise

This activity is presented at three levels of difficulty, all on the same activity sheet (see CW), ⌁ and is designed to teach pupils to think about subtraction as something other than 'taking away'.

Pupils use dice to generate two numbers to compare. They record the numbers as a subtraction number sentence and practise interpreting it as a subtraction, a difference problem and an equalising problem, before finding and recording the solution. This activity teaches children that finding the difference between two numbers can be viewed either as a subtraction or as a missing-addend problem. Switching between the different points of view and between the different ways of expressing the same problem mathematically will help reinforce a child's understanding of the relationship between addition and subtraction, and will also lay the groundwork for understanding complementary addition, which is the most useful subtraction strategy to teach any pupil who has difficulty with arithmetic.

The equipment needed will depend on which level of difficulty a pupil is working at: pupils working at the most basic level should be given counters or other small objects; pupils working at a higher level need Cuisenaire rods. All pupils need two 6-sided dice, one showing 0–5 and the other showing 5–10, and a pencil.

The activity sheet, which can be found on the CW, ⌁ should, at first, be folded before photocopying, so as to present each pupil with only the appropriate level of difficulty. Later, pupils can be given the whole sheet to decide for themselves at which level to work.

(Continued)

(Continued)

Compare the difference and equalise   A subtraction activity

Use two 6-sided dice, one showing numbers 0–5 and the other showing numbers 5–10.

<u>Step 1</u> Throw both dice and write the numbers separately in the two square boxes. Underneath, re-write the numbers in the form of a subtraction number problem. Read the question aloud, e.g. for **6 – 2** , read "Six minus two equals what?".

<u>Step 2</u> Set out the problem using counters at level A, or Cuisenaire rods at level B. At level C, the problem should be drawn on the number line. Now read the problem as a comparison and equalising problem, e.g. "How many more must we add to 2 to make it equal to 6?", or "What is the difference between 2 and 6?", or "How big is the gap from 2 to 6?"

<u>Step 3</u> Solve the problem. Write the answer on the dotted line. Read the whole number sentence aloud, e.g. "6 minus 2 is 4."

Activity   Throw the 5–10 die.
Write the number here. → ☐ — ☐ ← Throw the 0–5 die.
Write the number here.

Write the subtraction
problem. Read it aloud. ....

Level A

Set out the same number of counters as your first throw, one in each space of the top row. Set out the other amount underneath. How much more do you need to add to the lower row to make the amounts equal?

Level B

Put one Cuisenaire rod to match the
first throw on the top row of 1cm squares.
Put a single rod to match the number of
the second throw below it.
Find the difference.

Level C

Mark both the numbers on this empty number line.
Find the size of the gap.

© Ronit Bird

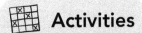 **Activities**

Hidden quantity subtraction

1. Take a small handful of small objects, such as buttons, bricks or pencils. Ask a pupil to count the objects into a bag, which can be transparent. While pupils look away, take some items out of the bag, keep them hidden but allow pupils to examine what remains in the bag. Pupils now record what just happened, on paper, as a missing-number subtraction problem, e.g. 9 – ☐ = 3. Finally, pupils must solve the problem and find what quantity was 'subtracted' or 'taken away'. Pupils could get into pairs to do this activity with each other.

2. Put a secret quantity of objects into a bag while pupils look away. The bag must not be transparent. Pupils look back, and while they are looking, take some of the objects out of the bag and display them, at the same time opening the bag to show how many items remain. Pupils must record this operation as a missing-quantity subtraction problem, e.g. ☐ – 6 = 3, before solving it.

Pupils may find these activities quite challenging, even when the numbers are kept below 10. A similar activity is recommended earlier for adding and subtracting 1 or 2. These activities should be practised until pupils can solve missing-number subtraction problems for numbers below 10, without the props.

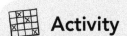 **Activity**

Teach complementary addition

Step 1

Take a small number of nuggets or counters, and ask the pupil to count them while moving them into a straight line. Decide on a small number to subtract from this quantity, and ask the pupil to remove this quantity from the start of the line, then from the end of the line, then from the body of the row. Each time, the pupil should count how many counters remain. Be explicit that it makes no difference to the solution whether an amount is subtracted from the beginning, or from the end of a quantity (or, indeed, from the middle). Have pupils repeat this exercise as many times as is necessary to convince themselves that this is always true.

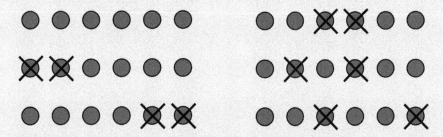

Working concretely helps prove that subtracting 2 from 6 leaves 4, no matter which two are removed.

(Continued)

(Continued)

Step 2

Explain to the pupil that step 1 has involved 'mechanical arithmetic', i.e. objects have been physically moved around after which an answer has been found by counting. Mechanical arithmetic does not help us to learn to perform mental arithmetic. Mental arithmetic involves keeping track in your mind as you work through the steps of a calculation until you reach the solution.

Step 3

Now set out a row of nine nuggets from left to right in a row, and tell the pupil you need to subtract six, and that you want to try to keep track of where you are in the calculation as you work through it, so as to learn the best way to solve this problem mentally.

Step 4

In your attempt now to take six away from the end of the row – the right-hand side – you will be involved in a complex double-counting procedure where you are counting up (1, 2, 3, 4, 5, 6) the amount that you need to subtract, while counting down (9, 8, 7, 6, 5, 4, 3) the amount that remains at each step. Make this performance as hard and as complicated as possible. As you subtract each nugget, move it slightly away from the rest in the row. Because the two counts are simultaneous, you will be saying something like: *I take one away, that leaves eight, now I'm subtracting two which leaves seven,* etc.

Step 5

Show how much easier it is to take away the six from the start of the row – the left-hand side. Now there are two single counts, not simultaneous counts, and both are going up in the same direction. Start from the left, moving each nugget away slightly as you touch it and count up 1, 2, 3, 4, 5, 6. Pause and say that these are the six you are taking away. Now continue counting up to find the answer: 1, 2, 3.

Step 6

Ask the pupil to explain back to you, with the nine nuggets, what you have just shown in the last two steps. Now hide the nuggets, and ask the pupil to work through the solution aloud, using only the second method, i.e. using complementary addition.

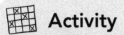 **Activity**

Complementary addition on a number line

Show how complementary addition can be modelled on an empty number line. To do this, label the beginning of the line with zero and encourage the pupil to scribble away part of the line, to represent the quantity that is being subtracted or taken away. But insist that the amount being subtracted is to be taken from the beginning of the line, as shown in the example.

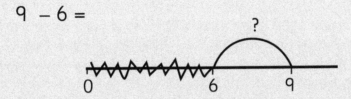

Subtraction by complementary addition allows us to work forwards.

There are two main benefits from working in this way. Firstly, pupils can always work in the forward direction. Except for very easy subtractions such as minus 1 or 2, when it would be normal to work backwards, encourage pupils to go forwards. Every pupil will find it easier to work forwards, and it is especially helpful for those with dyscalculia or other specific maths difficulties. It follows that work on a number line will always be in the forward direction, thus eliminating the need for arrows, which is a bonus for pupils with directional difficulties. Secondly, the same diagram models both $9 - 6 = \square$ and $6 + \square = 9$, thus reinforcing the relationship between addition and subtraction.

After practising this technique many times, pupils can skip the scribbling-out stage, if they are comfortable doing so, and simply start their labelling of the line at whatever number beyond zero they require.

$$9 - 6 =$$

Further work on complementary addition can be found in Section 2.

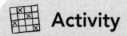 **Activity**

Use reasoning to find near-complements and near-doubles

Remind pupils of the earlier activities in which they regrouped number components set out as dot patterns, or investigated the 'Story' of each number with Cuisenaire rods, or when they first used a bead string. During all these activities, there will have been a lot of discussion, and some explicit teaching, about how the different facts about a particular number are related to each other. For example, during the work on components the teacher will have pointed out to pupils this important observation: as soon as one component becomes one unit larger, the other component must become one unit smaller to compensate, e.g. 4 + 5 = 3 + 6. While working with a bead string, pupils should have noticed that as soon as one bead is moved along the string from one group to the other, the first group is made smaller by one and the second group is automatically enlarged by one.

This kind of understanding allows pupils to derive new facts from the complement and doubles facts they already know. They learn to understand that they can adjust numbers to make a calculation easier for themselves, and to reason that any adjustment in one direction must be balanced by an adjustment in the opposite direction.

For example, if we know that 2 + 8 = 10 (which we do, because 2 and 8 are complements of 10), then we can reason that 2 + 7 = 9. Or that 3 + 8 = 11. Or that 7 + 2 = 8 + 1. Similarly, if we know that 3 + 3 = 6, we can derive the solution to the near-doubles facts: 2 + 3, 3 + 2, 3 + 4 or 4 + 3. Of course, the near-doubles facts up to 10 are already familiar to children who learned the 'key component facts' during earlier activities and games. In focusing on logical thinking in this activity, the emphasis is now on using reasoning as a calculation strategy, not on the facts themselves.

Put one of the known complements or doubles facts up on the board, and ask pupils to find the related near-complements and near-doubles facts that can be derived. It is more important, at this stage, to teach the pupils to recognise pairs of numbers that are almost doubles, or almost complements, than it is for them to find the actual answers to the sums.

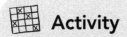 **Activity**

Identify the best strategy for different situations

Let the pupils throw dice to generate random addition and subtraction number problems, or present pupils with a page full of problems (an example can be found on the CW). Discuss with the pupils which are the best strategies to use for each problem. Counting up or down in ones is only considered a good strategy if there are no more than two steps to be counted.

Give points for identifying a good strategy, rather than for a correct answer. Note that some problems can be solved by more than one good strategy, e.g. the answer to 5 + 4 can be found because it is a known key fact or because it is a near-double fact (and so can be derived from 5 + 5 or 4 + 4) or because it is a near-complement fact (and so can be derived from 5 + 5 or from 6 + 4).

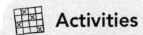 **Activities**

Use money for component work

Using money gives a new dimension to component work because coins come in specific denominations. These activities, therefore, give practice in splitting and recombining numbers in numerous new ways. However, remember that money is more abstract than base-10 materials: the 2 cent coin, for instance, is only worth twice the 1 cent coin because we say so, not for any logical or mathematical reason such as size or mass.

For all these activities, provide 1p, 2p, 5p and 10p coins (or 1 cent, 2 cent, 5 cent and 10 cent coins).

1. Take a small handful of 2p coins. The pupils must find the amount by counting in twos.

2. Take a few 2p coins and add to them a 5p coin. Show pupils how to start with the 5p and then count in twos starting from the odd number.

3. Teach pupils to count a collection of mixed coins by starting with the largest denominations.

4. Throw a 1–10 die. Match the throw with coins, first using the maximum number of coins (let children discover for themselves that this always means using 1p coins alone), then using the minimum number of coins.

5. Take a small handful of coins. The pupils must say how many 1p coins would be equivalent in value.

6. Take a small handful of coins that add up to an even number. How many 2p coins are equivalent in value?

7. Make small amounts of money out of different combinations of coins. How much does the pupil need to add to each collection to make 10p? (Let pupils discover for themselves that this is a complement question.)

(Continued)

(Continued)

8. Give pupils a 10p coin and send them 'shopping' for various small cheap items. For example, a pencil might cost 2p, or a rubber 3p. The pupils must work out the expected change after buying single items or combinations of items. Sometimes phrase the question as *How much money will you/do you have left to spend?* as pupils do not readily understand that this question means the same as the more common 'how much change' question.

   If one pupil buys small items while another gives change, the shopkeeper must give the change in the most efficient manner, i.e. using the smallest number of coins.

9. An extension of the shopping activity above is to ask the pupils to work out mentally how many pencils or rubbers they can afford to buy with only 10p to spend. Ask pupils to identify which prices use up the whole amount, and which result in change or money left over.

10. Give the pupils a small amount of money and challenge them to put together the same amount of money with a given number of coins. For example, give a 10p coin and ask the pupils to use five coins for the same amount, or five coins one of which is a 5p, or five coins none of which is a 5p.

11. Get pupils to make up problems modelled on the activity above for each other to solve on paper, as in the example shown here:

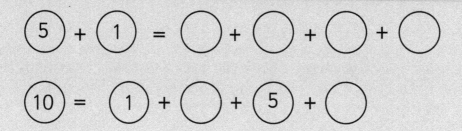

Basic calculation with numbers above 10

Overview

This section continues to focus on giving pupils techniques to replace the impractical strategy of counting in ones for basic calculations. Earlier activities have already targeted the 'counting trap': the situation in which children use counting inappropriately because they know so few basic facts by heart, which in turn becomes a process that is so laborious and prone to error that new facts cannot be stored in their long-term memory. Many pupils who have difficulties cling to their old habits when they cannot see the benefits of changing them. It is only at the stage when calculations involve larger numbers that pupils begin to accept the need to learn and practise different techniques that will lead to more efficient calculation strategies.

Concrete materials, and Cuisenaire rods in particular, continue to be used in this section of the book to help children build sound cognitive models. The emphasis should always be on the understanding that needs to underpin mental calculation, and never on using the materials to find any answer mechanically. Empty number lines, which were introduced in the previous section, appear frequently in the following activities as a transition between concrete and abstract work. The emptiness of the number lines in the transition stages is important: empty number lines have been shown by research to be a powerful and flexible tool for reflecting children's own informal strategies and for supporting mental calculation. Neither the concrete stage nor the transition stage can be rushed.

Children with dyscalculia and dyslexia may have severe problems with their short-term and long-term memory. It is therefore very important to minimise the amount that pupils have to know by heart, both in terms of facts and procedures. The activities and games presented here focus on those techniques that have the widest applications, such as bridging through 10 and subtracting using complementary addition. Alongside these key ideas, the activities teach pupils how to use logic and reasoning to derive new facts from those they already know.

You can find a video about this section of *The Dyscalculia Toolkit* on the CW.

What are the main problems?

▶ Poor number sense, i.e. no feel for the actual size of even small quantities, no feel for the numerical magnitude of a number or the relative sizes of different numbers, poor estimating abilities, no intuitive understanding of how the number system works and how the decade structure has repeating patterns, insecurity about the concept of place value, etc.

▶ Long-term memory difficulties, including weaknesses in sequential memory, auditory memory and memory for language-encoded facts, exacerbated by problems retrieving facts from long-term memory.

▶ Short-term working memory weaknesses, resulting in pupils going off on a tangent, or giving up before a full solution is reached, because they find it too difficult to keep in mind what the problem is asking at the same time as having to work on solving it.

▶ Confusion about whether adding or subtracting means counting the numbers, or the intervals between numbers.

▶ Not noticing patterns, relationships and connections between numbers, situations or other maths topics.

▶ Relying on cumbersome counting methods, resulting in memory overload and frequent errors.

▶ Using such inefficient calculation methods – in particular, counting in ones – that the connection between the question and the answer is lost. This means that new facts cannot be stored in long-term memory.

▶ Feeling overwhelmed when too much information is presented at once, for example a 100-square with 100 labelled numbers, or worksheets and textbooks with pages that are too busy and cluttered.

How to help

▶ Break each topic into tiny steps. Make sure the foundations are in place before trying to build on them. Do not move on too quickly to larger numbers. Include regular revision.

▶ Allow pupils as much thinking time as they need to complete any calculation, including oral work. Time constraints produce stress, which is the enemy of learning.

▶ Use concrete materials before introducing diagrammatic or abstract methods. Remember that the transitional stage between concrete and abstract work is pictorial or diagrammatic work.

▶ Continue to offer concrete materials until well after a pupil stops asking to use them.

▶ Use appropriate concrete materials that will help build cognitive models. At this stage, that means continuous material such as Cuisenaire rods and base-10 materials such as Dienes blocks. Discrete materials that have to be counted in ones should be phased out by the time pupils are working with numbers above 20.

▶ Let the pupils manipulate the concrete materials themselves. Do not use them only for demonstration purposes, or only to illustrate written calculations.

▶ Remember that recording the maths in writing should follow practical experience with concrete materials, not precede it.

▶ Allow informal jottings before teaching standard written notation.

▶ Avoid visual presentations that contain too much information. For example, introduce 100-squares carefully, as an extension of the number track. When making worksheets or choosing textbooks, ensure there is plenty of white space on the page.

▶ Ask lots of open questions. Encourage the pupils to explain and talk through everything they do, in their own words.

▶ Encourage the use of empty number lines, first as diagrammatic models and later as a model for pupils to visualise and manipulate in the mind's eye.

▶ After the individual numbers up to 10 are well understood, do not assume that pupils can make the connection to all larger numbers. Spend time on the numbers between 10 and 20, spelling out as many connections to earlier learning as possible, before moving on.

▶ Teach strategies to avoid counting in ones. Be explicit with pupils that the strategies deliberately encourage seeing numbers as being built out of component chunks, not ones.

▶ Teach component work in a way that reinforces the connection between partitioning and recombining, between adding and subtracting.

▶ Teach and practise bridging through 10, as soon as the foundation skills have been mastered. These include:

   – knowing the components of the numbers up to 10;

   – knowing the complements to 10;

   – understanding the relationship between addition and subtraction;

   – enough place value knowledge to be able to add any 1-digit number to 10 (without counting).

The idea of identifying and putting all the necessary pre-skills in place as part of a systematic approach to teaching the bridging technique is further developed, and explored in very great detail, in Part II of *Overcoming Difficulties with Number*.

▶ Teach subtraction as complementary addition. Tell pupils always to use complementary addition in preference to subtraction (unless there are only one or two backward steps).

▶ Minimise the number of facts that have to be known by heart.

▶ Teach explicitly how to reason from known or given facts.

▶ Do not overload pupils with too many strategies. Even if you demonstrate or explain several different strategies, allow each pupil to practise and learn only a minimum number of key strategies.

▶ Focus on the 'Basic 8' strategies and show pupils how to identify which kinds of problems can be solved by each strategy you teach.

▶ Pay attention to the vocabulary you use and be sure to vary the terms and sentence constructions.

▶ Encourage pupils to make up their own number problems and their own word problems.

⊞ Activity

Connect the numbers 10–20 with the numbers below 10

Remind pupils of their earlier work with dot patterns (see Section 1). Use dot pattern cards to make the numbers between 11 and 20, by using one 10-spot card and one other card representing a number of units.

Ask pupils to visualise one of the dot patterns, and answer questions about the number itself (which is revision) and about the number that is 10 more (which encourages pupils to make the desired connection). Vary the vocabulary and format of the questions. Using the dot pattern for 9, for example:

Put the pattern of 9 in your mind.

What must be added to 5 to make 9?

So, what do I need to add to 15 if I need 19?

What is left if you take 5 from 19?

How much bigger is 19 than 15?

How much more is 19 than 5?

If you have 19 sweets and I only have 5, how many more do you have than I have?

How far is 9 from 10?

So, how far is 9 from 20?

How much older is 9-year-old Tom than his sister who is 4?

Sally is 19 years old. How much older is she than the 4-year-old?

Game

Polka Dots

A traditional solitaire domino game, sometimes known as 'Twelves'.

Teaching points:

▶ The game provides practice in mentally adding small quantities to make larger quantities that, in turn, are combined to create the target number of 12.

▶ The game helps players make connections between addition, subtraction and missing numbers.

▶ During the game the player is not allowed to count in ones. Instead, the focus should be on using and visualising techniques based on the regrouping strategy.

Equipment needed:

▶ A set of dominoes from which the double-blank and double-six (0–0 and 6–6) have been removed.

Rules:

Turn the dominoes face down and mix them up. Pick six at random to start the game, arranging them face up in a row. Remove any pair of dominoes with a total value of 12, naming the value of each domino as you do so.

Make sure not to count in ones. Instead, try to visualise dots migrating from one side of the line to the other, or from one domino tile to another. For example, in the illustration, I can see that the two dominoes at the left add up to 12 because the two 3s at the top add up to 6, as does the 5 + 1 at the bottom. I can also see that the two dominoes at the right add up to 12 because each separate domino is worth 6.

As you match and remove pairs of dominoes, fill up the spaces with two more so that there are 6 dominoes always in play. The game is won if you can match and clear all 26 dominoes.

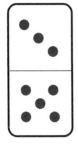 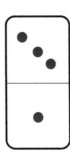 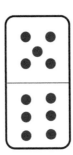 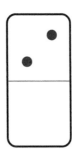 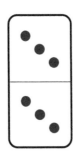 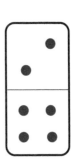

Game

Regroup

This game, for two players, is much harder than it looks. Children who have not had enough hands-on practice in exploring dot patterns and those with weak visualising skills will find this game particularly difficult (and might therefore benefit the most from playing it, often). A dice version of the game can be found in *The Dyscalculia Resource Book*.

Teaching points:

▶ The game is about using logic to derive a new fact that is one reasoning step away from a given fact. E.g. if we know that 4 + 4 is 8, we can mentally regroup to see that 3 + 5 must also be 8.

▶ The game gives practice in building the numbers below 20 out of two components.

▶ It highlights the connection between addition, subtraction and missing number problems.

▶ The game requires players to practise visualisation skills.

Equipment needed:

▶ A pack of dot pattern cards made up of two cards for the numbers 1–10, plus four extra cards for each of the numbers 2, 3, 4 and 5.

▶ A game board for each player (see CW, or sketch your own boards).

Rules:

Shuffle the pack and take turns to pick up two cards, keeping them hidden from your opponent. If the total value of both cards is less than 7 return the cards, one somewhere in the middle and one to the bottom of the pack, and try again.

On your turn, write the total value of both cards at the top of one of the triad shapes on your board. Next, imagine one – but only one – dot moving from one card to the other, to create two new components. Write these imagined quantities at the bottom of the triad. If your opponent can guess the two cards you hold in your hand from this written clue, your opponent wins both cards. An incorrect guess allows you to keep the cards. The winner has the most cards after six turns each.

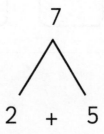

Visualise one dot moving from one card to the other, to find a new pair of components.

For example, if the cards I pick up are 3 and 4 I might, at first, imagine one dot moving from the 4 to the 3 but will soon notice that this creates exactly the same components as I have on my cards. I might therefore choose to imagine movement in the other direction, and record 7 on my triad as being created from 5 and 2. My opponent has to reason that my cards must be 6 and 1, or 4 and 3, and has an even chance of guessing the correct pair of numbers to win both cards.

Tip:

There is some strategy involved in having to consider both possible clues before recording one. For example, if one of your cards is a 2, decreasing that component to 1 would give your opponent an easy win (since there are no cards for zero in this game). Similarly, if you record a doubles fact as your written clue, your opponent cannot help but deduce which cards you have.

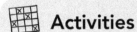 **Activities**

Focus on the 'teen' numbers

Point out to pupils that the names for the 'teen' numbers are inconsistent. Pupils need to be aware that in the numbers 13–19, the first digit one hears or says is the last digit one reads or writes.

1. Give lots of practice in *building* the numbers between 10 and 20 concretely from materials such as base-10 blocks, Cuisenaire rods, and coins.

   Give practice in *writing* teen numbers in digits, both by labelling amounts made from concrete materials, and from dictation.

   Provide practice in *reading* the teen numbers, presented in a random order.

2. Make the teen numbers using a spike abacus. Have pupils match these numbers with concrete materials. Pupils then record the number in digits.

3. Have pupils sketch the teen numbers, both as if they were made on a spike abacus, and as if they were made from Dienes blocks. Present the numbers to the pupils in words, in writing. Pupils complete their sketches with the number written in digits.

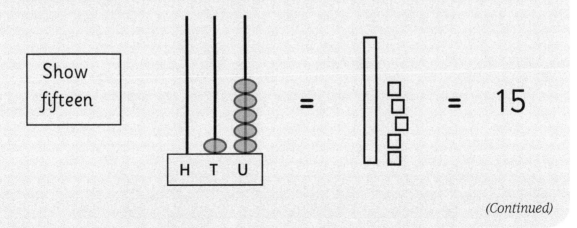

(Continued)

(Continued)

4. Let pupils practise adding 1 and subtracting 1 from all the teen numbers. Soon, extend this to adding or subtracting 2. Sometimes ask pupils to visualise the operations and answer orally, e.g. *Look at your sketch of 15 and tell me how many there would be if you had one less. What about 2 more than 15?* At other times, have pupils write the additions or subtractions as number problems, e.g. $15 + 1 = 16$, $2 + 15 = 17$, $14 = 15 - 1$.

5. Encourage pupils to make up varied word problems for the plus/minus 1 or 2 equations in the above activity.

6. Locate the teen numbers on a skeleton number line. Present pupils with a number line like the one below, on which round numbers (multiples of 10) are marked and labelled and on which there are marks but no labels for the numbers in between. As you can see from the illustration, it helps to minimise the need to count if each midpoint between round numbers can be easily distinguished. Pupils must locate a teen number, chosen at random by the teacher, and write it under the line as quickly as possible. Provide a fresh skeleton number line for every two or three numbers, so that pupils are forced to locate new numbers in relation to the round numbers or the midpoints, rather than from previous answers.

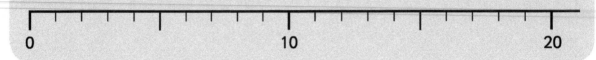

▦ Activities

Explore the numbers between 10 and 20 with Cuisenaire rods

1. Have pupils build a staircase out of Cuisenaire rods. Extend the staircase to 19 (or to 20 if large boxes of rods are available). Pupils are often surprised to see the familiar 1–10 staircase repeating itself.

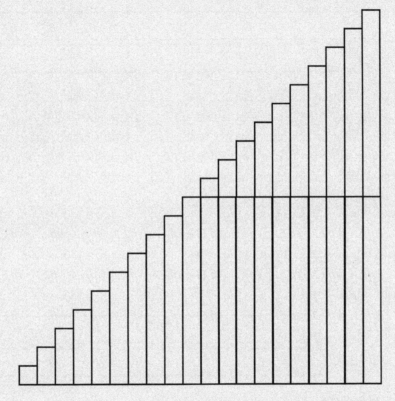

2. Pull out individual steps from the staircase for pupils to name orally and in writing. Show how these numbers can be laid out end to end, vertically (as in the staircase), horizontally, or side by side to emphasise their tens-and-units structure.

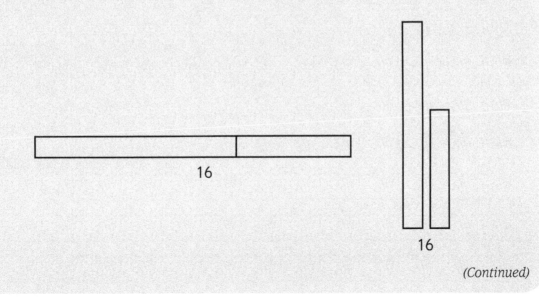

16

16

(Continued)

(Continued)

3. Ask pupils to solve simple additions by estimating the total of two rods and then measuring against other Cuisenaire rods. For example, for the question 8 + 8, pupils take out two brown rods and lay them end to end. Ask pupils to estimate whether the length of this 'train' is more or less than an orange 10-rod. More or less than two orange rods? At this stage, pupils should lay one orange rod under their sum, aligned at the left, and guess, or use trial and error to measure, what other rod exactly fills the gap.

8 + 8

[brown]	[brown]

[orange]	

Encourage pupils to notice during this exercise that just as the orange 10-rod is two units *bigger* than one of the original components, so must the gap-filling rod be two units *smaller* than the other component. This is the kind of reasoning approach that pupils first came across during the regrouping activity (in Section 1) and the Regroup game (above) and that they will find invaluable when they have to perform mental additions without concrete materials.

4. Pupils should 'read' the equation they make during the activity above, in just the same way as they read equations for Cuisenaire rods that totalled less than 10, in the Section 1 activities. As they speak, the pupils should point to each rod or quantity they mention. For example:

6 + 7

Six add seven is thirteen.

Seven plus six is thirteen.

Thirteen is equal to six and seven.

Thirteen minus seven is six.

Sometimes, pupils can record the equations in writing. Challenge them to find just as many subtraction formats as addition sums. For example:

6 + 7 = 13	13 − 6 = 7
7 + 6 = 13	13 − 7 = 6
13 = 6 + 7	7 = 13 − 6
13 = 7 + 6	6 = 13 − 7

5. You can introduce flexible thinking about partitioning (more on this later) by adding a final step to the equations activity above: treat the solution to the addition as a

tens-and-unit addition as well as a single 2-digit number. In the 6 + 7 example, this entails reading the equation as *six plus seven is equal to ten and three*, as well as all the other ways of reading it already listed above. There are two ways to record this in writing: for example, the 8 + 8 addition is recorded both as 8 + 8 = 10 + 6, and as 8 + 8 = 10 + 6 = 16 (or 16 = 10 + 6 = 8 + 8). This way of thinking encourages pupils to connect simple computation with the concept of place value.

This exercise also helps pupils understand the true meaning of the equal sign, which too many children believe to mean 'now find the answer' instead of actually meaning *everything on the left of the sign is equal in value to whatever is on the right of the sign.*

Game

It All Adds Up

A game for two or three players.

Teaching points:

▶ The game gives practice in adding small quantities.

▶ It requires players to exchange two smaller numbers for one larger number of equal value.

▶ The focus of this game is on creating the teen numbers out of two components.

Equipment needed:

▶ A pack of digit cards (see CW) or playing cards made up of four cards each for the numbers 3–9.

▶ Small Post-It notes (or pieces of card or paper) and a pencil.

▶ A game board for each player (see CW, or sketch your own game boards).

Rules:

Take turns to pick up a card from the shuffled pack. On your turn, copy the number from the card onto a Post-It note. Keep the Post-It on or near your board. Replace the card at the bottom of the pack. Before play passes to the next player, you may exchange two smaller numbers for the sum of both numbers, by writing the new total onto a new Post-It note and destroying the Post-Its for the two smaller numbers. Explain what you are doing to your opponents so that they can check your addition and ensure the smaller numbers are discarded as soon as their combined value has been recorded on a new Post-It.

You may make as many exchanges as you like when it is your turn, but you may not reverse the process by splitting any number into two smaller components.

(Continued)

(Continued)

The winner is the first player to position six Post-It notes to create sums that result in any three consecutive numbers within the range 13 to 18.

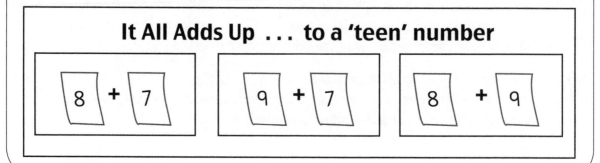

It All Adds Up ... to a 'teen' number

8 + 7   9 + 7   8 + 9

Activities

Locate 2-digit numbers and put them in context

1. Locate individual numbers on a 100-bead string. 100-strings that are sold commercially usually have a colour change after every 10 beads, but I prefer to use bead strings of my own making with a colour change after every 5 beads. Call out a 2-digit number. Pupils race to touch the bead that represents that number. Some counting is inevitable in this exercise but, by making it a race, pupils will have to find the most efficient counting strategies, e.g. counting first in tens and then in twos, or counting back from the next round ten for locating a number ending in 8 or 9.

2. Locate numbers on a number track made of labelled squares on paper. Start with numbers up to 30 or up to 50, before extending the activity to numbers up to 100. Note that tracks that are long enough for 50 or more numbers are cumbersome to use, a fact you should point out while doing this activity, so that pupils will see that there are advantages to using 100-squares instead.

1	2	3	4	5	6	7	8	9	10	11	12	13	14	15	16	17	18	19	20	21

As an additional exercise, once the number is located pupils must say which are the two nearest round numbers (multiples of 10) that lie on either side of the targeted number.

3. Sometimes, ask pupils to locate numbers on tracks on which most of the numbers are blanked out, so that pupils have to find numbers in relation to others, with a minimum of counting.

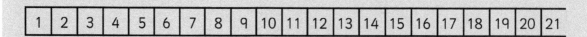

			4				10						17			21

4. Locate numbers in a 100-field. Note that 100-squares are not popular with children who have maths difficulties, because there is an overwhelming amount of information on them. To introduce the 100-square gradually, while also demonstrating the logic behind it, get pupils to construct their own. Give pupils a number track like the one described in step 2 above, i.e. a paper track made of numbered squares. Have pupils cut the track after every 10 numbers. Show pupils how to reassemble the strips into the top part of a 100-square (using a 1–30 track or a 1–50 track). At a later stage, have pupils make a whole 100-square by cutting up a 1–100 track.

Pupils should practise locating individual numbers as quickly as they can. Ask pupils also to find and name the two round numbers between which the targeted number lies.

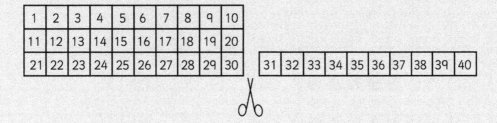

5. Make an overlay to fit the 100-square. The overlay should be opaque and should show all the squares but not their number labels. Cut out a few squares through which the numbers on the labelled 100-square can be seen. Ask pupils to locate numbers that are hidden, by reasoning in as few steps as possible – i.e. not counting in ones – from the numbers that they can see through the cut-outs. Rotate the overlay to produce four different positions for the cut-outs.

Laminated paper overlay for a 100-square. The shaded squares have been cut out so that the numbers beneath can be seen.

(Continued)

(Continued)

6. Locate numbers on a Slavonic abacus. A Slavonic abacus is an abacus made of 100 beads on ten horizontal spokes, in two colours arranged so that there is a colour change after every five beads and five rows. The number tracks with Slavonic shading that I use (see Section 1 and the CW) are based on a single row from an abacus of this type. Locating an individual number on a Slavonic abacus is very similar to using the 100-square above, the difference being that there are no number labels on an abacus. Despite this, counting is kept to a minimum because of the colour changes. For children already familiar with a Slavonic abacus, you can provide a paper abacus for further practice, like the one illustrated below.

Lots of interesting ideas about using a Slavonic abacus, or a paper abacus, can be found in Eva Grauberg's book *Elementary Mathematics and Language Difficulties.*

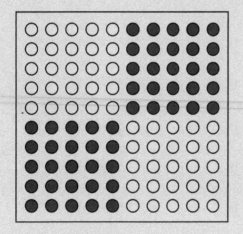

Paper Slavonic abacus

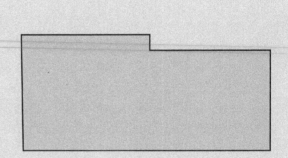

Translucent overlay used to locate and read numbers on the paper abacus

7. Locate numbers on an empty number line. Give pupils a number below 100 to put anywhere on an empty number line. Pupils should mark on the number line the two round numbers, i.e. multiples of 10, on either side of the number.

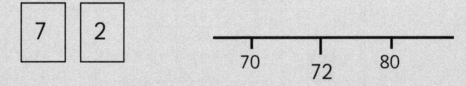

To make sure pupils understand that 100 is a multiple of 10 (as well as a multiple of 100), include several numbers in the nineties for this activity. It is equally important that pupils understand that the two 'round numbers' between which all the numbers from 1 to 9 lie, are zero and 10.

🔲 Activities

Complements to 20

Look back at the activities on learning complements to 10, in Section 1, before trying these.

1. Give each pair of pupils two of the 10-bead strings, with which they are by now familiar from earlier activities. One pupil hides some beads in their hand while leaving the others on show. It is very important that only one string is split into components: to show 6, for example, keep one whole string in the hand as well as four beads from one end of the second string; to show 16, keep only 4 beads in the hand while dangling the whole of one string and 6 beads from the other, etc. An important part of this activity is to help pupils realise that complement problems only require that one set of ten numbers is 'broken into', leaving the other decade(s) undisturbed. For this reason, it is better to use two 10-bead strings for this activity than a 20-bead string.

The second pupil in the pair must 'read' the number of beads on show, by subitising instead of counting, as far as possible, and must deduce – using knowledge of complement facts, not by counting – how many beads have been hidden.

2. Use the bead strings to reinforce the regrouping reasoning strategy, namely the important logical idea that as one component increases, the other decreases by the same amount, and vice versa. With the two bead strings lying end to end, let pupils make a number between 1 and 20, e.g. 16. Pupils should be able to demonstrate that if they move a bead from the large group to the smaller group, one component decreases from 16 to 15 and therefore the other must increase by the same amount from 4 to 5.

$$20 \ = \ 16 \ + \ 4$$

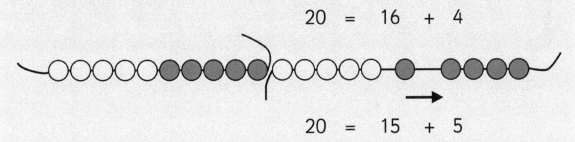

$$20 \ = \ 15 \ + \ 5$$

3. Give pupils enough Cuisenaire rods to make a staircase to 20, and then to add rods to each step to make a 'wall' as they did in an earlier activity in this section. Examining and discussing the wall helps pupils to understand how two components can be adjusted in opposite directions to add up to the same amount. Working from the fact that $20 = 7 + 13$, we can use logic to predict how other rows in the wall are built, for example that 20 must also equal two more than 7 plus two less than 13, which is $9 + 11$, or one less than 7 plus one more than 13, which is $6 + 14$, etc.

4. Make 'complement of 20 sandwiches' out of Cuisenaire rods. In the lid of the rods' box, have pupils set out four orange 10-rods, as illustrated below, leaving enough space between the layers to fit another row of rods. The teacher calls out a random number between 1 and 20. Each pupil makes that number out of the minimum number of rods,

(Continued)

(Continued)

and sandwiches it between the two layers, aligning the rods at the left. Pupils must first predict, then check by measuring (again using the minimum number of rods) which number exactly fits the remaining gap. Alternatively, use a 20 cm ruler that has a special 1 cm channel to take rods or Dienes blocks for this activity.

[orange]	[orange]

[orange]	[orange]

5. The sandwich or ruler activity above represents the number 20 as a 'train' measuring 20 cm long and 1 cm wide. However, it is also useful to repeat the activity with an alternative shape: a rectangle of 10 cm × 2 cm. A net for making a shallow cardboard tray in which two Cuisenaire 10-rods fit exactly side by side can be found on the CW. When using the tray for this activity, sometimes position the tray vertically and at other times horizontally.

6. Play a brisk game of Complements Ping-Pong, for pairs of numbers totalling 20. In response to a random number between 1 and 20 being called out, each pupil in turn has to 'bounce back' the complement to 20, without pausing to calculate it. A pupil who takes too long is deemed to have 'dropped the ball', and must sit out the rest of the round.

7. Make number searches for pupils to find adjacent complements to 20, as described in Section 1 for complements to 10. Pupils can learn as much about complementary pairs when they are the ones to create the number puzzle as when they are the ones to solve it.

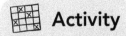 **Activity**

Complements to larger multiples of 10

Step 1

Use a partially labelled number track on which each number is represented by a 1 cm square. The track can be created by the pupils by cutting it out of 1 cm squared paper (see CW). Pupils should label the minimum number of squares that they feel comfortable with, e.g. every tenth or fifth number. Next, pupils cut the track into strips of ten numbers, and arrange the strips to form the top of a 100-square, just as they did in the earlier activity on locating and putting into context various 2-digit numbers.

Step 2

Pupils generate a 2-digit number by turning over two digit cards from a shuffled pack. Pupils use Cuisenaire rods to match the number, placing the rods on the 100-square. The illustration shows the number 27, with two orange 10-rods covering the top twenty numbers, and a black 7-rod covering the first seven squares in the third row. Pupils must now use their complement knowledge, together with an examination of how many rows are left uncovered by rods, to find the complement to 50, i.e. the number that must be added to 27 to make 50. (See also the activity later in this section on complements to 100.)

The problem posed by this activity can be recorded both as a missing-number addition, and as a subtraction sentence, e.g. 27 + □ = 50 and also as 50 − 27 = 23. After trying the activity for several numbers, pupils should make up at least one word problem.

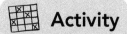 **Activity**

Complements on a number line

Pupils draw an empty number line. Two-digit numbers are chosen by the teacher, or generated at random using dice or cards. The number is marked anywhere along the line. Pupils draw a jump on the number line towards the next multiple of 10. Pupils must label both the name of the next multiple of 10 (which they practised in earlier activities in this section) and the amount of the jump (which they should recognise as a complement fact).

This activity can be usefully extended by also asking the pupils to record the previous multiple of 10 and its distance from the target number.

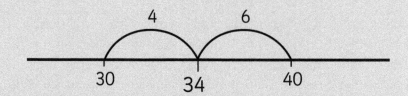

After trying this activity for various 2-digit numbers, encourage pupils to answer some of the same questions again, orally, by visualising a blank number line in their mind's eye.

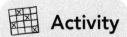 **Activity**

Introduce bridging through 10 with Cuisenaire rods

Bridging through 10 is the single most useful mental calculation strategy that pupils can learn. Pupils will need to practise the technique in a variety of ways until they can perform bridging calculations without the help of concrete materials or paper and pencil.

Several of the activities and games in this section of *The Dyscalculia Toolkit* are designed to teach and practise this important strategy, but for even more about bridging, see *Overcoming Difficulties with Number*, in which three whole chapters are devoted entirely to teaching and learning bridging strategies.

Start by using a Cuisenaire 10-rod sandwich to explore when to use bridging through 10. For example, put a blue 9-rod between the two orange 10-rod layers of the sandwich. The rods now represent the starting position of any addition that begins 9 + □. Explore with pupils what numbers added to 9 do not require bridging (only 1 or 10) and which do require bridging (any number between 2 and 9).

10	[orange]
9	[blue]
10	[orange]

Next, substitute another rod for the blue rod, and repeat the investigation.

Here is how I might talk through an addition such as 9 + 7: *To add 7 to 9, let's set up a sandwich. We can see straight away that we will need to bridge through 10. Our first number is 9 and the complement of 9 is 1. So we need to split the second number, the 7, into 1 and what's left. Let's take a 7 and do it. When we break 7 into 1 and what's left, we get 1 and 6. The 1 can attach itself to the 9 to make 10, and 6 more makes 16. So, 9 + 7 is the same as 9 + 1 + 6, which is 16.*

The pupil should be the one to split the 7 into its components. Quite often pupils will revert to their earliest ideas about components and tell you that the 7 should be split into 3 and 4. Your response will be that these components are not wrong, but are not helpful in this situation. Pupils may need several reminders that the split that is needed for bridging is: *the complement of the first number, and whatever is left of the second number.*

(Continued)

(Continued)

10 [orange]	
9 [blue]	7 [black]
10 [orange]	

7 [black]	
1	6 [dark green]

10 [orange]		
9 [blue]	1	6 [dark green]
10 [orange]		

Some children find it easier to work through a concrete bridging calculation on a prepared outline drawn on 1 cm paper, as illustrated below. This has the advantage of eliminating any possible confusion about which rods are part of the calculation and which are being used just to measure against. It also provides a template that is easily recognised and easily visualised, which helps children notice what all bridging calculations have in common. This, in turn, helps children see the connection between concrete bridging with rods and abstract bridging on an empty number line (see the next activity).

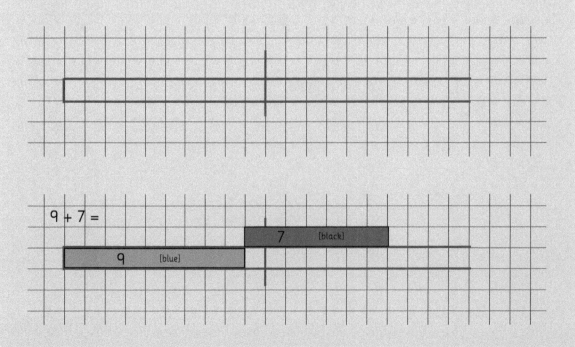

9 + 7 =

7 [black]

9 [blue]

Game

Five and What's Left

A game for two or three players.

Teaching points:

▶ The game gives practice in bridging through 10.

▶ It teaches when to use the bridging through 10 strategy.

▶ It incorporates revision for the complements to 10 facts.

Equipment needed:

▶ A game board (see CW, or draw and shade a rectangle on 1 cm squared paper).

▶ Cuisenaire rods.

▶ A 0–9 die.

Rules:

Start with a yellow Cuisenaire 5-rod placed on a 1 cm × 10 cm rectangle. Take turns to throw the die and take the rod to match the throw. If adding the two numbers (5 plus the number thrown) gives a total of 10 or less, you cannot proceed and you win nothing on that round. If the total is more than 10, you must use rods to explain how to use the bridging through 10 technique to find the total, and must exchange the added rod for two rods: a 5 and what's left. Keep the second rod – the rod representing 'what's left' – as winnings. The winner of the game is the player who has won the most after five rounds.

Tips:

The most valuable part of this game is the talking aloud while it is being played. To maximise the bridging practice, use a pack of digit cards in which there are more of the numbers 6–9 than of the numbers 5 and below, rather than a die.

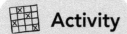 **Activity**

Bridge through 10 on a number line

Bridging is a very powerful technique, both for addition and subtraction. Several of the activities and games in this section of *The Dyscalculia Toolkit* are designed to teach and practise this important strategy, but for even more about the bridging technique, see *Overcoming Difficulties with Number*.

When demonstrating how to bridge abstractly, on an empty number line, pupils can be shown two slightly different ways of recording the calculation. Once they have experimented with both, each pupil should be allowed to choose which way to adopt and practise.

Take, for example, 8 + 7.

Method 1

Draw an empty number line. Mark 8 anywhere on the line. Bridge from the 8 to 10. Explain that we know (because we know the complements, or because we know that alternate numbers are even or odd) that this is a 'jump' of only 2. Label the size of the jump either inside or above the arc. Because this number indicates size, which is always a positive number, there is no need for a plus sign before the 2. Looking back at the question, we see that we need to add 7 and so far we've only added 2. Therefore, we need to add 5 more. Draw a jump of 5, label its size, and label the point at which the end of the jump meets the number line. Now we can see that the answer is 15.

8 + 7 =

Method 2

Draw an empty line. We have 8 and need to add 7. We can show this on a number line by marking the 8 and adding, or 'jumping' forward, 7. But we cannot immediately see where this lands on the number line. So, to make life easier for ourselves, we will split our addition jump into two steps and bridge through 10. The first step must be 2, because 2 is the complement of 8. We have taken care of 2 out of the 7; that leaves another 5 to add. Five more than 10 is 15.

8 + 7 =

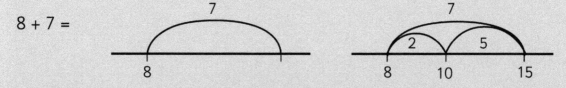

The advantage of the second method over the first is that the whole question is notated on the number line immediately, making it less likely that pupils will lose their place and forget what they are supposed to be doing after completing the first step of the calculation. The disadvantage is that it can look messy, especially if pupils leave insufficient space for a jump to be subdivided.

Whichever method is chosen, make sure that at the early stages children are only asked to record a bridging calculation that they have just performed concretely. With the rods still in front of the child, it is easy to see that each jump on a number line corresponds to each of the components being added.

More practice of this kind can be achieved by playing the Frame an Addition game (below).

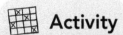 **Activity**

Practise bridging and reinforce the commutativity of addition

Arrange pupils into pairs or into two groups. Give all pupils the same addition problem for them to solve on a number line, using a bridging strategy as described in the activity above. Half of the pupils are asked to solve the problem as it is given, for example 9 + 7, while the other half must switch the order of the numbers before proceeding, i.e. 7 + 9.

Number line work is a good opportunity to reinforce the commutative property of addition, and this activity promotes discussions between pupils about whether one approach is better, or faster, than another. For example, the number line calculation for 7 + 9 is just as easy as 9 + 7, as you can see from the illustration below. However, the same is not true when one addend is a 2-digit number (see the next activity on bridging through multiples of 10).

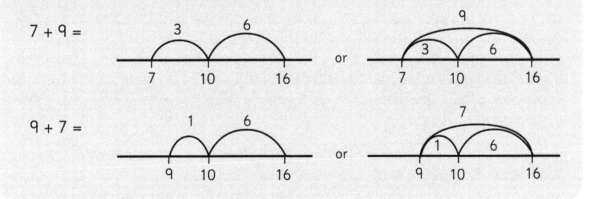

Game

Frame an Addition

A game for two or more players. You can find a short demonstration video of this game, and the related Frame a Subtraction game, on the CW. ⌨

Teaching points:

▷ The game is about bridging through 10.

▷ The game makes players think about which calculations do, and do not, involve bridging.

▷ The game supports the transition between concrete and abstract work by requiring players to perform the same calculation first with Cuisenaire rods and then on an empty number line.

Equipment needed:

▷ Cuisenaire rods.

▷ A frame or tray surrounding a space measuring 2 cm × 10 cm for each player. This can be made of paper or card (see CW) ⌨ or a more durable frame can be cut out of craft foam or kitchen sponge.

▷ A 1–6 die on which the 1 has been overlaid by a sticker showing the number 7.

▷ Paper and pencil.

Rules:

Take turns to throw the die twice in succession. After the first throw, take one rod to match and put it inside your frame. When you throw the second time, take the rod to match and say (before you try it in the frame) whether it will fit into the same row.

If it cannot fit into the same row, exchange it for two smaller rods so that one fills the gap. You may only start a new row after the first is complete. As you make the exchange, explain every step of the process aloud. Record the bridging calculation on an empty number line. If you have already recorded an identical calculation earlier in the game (i.e. the same pair of numbers, added in the same order) cross out one calculation, so that only one is included in the scoring.

If the total of both dice throws is equal to or less than 10, demonstrated by the fact that both rods can fit within a single row in your frame, announce the total value of both rods and exchange them for a single larger rod. Before the end of your turn, you now have a decision to make: either to keep the rod in your frame and add to it on your next turn by throwing the die once, or to return the rod and start your next turn with an empty frame and a double dice throw.

The winner is the first player who has sketched five number lines that record five different bridging calculations.

Tip:

The winner is usually the player who has the first turn, so let the child go first when playing against an adult or make sure children take turns to start the game when playing with each other.

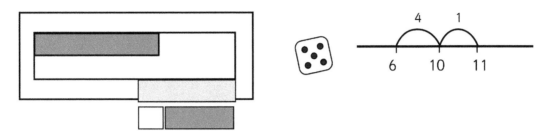

Frame an Addition demonstrates numbers being added as two separate chunks, by bridging through 10.

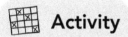 **Activity**

Bridge through multiples of 10 on a number line

Set up additions where a 1-digit number is added to a 2-digit number. Make the connection with earlier work explicit, i.e. that the second addend must again be split into *a complement and whatever is left*, just as before. What is new is that now larger multiples of 10 are used as stepping stones on the way to the final total. Encourage pupils to set out their calculation on an empty number line, as before. For example:

38 + 7 =

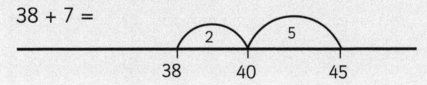

After trying a few additions like this, challenge pupils to solve the same questions without paper and pencil, by visualising the number line in their mind's eye.

Game

Race Along a Number Line and Bridge

A game for two players.

Teaching points:

▶ The game focuses on the bridging through 10 strategy.

▶ It gives practice in using an empty number line for addition.

▶ It gives practice in visually estimating the size of numbers below 10, relative to a whole 10.

▶ It makes pupils notice which sums need the bridging through 10 strategy and which do not.

Equipment needed:

▶ A game board and pencils (see CW, or sketch number lines on paper to create a game board).

▶ A die. A 10-sided die makes for a faster game than a 6-sided die.

Rules:

Players have their own number lines and agree on a round number to start (not always zero). Mark the next four multiples of 10 on your line, then take turns to progress in jumps along the number line according to the throw of a die. You can win points only if you bridge through a multiple of 10. The game ends as soon as one player reaches, or passes, the end of the line. The score is one point for finishing first, and two points for each time the bridging technique was used (so 9 is the maximum score).

Tip:

Insist on clear and neat recording, with the amount of the addition labelled in or above each jump, and the running total marked beneath the number line at the end of each jump.

Game

Race to the End of the Number Line

A game for two players.

Teaching points:

▶ The game practises the use of an empty number line for addition.

▶ It brings into sharp focus the difference in quantity between a ten and a unit.

▶ It gives practice in visually estimating the size of 1 in relation to 10.

▶ The game teaches that adding single 1s or whole 10s does not require the bridging through 10 strategy, even though adding a 10 always crosses a decade boundary.

Equipment needed:

▶ A game board and pencils (see CW, or sketch number lines on paper to create a game board). ⓚ

▶ A die with three sides labelled '+ 1' and the other three labelled '+ 10'.

Rules:

Take turns to throw the die and to race along the number lines, recording each turn as a single jump, and labelling your line as you move forwards.

Tip:

A game board is provided on the CW, ⓚ but if you decide to sketch your own game boards, it is best to vary the length of the number lines and the spacing of the numbers on the line each time the game is played, so that pupils begin to see that number lines are flexible and can represent whatever sequence of numbers they wish.

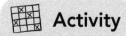 **Activity**

Complementary addition, or subtraction by adding

Step 1

Remind pupils of the work they have already done on complementary addition with small numbers (see Section 1). Ask pupils to explain it back to you, and to each other, first by using counters and then on a number line.

The key idea is that the number to be subtracted is taken away from the beginning of the array of counters, or from the start of the line, so that the whole calculation moves in the forward direction.

Remind pupils that they can physically cross out the amount to be subtracted on a number line beginning at zero, and only begin to use an empty number line that does not start at zero when they are completely convinced that both representations model the same problem. For example:

19 – 13 =

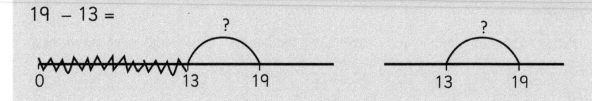

Step 2

Give pupils lots of practice in using number lines for problems like the above, where both the numbers in the question are 2-digit numbers, but where the answer is below 10.

Step 3

Ask pupils to use their number line solutions to the problems in the previous step, and to rewrite the problems as an equalising (or difference) problem, using the missing-addend notation, e.g. 13 + ☐ = 19. This part of the activity reinforces the relationship between addition and subtraction. It also shows pupils that, because work on a number line is in the forward direction, there is no need for arrows on the jumps or operation signs for the quantities.

Step 4

Give pupils the same kinds of problems as above, but without paper and pencil. Pupils must practise putting an empty number line in their mind's eye and working forwards along it. You should provide the actual question in writing, as it might put too great a strain on a pupil's memory to have to keep hold of the numbers of the question, while mentally calculating the answer. This kind of activity should not be timed. However, these problems can be answered in only two steps, so check that pupils who are very slow are not finding the solution by counting in ones.

Game

Frame a Subtraction

A game for two or more players. You can find a short demonstration video of this game, and the related Frame an Addition game, on the CW. ⊾

Teaching points:

▶ The game is about subtraction by complementary addition using bridging through 10.

▶ The game targets those subtractions that arise from using decomposition methods to solve column subtraction: teen numbers minus single-digit numbers.

▶ The game supports the transition between concrete and abstract work by requiring players to perform the same calculation first with Cuisenaire rods and then on an empty number line.

▶ During the game, players model the idea that subtraction can be expressed as 'difference' and that finding the answer to a subtraction does not necessarily involve working backwards.

Equipment needed:

▶ Cuisenaire rods.

▶ A frame or tray surrounding a space measuring 2 cm × 10 cm for each player. This can be made of paper or card (see CW) ⊾ or a more durable frame can be cut out of craft foam or kitchen sponge.

▶ A spinner with a base showing the numbers 11–15.

▶ A 4–9 die.

▶ Paper and pencil.

Rules:

Start every turn with an empty frame. On your turn, spin the spinner and take two rods (one of which must be an orange 10-rod) to match the spin. Put the rods inside your frame. Roll the die to find out how much to subtract. If you have enough rods to carry out the subtraction without touching the 10-rod (i.e. 15 minus 4 or 5, or 14 minus 4) that is the end of your turn.

If the solution to the subtraction problem is less than 10, you must demonstrate how to find the answer by exchanging the orange 10-rod for two smaller rods. Make the exchange in such a way that you can subtract – by physically removing – a single rod that matches the number on the die. For example, in order to subtract 7, the orange rod that represents the 10 of the teen number must be exchanged for 7 + 3 so that the black rod can be removed. The answer to the subtraction is found by adding the two rods that remain in the frame after the subtraction has been performed. As you carry out the exchange and subtraction, explain aloud every step of the process.

(Continued)

(Continued)

Record the bridging calculation on an empty number line as complementary addition. This entails finding the difference between the two numbers and working forwards on the number line. Finally, empty your frame of rods, ready for your next turn.

If you spin and throw the same pair of numbers again at any point during the same game, cross out the duplicate calculation so that only one is counted during scoring.

The winner is the first player with five number lines recording five different calculations showing solutions achieved by complementary addition and bridging.

Variation:

Go on to have an extra turn whenever the answer to your subtraction problem is 6 or 7. This extra rule makes players embrace what are often regarded as the more difficult subtractions presented by this game.

Tips:

The winner is usually the player who has the first turn, so let the child go first when playing against an adult or make sure children take turns to start the game when playing with each other.

Encourage beginners to scribble out the start of the number line, as illustrated in the previous activity. Confident players should be allowed to omit this step, if they prefer, as illustrated here.

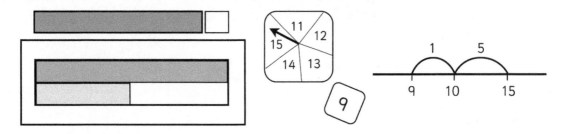

Frame a Subtraction demonstrates subtraction as complementary addition, with bridging through 10.

Activity

Complementary addition for subtracting round numbers

This activity provides an important transition between the previous activity and game (beginning to use complementary addition) and the next activity ('harder' complementary addition). This activity teaches pupils to subtract multiples of 10 in one chunk where possible, or, later, in two steps where bridging through hundreds is necessary.

Step 1

Use Cuisenaire rods, or Dienes blocks, in conjunction with an empty number line.

Set up subtraction problems for pupils to answer, where the minuend (the first number) is not a round number, e.g. 75, and the subtrahend (the number to be subtracted) is any multiple of 10 that is easy to subtract from the tens digit in the minuend, e.g. 40. Other examples are 72 – 60, 86 – 20, 99 – 50, 264 – 30, etc.

Step 2

Have pupils build the first number out of concrete materials, and model the subtraction by covering the number of tens in the subtrahend with a translucent overlay (e.g. a piece cut out of a plastic wallet). The answer can clearly be seen as all the tens that have remained uncovered, together with all the units that have remained untouched.

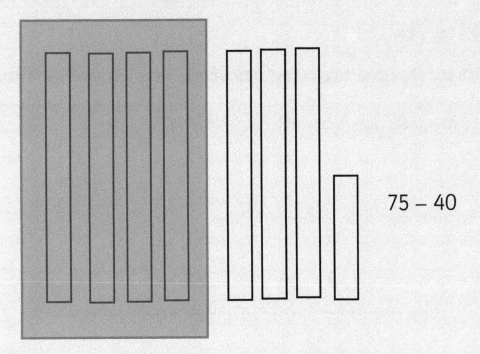

75 – 40

Step 3

Pupils draw two number lines and mark both numbers on them. On the top number line, the pupil makes one bridging jump for the tens, talking it through aloud, e.g. *I have 4 tens*

(Continued)

(Continued)

and I'm moving forwards to 7 tens, that means I move 3 tens which is 30, or once they are more practised, *40 to 70 is 30.* Pupils draw a second jump for the units and say: *70 to 75 is 5.* Immediately underneath, the pupil repeats the subtraction but drawing only one jump and saying aloud: *From 40 to 75 is thirty … five.*

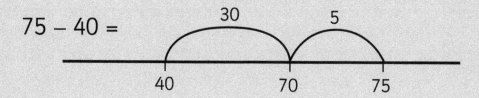

$75 - 40 =$

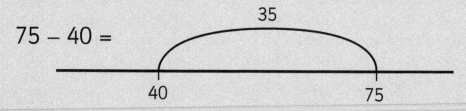

$75 - 40 =$

Step 4

Pupils practise these kinds of subtractions mentally, by visualising a number line.

▦ Activity

Harder complementary addition on a number line

Do not attempt this activity until pupils are secure with the earlier activity in which there were only single-digit answers, and with the previous activity in which they practised subtracting multiples of 10.

The technique is basically the same as any other complementary addition, but the aim of this exercise is to encourage pupils to minimise the number of steps. For example, a subtraction such as 76 – 28 can be done in two steps.

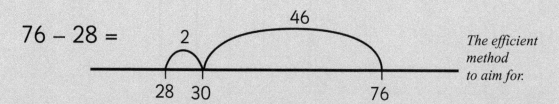

$76 - 28 =$

The efficient method to aim for.

Pupils who can get the correct answer only by doing the calculation in lots of small steps should be given plenty more practice of the earlier activities. The benefit of using a number line is completely lost if the pupils need to add too many jumps to reach the solution, or if they end up doing lots of counting in single units of one or ten.

76 − 28 =

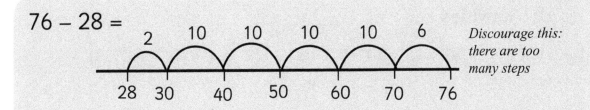

Discourage this: there are too many steps

76 − 28 =

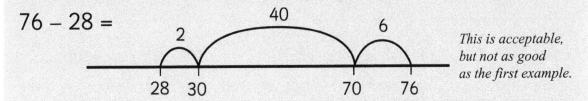

This is acceptable, but not as good as the first example.

The hardest subtractions involve successive bridging: through a multiple of 10, and through a multiple of 100. It can be done efficiently on a number line, but only if pupils can subtract a round number of hundreds from a 3-digit number, e.g. 364 − 200.

364 − 177 =

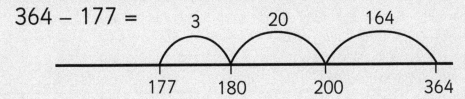

My general rule is that if the number of steps on a number line exceeds four, the number line method should be abandoned in favour of written column addition or subtraction, or using a calculator. It is also worth noting that it is easier to use column arithmetic for subtractions in which no decomposition is required (e.g. 45 − 22), whereas complementary addition on an empty number line is most successful when used for subtractions for which decomposition would otherwise be required (e.g. 42 − 25).

▦ Activity

A flexible approach to partitioning

Dictate a 2-digit number between 20 and 100 for pupils to build out of Cuisenaire rods. Pupils must find as many different ways of partitioning the number into two components as possible, by moving only one rod at a time from one component group to the other. For example, 35 is built with three orange 10-rods and one yellow 5-rod, and so can be partitioned into 30 + 5, into 20 + 15, and into 10 + 25. This activity reinforces an understanding of partitioning that will be useful for subtractions requiring decomposition.

As an extension of this activity, challenge pupils to determine whether different solutions are possible by moving, say, all the tens before the units rod, or altering the order of the movements in other ways. Pupils will find that different solutions are not possible for the same number. This extension activity, therefore, also reinforces the commutative principle of addition, i.e. that 20 + 15 is the same as 15 + 20.

▦ Activities

Explore partitioning methods for 2-digit mental additions

These activities should not be tried until pupils have some understanding of place value (see the activities in Section 3). Note that in contrast to column addition, the actual values of the numbers are kept throughout, i.e. 20 remains twenty, never two (although it could be thought of as two tens).

1. Add a 2-digit number to another 2-digit number by partitioning, using Cuisenaire rods.

   For example: 45 + 23. Make 45 out of four orange 10-rods and a yellow 5-rod. Make the number 23, separately, out of two orange 10-rods and a light green 3-rod. Push the orange rods together into one group and name the quantity *(sixty)*, then do the same for the units and name the running total: *sixty … eight.*

   When adding two numbers whose units add up to more than 10, there is an extra step. For example: 45 + 28. Make the numbers out of rods as before, and combine the tens together, naming the amount *(sixty)*, then do the same for the units and name the amount *(thirteen)*. Finally, teach pupils to say aloud not the sum, but just the running total: *sixty … seventy … three.*

2. Show pupils how to record the mental partitioning method informally. Take an example that has been set out with concrete materials, like the one above, and show how both the 2-digit numbers have been split into tens and units, so that the original question 45 + 23 has been turned into the question 40 + 5 + 20 + 3 (do not write this down; explain orally while pointing to the relevant rods). Combining the tens before combining the units results in a question that can be expressed as 40 + 20 + 5 + 3 (again, do not write this down, but explain orally). Now show the two best ways of writing and reorganising the sum, as follows:

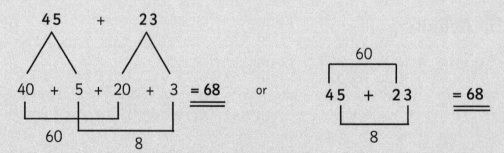

Pupils should try both ways a few times, before settling on the one they like best. Although the method at the left looks more complicated, it provides good support for the mental reasoning process, especially for pupils whose weak understanding of place value might lead them to treat 6 tens as if it were 6 (see Section 3).

3. Practise the above activity including some additions that require carrying. In the example 36 + 88, illustrated below, the sequential calculation steps at the left reflect what a pupil might say while visualising the quantities and mentally manipulating them (do not

write these steps down or ask pupils to write them down). The notation at the right is an informal way to support the mental process and record the calculation.

$$36 + 88 \quad = 30 + 6 + 80 + 8$$
$$= 30 + 80 + 6 + 8$$
$$= 110 + 14$$
$$= 124$$

11 tens = 110

3 6 + 8 8 = 124

14

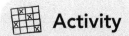 **Activity**

Teach an alternative written method for column addition

Teach pupils a non-standard column method that avoids the two main problems that pupils have with the standard algorithm: it (practically) eliminates 'carrying', and the sum can be worked from left to right, i.e. starting with the largest values, just as for mental addition.

The method, which you can read more about in Chapter 14 of Ian Thompson's *Issues in Teaching Numeracy in Primary Schools*, works by collecting a subtotal 'under the line' for each column, before adding the sub-totals to produce the final solution. For example:

```
                36
            +   88
tens          110
units          14
              124
```

```
           473
        +  102
            56
   H       500
   T       120
   U        11
           631
```

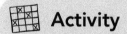 **Activity**

Avoid decomposition in subtraction

This activity shows pupils how much easier it is to use complementary addition than to use columns for those subtraction problems that would otherwise require decomposition.

Set up some subtraction problems where there are one or more zeros in the minuend (the first number), e.g. 200 – 56 or 104 – 78. Demonstrate both ways of solving, first by column arithmetic, then by complementary addition on a number line. For example:

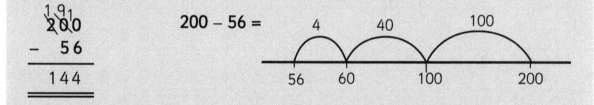

Give pupils practice in solving subtractions that normally require 'borrowing' or decomposition (whether or not the numbers contain zeros), on a number line as well as in columns. Many pupils will find the number line method much quicker and easier, especially if they have already had plenty of practice using number lines to support or record mental calculations. Pupils who prefer to use the standard written algorithm for these difficult subtractions can still use complementary addition to work out their answers to each separate column and to check their final answer.

A simple way to avoid decomposition when subtracting from a round number of hundreds or thousands – a situation that often arises when working with metric measurements or money – is to rewrite the minuend (the first number) as two components, the second of which is 1. Perform the subtraction on the first component, an easy task now that no decomposition is required, and make sure the 1 is added back into the final answer.

$$
\begin{array}{r}
199 + 1 \\
-\quad 56 \\
\hline
143 + 1 \quad = 144 \\
\end{array}
$$

You can find more about this type of compensation strategy, together with a variety of other reasoning methods, in Chapter 9 of *Overcoming Difficulties with Number*.

⊞ Activities

Complements to 100

Complements to 100 should be given lots of practice because knowledge of these facts will be needed for calculations to do with money and metric measurements. Of course, the five complement facts to 10 must be known by heart first (see Section 1).

1. Build Cuisenaire rods on top of a Dienes 100-block or in a shallow cardboard tray that measures 10 cm × 10 cm (see CW). This is an extension of the earlier activity in this section on complements to multiples of 10.

   Have the pupils generate a random 2-digit number by throwing a set of tens and units dice. Pupils take the Cuisenaire rods to match the dice throw and arrange them on top of the 100-block, aligned at the left. Pupils then cover the remaining space on the block with one coloured rod and some orange 10-rods. For example, the following illustration shows what the rods would look like if 40 and 6 were the dice throws.

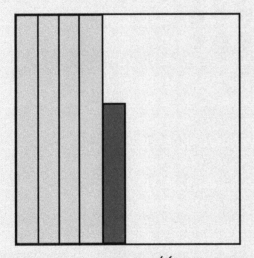

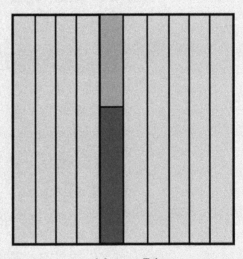

Finding complements to 100: **46** *on a 100-block*   **46** *and* **54**

   Pupils now 'read' the rods they have added to find that the complement of 46 is 54. It is important for pupils to notice that only one of the ten orange rods that could build up to 100 has been 'broken' into components. *Nine* orange rods remain, the *tenth* being built out of two smaller coloured rods. This is the crucial understanding that is needed to avoid the very common error when children name as complement pairs numbers that actually add up to 110.

   Remind pupils that rods are tools for building mental models, not for getting answers mechanically, and challenge them to answer some of the same problems without using rods (or fingers), but perhaps while having a 100-block in view.

2. Use a Slavonic abacus and later a paper abacus. Both of these are described in the earlier activity in this section on locating 2-digit numbers and putting them into context.

   As in the activity above, pupils generate random 2-digit numbers using tens and units dice. With all the beads on the abacus aligned on one side, have the pupils slide as many beads as are shown on the dice to the other side. Make sure the pupils do not count in

(Continued)

(Continued)

ones, but slide whole tens across, and then all the units in one sweep. The pupils can now find the complement to 100 by reading the beads that have not been moved.

As before, draw the pupils' attention to the fact that on nine of the abacus rows the beads remain in unbroken groups of ten; it is only one row where the group of ten has been split into two components, which are, of course, a pair of complements.

If the pupils are using a paper abacus, show them how to use the translucent overlay to cover just the right number of dots, without counting in ones. The overlay on a paper abacus can be used in any orientation that suits the pupils: horizontally from the top down or from the bottom up, or vertically from the left or from the right.

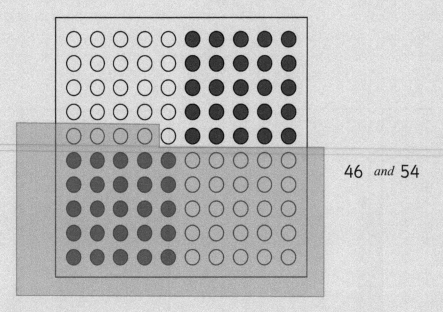

46 *and* 54

3. Earlier activities have described complementary addition on a number line in great detail, so pupils should be able to use the method for complements to 100 without any special introduction.

   Give pupils 2-digit numbers, or have them throw dice to generate numbers. Pupils should only draw the number lines if they feel they need to. If they can find the answer by visualising a number line in their mind's eye, so much the better. Pupils must practise doing the calculation in only two steps: first to the next multiple of 10, and then in one jump to 100, as shown in the illustrated example.

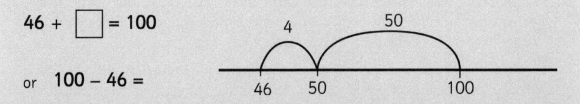

4. Give children practice in solving complements to 100 problems against the clock. They should be able to choose whichever of the above methods they like best to support their mental thinking. Challenge pupils to see how many sums they can do in one minute, or

time them, giving them the opportunity to beat that number or that time on the next occasion. An example of an activity sheet can be found on the CW.

5. Give pupils money problems of the 'how much change' sort, telling them explicitly to use their knowledge of complements for the solutions. An example of an activity sheet can be found on the CW.

6. Tracking complements to 100. Make a tracking sheet on which are several rows of 2-digit additions, some of which add up to 100 and others that add up instead to other numbers, especially totals of 90, 99, 101, or 110. Pupils, working as fast as they can, against the clock, must circle only the pairs of numbers that add up to 100. An example of a tracking sheet to practise complements to 100 can be found on the CW.

Game

Keep the Change!

A game for two players or a small group.

Teaching points:

▶ The game gives practice in complements to 100.

▶ It shows pupils that it helps to know complement facts when solving problems about money.

▶ It gives practice in making amounts out of coins, and in counting amounts in coins.

Equipment needed:

▶ Coins.

▶ A pair of tens and units dice.

Rules:

Each player starts the game with £5 (or €5) to use to 'go shopping' to buy five (virtual) items. Take turns to throw both dice, five times each, to see how much each item costs. After buying each item, keep the change from £1 (or €1). The winner is the player with the most money at the end of the game.

Tips:

The £1 or €1 coins will probably need to be made of plastic or card, but try to provide real coins for the lower denominations if possible, as it makes the game more exciting for the children to collect and count real money.

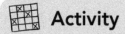 **Activity**

Learn the doubles up to 10 + 10

The doubles facts to 5 + 5 should already be known by heart (see Section 1).

Have pupils make a doubles pyramid out of Cuisenaire rods, like the one shown below. It can also be drawn onto squared paper, preferably 1 cm squared paper (see CW), ⌕ so that the rods fit exactly on top. Make sure that when pupils build the models out of pairs of rods, or when they draw them, the line of symmetry is clearly visible. Use a mirror in the middle to reinforce the symmetrical structure, as this will help pupils think of doubling as 'twice as much' instead of the less useful 'add one more group'.

Show pupils exactly how they can use this visual model to find doubles facts: each double is visibly 2 more than the previous fact – *one on each side* of the pyramid – and 2 less than the next double fact. The hardest doubles to remember are, traditionally, 8 + 8 and 9 + 9. However, children who can easily visualise the pyramid and know that 9 + 9 is the step before 10 + 10, are able to reason back from 20.

Pupils who find it difficult to visualise this model may use a bridging through 10 technique instead. For example, 'double 8' becomes 8 + 8, which becomes 8 + 2 + 6 on a visualised number line, to give 16.

Encourage pupils to 'read' the rows of the pyramid, using the words 'double' or 'twice'.

🪟 Activities

Practise and extend the doubles facts

1. Give pupils dice to generate random numbers to double: a normal die will give practice up to 6 + 6 and a 1–10 die will give practice up to 10 + 10.

2. Play a game of Doubles Ping-Pong. The teacher calls out a number between 1 and 10. Each pupil in turn has to 'bounce back' the double as quickly as possible. A pupil who takes too long is deemed to have 'dropped the ball', and must sit out the rest of the round.

3. Play a game of Double Take (below).

4. Use rods to demonstrate to pupils how their existing doubling knowledge can be extended to larger numbers. Note that pupils must have some understanding of place value first (see Section 3). For example, for double 24, make the number out of rods and put it in a tens-and-units formation on one side of a piece of paper that has been folded, or clearly marked, in half.

If necessary, allow the pupils to make the number again on the other half of the paper, but as soon as possible encourage pupils to imagine that the fold line is a mirror so that they can visualise the doubling, without having to actually see two groups of rods. At this stage, show pupils how to make an informal notation, like the one illustrated, with separate arrows descending from each digit. Notice that arrows are being used here to denote that something has to happen to these numbers (doubling, in this case). By contrast, the triad notation is without arrows, to indicate a static description of number relationships rather than an active operation. If you think pupils might confuse the two notations, do add a small '× 2' along each arrow.

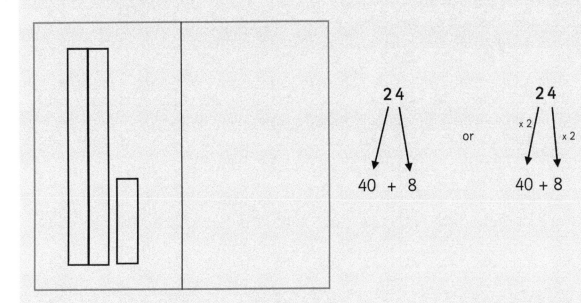

(Continued)

(Continued)

Next, do the same for numbers where the units are between 5 and 9, e.g. double 36.

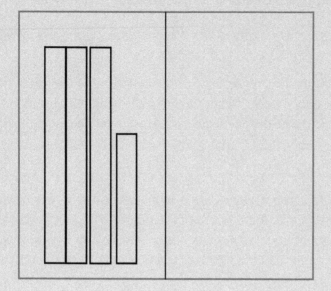

36

60 + 12

Activity

Halving is the opposite of doubling

Halving is much harder than doubling, quite apart from the problem of halving odd numbers. The main difficulty is that halving does not declare itself in the same way as doubling. For example, all pupils can see that 19 + 19 is a doubling question even if they do not know how to find the answer, whereas 38 − 19 does not signal to the solver that there is any doubling or halving involved.

Therefore, a good way to start halving practice is to set up a situation where pupils have to find half of a number that they have only recently doubled, and vice versa. An exercise that helps pupils connect the two ideas and the two procedures can be found amongst the activity sheets on the CW.

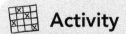 **Activity**

Find half of round numbers

Use Cuisenaire rods to find half of round numbers. Start with numbers that have an even number of tens. Have the child name the amounts both as a quantity of 10-rods and as a multiple of 10, e.g. *These 6 tens are 60, so half is 30, or 3 tens.*

Numbers that have an odd number of tens will require much more practice. Do not let the child split every rod in half by exchanging all the orange rods for yellow rods. Instead, show how moving one orange rod aside creates two groups that the child already knows how to halve separately: an even number of orange rods, and a single orange rod. At first, you could allow pupils to physically split the single orange 10 into two yellow 5s. Soon pupils should be able to find the answer by just looking at the rectangle of long rods and introducing judicious spacing, as shown here.

Finally, give pupils problems to solve mentally, without rods.

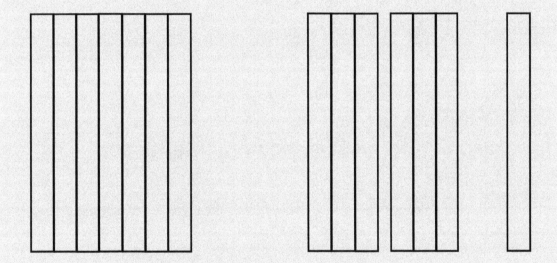

To halve an odd number of 10s, first rearrange them as an even number of 10s, plus one single 10.

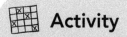 **Activity**

Function machines for doubling and halving

Introduce pupils to the idea of a function machine: a 'machine' that performs the same, pre-agreed, operation on any number that enters the machine.

Introduce a doubling machine by drawing something very simple, like the example illustrated here. Make sure that the operation the machine performs, and the direction of movement from left to right, are both very clear. Label the machine either '× 2' or 'double'.

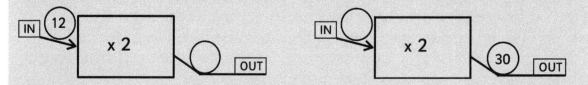

Pupils are given numbers that sometimes go into the machine, and sometimes come out of the machine. Repeat the activity for halving machines, to emphasise the connection between doubling and halving. To avoid one of the more common problems, do not ask pupils to halve odd numbers yet.

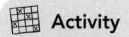 **Activity**

Use reasoning to find near-complements and near-doubles

Remind pupils of the key reasoning idea that you will already have introduced them to in previous activities: that when a number has two components, as soon as one component is increased or decreased by an amount the other component must be adjusted by the same amount in the opposite direction, if the total is to stay the same.

This work can now be extended to using complement facts and doubles facts with larger numbers. For example, because you know 20 + 80 = 100, you can work out what to add to 22 to make 100, without treating it as a new and separate problem. A doubles example might be: work out 16 – 7 from your knowledge that double 8 is 16.

Put one of the known complements or doubles facts up on the board, and ask pupils to find and write down some near-complements and near-doubles questions that can be derived from these facts. Pupils swap papers and answer each other's problems.

Two pages full of examples designed to give pupils practice in reasoning from complement facts and doubles facts can be found amongst the activity sheets on the CW.

Game

Double Take

A solitaire or patience game.

Teaching points:

▶ The game provides practice in the doubles facts up to 10 + 10.

▶ The game provides practice in deriving a near-doubles fact from a known doubles fact. For example, you can find 7 and 6 by reasoning from double 6 or from double 7.

Equipment needed:

▶ A pack of 36 digit cards (see CW) or playing cards, made up of four cards for each of the numbers 2–10.

Rules:

Shuffle the cards. Place one card face down in the centre and then set out 9 cards, face up, in a 3 by 3 array, positioning the middle card of the array on top of the face-down card. Clear away the cards in pairs according to the following rules: the two cards must be either doubles (i.e. two cards for the same number) or near-doubles (i.e. cards for consecutive numbers); also, both cards must lie in the same row or column. As you clear the cards, announce the total value of the pair aloud.

You must calculate the total value by using doubles facts and reasoning strategies. For example, once you identify 7 and 6 as a near-double, you can find the total by thinking, *Double 6 is 12, so 7 + 6 must be one more, which is 13,* or *Double 7 is 14, so 7 + 6 must be one less, which is 13.*

As soon as cards are removed from the array, replace them with new cards from the pack. After all the cards in the pack have been used, you may turn over the face-down card as soon as it is exposed, to bring it into play.

The game is won when all the cards have been dealt out. It is rare to be able to clear all the cards: a remainder of four cards, or two cards, at the end can be considered a good, or a very good, outcome. Make a note of how many cards remain and try to beat this score next time; alternatively, keep a record of the total face value of the cards remaining at the end and try to beat that score next time.

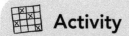 **Activity**

9 is almost 10

Using Cuisenaire rods, show the following two ways of adding 9 to a number, for example, 6 + 9 (or 9 + 6). Put a 6-rod and a 9-rod end to end. Put a 10-rod immediately under the 9-rod, aligning both at the right.

In language that should already be familiar to them, show pupils that because the 9 is being increased by one unit to 10, the other component must be decreased by one unit, in this case from 6 to 5. So, the problem 6 + 9 becomes 5 + 10.

The other, slightly different, way is to put an orange 10-rod under the 9-rod so that the extra unit is sticking out. This time the explanation points out that because 10 is one more than 9, adding 10 will overshoot the target by one unit, which must then be adjusted by 1 in the opposite direction. So, the problem 6 + 9 becomes 6 + 10 − 1.

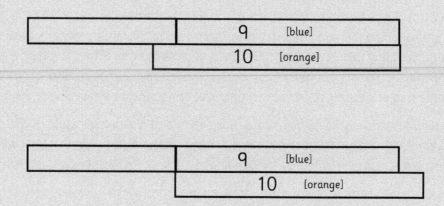

After making sure pupils understand the logic of both these slightly different methods of adding 9, pupils should be allowed to choose only one of the methods for themselves. Set up lots of problems for adding 9 to 2-digit and then 3-digit numbers for pupils to practise their own chosen method.

The techniques can also be adapted to + 99: either pupils can decrease the first addend by 1 so that they can use the 1 to combine with 99 to make 100 (pupils quite enjoy the idea of 'pinching' 1 from one number and attaching it to the other); or pupils can add 100 to the first addend and then subtract 1.

⊞ Activity

The Basic 8 strategies

The 'Basic 8' strategies are the most useful, and most important, mental arithmetic strategies for addition and subtraction. It is often a relief to pupils to learn that there are only eight strategies they need to know for basic competence. What is more, they already know them.

Details of all these strategies can be found in earlier activities, both in this section and in the previous section. What is new about this activity is that the pupils are being explicitly told about the Basic 8 strategies and are taught to focus on when each strategy is helpful. The Basic 8 strategies are:

▶ Plus or minus 1

▶ Plus or minus 2

▶ Plus or minus 10

▶ Complements to 10 and near-complements (alternatively 'almost complements')

▶ Doubles and near-doubles (alternatively 'almost double')

▶ 9 is almost 10 (alternatively 'almost 10', or 'nearly 10')

▶ Bridging through 10

▶ Complementary addition (alternatively 'subtraction by adding').

Make cards to give to pupils, or have the pupils make a set of cards for themselves, with the strategies written on them, one strategy per card. See the CW ⌖ for cards that you can photocopy and distribute to pupils. I tend to use ten cards for the eight strategies, but you could combine the 'complements and near-complements' and the 'doubles and near-doubles' if you prefer the logic of eight cards for eight strategies.

Present the cards to the pupils one at a time (probably not all at the same lesson), reminding them that they already know the strategy, and invite examples from the group to demonstrate the strategy. Collect some examples on the board. For example, give all the pupils the card labelled 'plus or minus 1', explain the sign ± , and say: *Who remembers this strategy? How can we find the answer to a number plus or minus one? Give me an example of a number question that asks us to add or subtract one.* After collecting a number of suitable examples, wipe them off the board before asking pupils to write one example for themselves on the back of their card, so that they will be able to remember what the label on the front means.

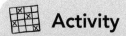 **Activity**

Identify which strategy works best in different situations

Together with the pupils, examine a page full of easy mixed addition and subtraction problems to give children practice in determining when any of the Basic 8 strategies can be helpful. On the CW you will find a blank activity sheet called *Which Strategy?*, that can be adapted by including some or all of the Basic 8 in the list of known strategies, and by using larger or smaller numbers in the addition and subtraction problems, depending on what best suits the learners' needs and capabilities.

Pupils can win a point for identifying a good strategy, and another for a correct answer. Remind pupils that counting up or down in ones is not considered to be a good strategy unless there are only one or two steps. Note that some problems can be solved by more than one good strategy, e.g. the answer to 60 – 31 could be found because it is a near-double fact or by complementary addition (which requires knowledge of complement facts, therefore 'using complements' cannot be named as a third strategy). A pupil who identifies both strategies, and gives the correct answer of 29, can score three points.

SECTION 3

Place value

Overview

This third section collects together the activities that help teach the concept of place value, i.e. that the value represented by a numeral depends upon its position within a number. This concept cannot be left until all the activities in the previous two sections have been completed, but must be introduced alongside the earlier work on basic calculations.

Place value is an abstract idea that many children find confusing. An understanding of the place value system is best cultivated by activities that focus on the notion of exchange.

In addition to the regrouping and conversion ideas that are fundamental to the concept of place value, pupils must learn that in the decimal system the base is 10 and that the column positions therefore represent powers of 10.

A note about the threefold nature of the column labelling system

Most children are first introduced to single-digit numbers, and, as they grow older, to 2-digit numbers (which we teach them to call tens and units) and then to 3-digit numbers (introducing the hundreds) and later still to 4-digit numbers (introducing thousands). This gradual introduction leads many children to assume that every column in our place value system has a completely new name. This misconception is at the root of the very common mistake in which pupils 'lose' or merge one or more of the columns, especially those denoting tens of thousands and hundreds of thousands.

It is, therefore, important to tell pupils explicitly that entirely new labels are given, not to every column, but to every group of *three* columns. Each new 'family' of place values – ones, thousands, millions, billions, etc. – consists of subsections of units, tens and hundreds, each in their own column. Thus, multi-digit numbers have (starting at the right): units, tens and hundreds of *ones*, then units, tens and hundreds of *thousands*, then units, tens and hundreds of *millions*, etc.

My experience is that a clear explanation of the threefold logic behind place value column labels often comes as a complete surprise and revelation to students of all ages.

You can find a video about this section of *The Dyscalculia Toolkit* on the CW.

What are the main problems?

▶ Confusing the absolute value of the numbers 1–9 with the symbolic value of numerals in multi-digit numbers.

▶ Not appreciating that our place value system has a decimal structure, i.e. it is based on powers of 10.

▶ Being unaware of the threefold pattern of 'units, tens, hundreds', or that it is a repeating pattern.

▶ Not understanding how zero works as a place holder.

▶ Having no feel for the actual value of large numbers.

▶ Making no connections between place value work and mental calculation.

▶ Not recognising that multi-digit numbers can be partitioned into tens and units in more than one way.

How to help

▶ Do not rush the early work with concrete materials. Progress in very small steps. Revisit early activities often.

▶ Do not insist that everything is recorded in writing. Practical experience comes first.

▶ Remember that concrete materials are best used to help build cognitive models and should not be used simply to find an answer mechanically.

▶ Let the pupils manipulate the concrete material themselves, to explore new ideas. Do not restrict the use of apparatus to demonstrations only, or just to illustrate a written algorithm.

▶ Use continuous materials that showcase 10 as a single unit, in preference to discrete materials that require sequential counting and consequently encourage pupils to see 10 only as a group of ten ones.

▶ Use proportional concrete materials such as Cuisenaire rods or Dienes blocks, before using more abstract representational materials such as a spike abacus, colour-coded chips, or money.

▶ Use concrete materials before diagrams. Use pictures and diagrams as a transitional stage between concrete and abstract work.

▶ Emphasise the repeating pattern of units, tens and hundreds (see the overview to this section). In column work, always set out columns in groups of three. For example, even when working with numbers of four digits, show six columns (i.e. including all three of the thousands columns). Similarly, use three or six, never four, spikes on a spike abacus.

▶ Be explicit about what is happening at every step. Encourage pupils to talk aloud about what they are doing and why. When you are doing the talking, vary your vocabulary.

▶ Use hypothetical questions to encourage visualisation and mental work.

▶ Explain to pupils explicitly that place value is a kind of shorthand to save time. Experiment with longhand writing of numbers and informal jottings to highlight the efficiency of the standard place value system.

▶ Play games that help teach place value. Set games for homework practice.

▶ Spend at least as much time on subtraction as on addition. Concrete activities and games that help illuminate decomposition are especially valuable.

▶ Teach pupils how to split numbers into components in a variety of ways, e.g. 32 = 2 + 30 and also 12 + 20.

▶ Be explicit about the connection between the mental calculations that pupils are already familiar with and the more condensed notation and procedures of column arithmetic.

▶ After showing pupils different ways of splitting and recombining numbers in order to solve addition and subtraction problems involving 2-digit or 3-digit numbers, allow each pupil to settle on only one or two methods to practise and adopt.

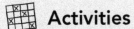 **Activities**

Exchange units into tens

1. On different occasions, use different objects that you designate as 'units'. From a large heap of units, pupils must sort out ten and find ways to keep the ten in a separate group, e.g. by using saucers, boxes, small transparent plastic bags, rubber bands, or sticky tape. The objects could be bricks, cubes, hairpins, lolly sticks, plastic shapes, games tokens, counters, beans, beads, pebbles, nuggets, buttons, paper-clips, shells, straws, toothpicks, spaghetti shapes, bolts, strips of paper, lengths of ribbon, cards, pencils, etc. At the end of the activity, pupils must say how many tens they have and therefore how many units are contained in the bundled groups.

2. Set up activities like the one above, where there is a banker who will exchange ten units for a packaged ten, and where children can accumulate items according to the throw of a die, or the spin of a spinner. After practising this activity with some of the objects suggested above, pupils can also exchange ten white Cuisenaire cubes for an orange rod at the bank, or ten unit cubes for a Dienes long, or ten pennies for one 10p coin, or ten 1 cent coins for a 10 cent coin.

3. Set up a bank for making exchanges like the activity above, but where the exchange is not measurable. Instead, it is the result of a previously made agreement. For example, pupils can exchange ten small shirt buttons for a fancy button, or five dull-coloured counters for a shiny one, or five beans for a small marble and ten beans for a large marble. This activity emphasises that exchange is about equivalent value.

Activities

Concrete counting on place value mats

Cuisenaire rods are excellent for place value work if you use only the white and orange rods (except for step-counting). Dienes blocks, or other base-10 materials, are just as good (again, except for step-counting).

You can enlarge, photocopy and laminate the mats provided on the CW. But it is also useful practice for pupils to make their own mats. Note that the hundreds column must be at least 10 cm wide to accommodate base-10 material, and that it is logical to make each column the same width.

In the following counting activities, do not always start the count at zero or one.

1. *Count up and exchange.* A pupil takes or makes a place value mat (see CW). The pupil takes one white cube at a time out of the Cuisenaire box and puts it on the mat, keeping a count of the running total. As soon as there are 10 white cubes, they must be exchanged for an orange 10-rod which is put in the tens column. The pupil explains the exchange procedure, and the reason for it, aloud.

2. *Decomposition is the inverse of exchange.* Reverse the process described above, so that a pupil starts with a random amount on the mat made up of white and orange rods and returns one cube at a time to the Cuisenaire rods box, counting down as every cube is returned, and explaining aloud the decomposition procedure when a ten must be exchanged for units.

3. *Group work, counting up.* A small group uses one place value mat (but it is very important that all members of the group are looking at it the right way up). Pupils take it in turns to add one white cube to the group's collection and announce the total so far. The pupil who puts a tenth cube onto the unit side of the mat is responsible for making the exchange and explaining aloud what is happening and why. The size of the groups should be planned so that the exchanges do not always fall to the same pupils. Do not always start the count at 1.

4. *Group work, counting back.* Reverse the process described above so that members of a group are removing rods one at a time and counting backwards. Ensure that it is not always the same person who has to perform and explain the decomposition procedure.

5. *Hundreds, tens and units.* All the activities above can be adapted for a three-column mat (see CW). The counting up and down is now done in tens, so the unit column will remain empty throughout. The exchange, and decomposition, procedures must be explained aloud.

6. *Cross-counting.* Pupils in a small group use one three-column place value mat between them, with all viewing the mat the right way up. Just as in the activities above, pupils take turns to add one rod to the mat, announce the accumulated total, and perform any exchange or decomposition that is necessary on their turn. What's new in this activity is that a randomly timed noise, like a teacher's hand-clap, becomes the signal for the pupils to change from counting in ones to counting in tens, and then back again at the next clap.

7. *Cross-counting up and down.* Extend the above activity by having someone call out what kind of counting the group must perform, and changing the instructions frequently:

counting up or counting down, combined with counting in ones, tens or hundreds. It is very useful for pupils to be able to do this concretely before they are expected to cross-count abstractly without supporting materials.

8. *Use money on place value mats.* The activities above can be performed with money, instead of rods, on the place value mats. For two-column work, use 1p and 10p coins (or 1 cent and 10 cent coins) and count in ones, or use a 1–3 die to accumulate different amounts at each step. For three-column work, use £1 (or €1) coins in the hundreds column in conjunction with a 1–10 or a 1–20 die. As already mentioned, it is important for the pupils to articulate aloud exactly what is happening when exchanging coins and moving them from one column to another on the place value mats.

Game

Magic 10s

This is one of Professor Sharma's games, for two or three children (see his 1993 articles on the *Place Value Concept*).

Teaching points:

▶ The game teaches that ten units, when grouped together, form a single unit of 10 times the value, i.e. that 10 is ten ones, and at the same time, is also one ten.

▶ It teaches that quantities set out in a tens and units pattern can be determined without having to start counting from 1.

▶ It reinforces the connection between our spoken names for 2-digit numbers and their tens-and-units structure.

Equipment needed:

▶ A place value mat for each player, showing two columns labelled 'Tens' and 'Units'.

▶ Unifix cubes, or any unit cubes that can be attached together end to end.

▶ A die or spinner.

Rules:

Take turns to throw the die or spin the spinner, and accumulate single cubes on the units side of your mat to match the number thrown. The rule is that 10 is the magic number, so cubes can only be clicked together when there are ten of them. As soon as you make a 10, move it onto the tens side of the mat. Play continues for a certain number of turns, or a certain length of time, before the winner is found, or until one player reaches a target number, say 30.

Tips:

It is a good idea for players to call out how much they have accumulated so far at the end of every turn. At first play with a 1–3 die or spinner; later play with larger numbers, e.g. 1–6 or 4–9 dice or spinners.

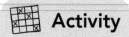 **Activities**

Make a 20-step staircase and explore the 'teen' number names

1. Have the pupils make a staircase from 1 to 10 out of Cuisenaire rods and then extend the staircase to 20. This activity, which is described and illustrated in Section 2, highlights the way that the 'teen' numbers are constructed out of tens and units.

2. Use the staircase to help pupils connect the spoken names for the numbers 11–19 with the actual values. Tell pupils explicitly that the 'teen' numbers are irregular. The words eleven and twelve seem to have no connection with the tens-and-units combinations, while in the numbers 13 to 19 there is a discrepancy between the order in which we read or write the digits and the order in which we hear or say them. By contrast, the numbers above 20 are more consistent because tens come first in both spoken and written formats.

Activity

Cover 20

Make a shallow tray measuring 10 cm × 2 cm out of card (see CW) for each pupil. The pupils' aim is to fill their tray with rods. Pupils throw a 6-sided die, take a single rod to match the throw, and place the rod in the tray. As the total value of the rods approaches 10, pupils (usually) have to exchange a new rod for two smaller rods in order to fit them into the tray. Pupils then swap their collection of smaller rods for a single orange 10-rod. They must talk through all the decompositions and both of the exchanges needed to fill the tray. (See also the Frame an Addition game in Section 2.)

Game

Race to Cover 100

A game for two or more players. You can find a short demonstration video of this game on the CW.

Teaching points:

▶ The game focuses on the principle of exchange that underlies place value.

▶ It provides a concrete model of 100 that pupils can later connect to the abstract 100-square format.

Equipment needed:

▶ A 10 cm square tray or frame to fill (see CW) for each player, or a Dienes 100-block each as a base to cover.

▶ Two 1–6 or 1–10 dice.

▶ Cuisenaire rods, including 10 orange rods for each player.

Rules:

Take turns to throw the dice and take as few rods as possible to match your throw (i.e. not a pile of ones). Put the rods in columns, working from left to right across the 100-square. As each column fills, you may have to exchange a single rod for two smaller rods, so that each column is filled before a new column is started. Exchange any whole column of rods for an orange rod. Keep a running total, both spoken and written, of how much you have after each turn. The winner is the first player to fill their tray, or square, with ten orange rods.

Game

Four Throws to Reach 100

This game for two or more players is proposed by Ian Sugarman in *Teaching and Learning Early Number*, edited by Ian Thompson.

Teaching points:

▶ The game helps build a sense of the magnitude of numbers up to 100.

▶ The game teaches base-10 place value.

▶ It shows the connection between column value (e.g. three tens) and quantity value (30).

Equipment needed:

▶ A board (see CW⬏) or a place value mat for each player.

▶ White and orange Cuisenaire rods, or units and tens from a set of Dienes blocks or other base-10 materials, or coins with values of 1 and 10.

▶ A 1–6 die.

Rules:

Take turns to throw the die. No player may miss a turn and the round ends when each player has had four throws. On your turn, you must decide immediately whether to take a matching number of single units or of tens. Any player whose total goes over 100 is out. The winner of the round is the player whose total is nearest 100. Play several rounds, or play for 5 minutes, to find the overall winner of the game.

Variation:

Use tens and hundreds blocks, or equivalent coins, for a target of 1000.

🔲 Activities

Make and read numbers made of Cuisenaire rods or base-10 materials

Cuisenaire rods can be supplemented by 10 cm × 10 cm × 1 cm flat blocks in plastic or wood, to represent 100. Large cubes to represent 1000 can also be bought, but are expensive. You could make cardboard 1000-cubes, and even glue ten such cubes together to make a 10,000 'long'.

1. Give pupils 2-digit numbers to make with concrete materials. At first, the numbers can be built on place value mats, to get pupils used to the idea that the tens are grouped together at the left (and not arranged into a long train, as they were in earlier activities with smaller numbers). Later, numbers can be made without the mats. Pupils should read the number they have made, and can also record it on paper, as illustrated. Give plenty of practice with the teen numbers as well as the larger numbers.

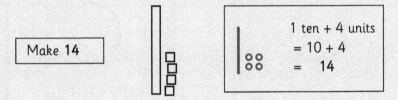

2. Pupils pick two single-digit cards from which they must build the larger of the two possible 2-digit numbers. When the rods are laid out, the pupil takes the card representing the tens digit and puts it on the orange rods, and puts the unit card as close as possible to the white rods. The pupil then repeats the exercise with the same cards now arranged to make the smaller 2-digit number.

3. Pupils take a small pile of mixed white and orange rods. They must arrange them in a tens-and-units pattern and read the pattern to find the total value of the rods.

4. In any of the activities above, it is useful for the teacher to ask hypothetical questions – such as *What if you had … one more ten*, or *one less unit* – so that pupils learn to visualise the concrete materials and manipulate the quantities in their mind's eye.

5. The four activities above can be repeated with 3-digit and 4-digit numbers.

6. Pupils make multi-digit numbers in groups, with one pupil responsible for the tens, another for the hundreds, etc. All pupils read the number. Pupils swap roles after a few numbers.

Games

Dice and spinner games

Dorian Yeo gives a good selection of place value games in her book *Dyslexia, Dyspraxia & Mathematics*. Most of them are played on place value mats with concrete base-10 materials. Spinners, labelled 'ones' and 'tens', or 'H', 'T' and 'U', are used on their own or in conjunction with dice to produce instructions to add, or subtract, amounts from one column at a time. The most valuable aspect of these games is the focus on *change* in the values of the concrete materials, rather than on a static amount. An integral and important part of each game is that players record quantities in columns at the end of every turn.

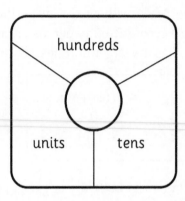
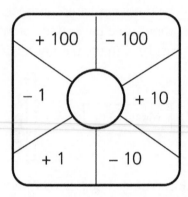

Activities

Practise subtraction and decomposition with concrete materials

1. Have the pupils build any 2-digit number below 25 on a place value mat using Cuisenaire rods or Dienes blocks or similar base-10 materials. Use a 1–3 die to decide how much is to be subtracted at each turn. The pupils must say, before touching any of the materials, whether an exchange will be necessary. At every decomposition, the teacher supervises the exchange, and encourages the pupils to talk through what they are doing and why. Pupils must write down what remains after each subtraction.

   At the end, pupils should be asked to look back at this list of numbers, and deduce the die throw. Pupils can be asked to write down some of the subtractions both as horizontal equations and as vertical subtractions in columns.

   It is really important not to let pupils carry out this activity without supervision. (After all, if they can do it without any muddle on their own, they do not need to practise the activity at all.) Here is how to manage the all-important exchange: the 10-rod should be taken off the mat, and placed in a designated exchange area, e.g. the lid of the box of rods, or a piece of paper. The ten units are counted up or lined up and measured alongside the 10-rod, and then taken by the pupils, as a whole group, back to the mat. The units should be put initially into the tens column, or along the line that separates the tens from the units column, and then immediately moved into the units column. During all these procedures, the pupils should commentate in detail on every action.

2. Repeat the activity described above, starting with 2-digit numbers above 25 and using a die showing larger numbers, e.g. 0–9 or 4–9.

3. Repeat the activity with 3-digit numbers between 100 and 200, on a place value mat, with a 0–9 die. Later, use larger numbers and a 1–20 die.

4. Repeat the activity with 3-digit numbers, but use a die to show how many tens, not units, are to be subtracted. It is now the hundreds that will be decomposed and exchanged.

5. Try some of these activities using money instead of base-10 blocks or rods.

All five activities can be adapted into games where pupils compete with each other.

Game

Spot the Decomposition

A game for two players, or a solitaire activity.

Teaching points:

▌ The game familiarises pupils with the (sometimes inverted) vocabulary of subtraction.

▌ It teaches pupils not to assume that subtraction means a smaller amount taken away from a larger one, e.g. when taking 6 from 23 vertically, not to fall into the common error of reversing the units and finding 6 – 3.

▌ It gives practice in identifying the situations where decomposition will be necessary.

Equipment needed:

▌ Cards, made by the teacher, on which are written various subtraction problems, some of which require decomposition to solve and others that do not. Present some problems vertically, some horizontally, and some using words, as in the examples below.

18 – 5	23 – 6	Take 14 away from 16	27 minus 11	41 subtract 7	125 – 22

Rules:

Players race to sort all their cards into two piles: 'decomposition needed' or 'no decomposition'.

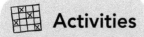 **Activities**

Use a spike abacus

There are so many sources for ideas on using a spike abacus to teach place value that I do not detail any here. However, there are some important considerations to bear in mind.

When working on place value, avoid using an abacus with four spikes. Start with two spikes for 2-digit work, followed by three spikes for 3-digit work. Use six spikes for 4-digit, 5-digit and 6-digit numbers. This is so as to emphasise the threefold nature of our place value system, as explained at the start of this section.

Abacus work is more abstract than work with rods. It may be helpful to use different coloured beads for each place value spike at first. Abacus work makes a useful transition between concrete and pictorial or diagrammatic work.

Be aware that some children who struggle with arithmetic have directional confusion. It is therefore crucial for pupils to have a front view of the abacus at all times.

Game

Win Counters on a 100-Square

A game for two or three players.

Teaching points:

▷ The game highlights the place value structure of the numbers below 100.

▷ It familiarises pupils with the 100-square format.

Equipment needed:

▷ A 100-square, i.e. a paper square showing all the numbers from 1 to 100 (see CW).

▷ 17 counters, each of a size to cover one of the squares.

▷ Two 0–9 dice.

Rules:

Players sit facing the 100-square and place the counters at random over the square, so that each counter covers and hides one number. Take turns to throw both dice. On your turn, arrange the digits in whatever order you choose to form a 2-digit number. The aim is to match a number hidden by one of the counters by adding (or subtracting) either 1 or 10 to (or from) the number created on the dice. If successful, remove and keep the counter. The winner is the player who has won the most counters.

Tips:

Do not allow players to look underneath the counters to see the hidden numbers. Because the game gets slower as there are fewer counters on the board, play for a certain number of turns, rather than until all the counters have been won.

1	●	3	4	5	6	7	8	9	10
11	12	13	14	●	16	17	18	19	20
21	22	●	24	25	26	27	●	29	30
●	32	33	34	35	36	37	38	39	●
41	42	43	44	●	46	●	48	49	50
51	52	53	●	55	56	●	58	59	60
61	62	●	64	65	66	67	●	69	70
71	72	73	74	75	●	77	78	●	80
81	●	83	84	85	86	●	88	89	90
91	92	93	94	●	96	97	98	99	100

Game

Race through a 100-Square

A game for two or three players.

Teaching points:

▶ The game highlights the place value structure of the numbers below 100.

▶ It familiarises pupils with both the horizontal and vertical formats of the 100-square (see CW).

Equipment needed:

▶ An unnumbered paper 100-square (see CW for game boards or 100-squares) and pencils.

▶ A token for each player.

▶ A pair of tens and units dice.

Rules:

Take turns to throw the dice and to move your token accordingly. At each turn, you must find your new position with as little counting as possible. Write the correct number in the blank square on which you land. If the square has already been numbered by an opponent, move your token to the first available blank square and record that number. The first player to reach, or pass, 100 is the winner.

Tip:

Before the game starts, players must decide if the numbers will run from left to right in rows or from top to bottom in columns. Choose the alternative format for the next game.

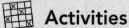 **Activities**

Practise adding and subtracting 10 and 100

Set up paper-and-pencil exercises that give pupils practice in adding and subtracting 10. If you see pupils using their fingers to count, they will need more time exploring the earlier activities that use concrete materials, before returning to these abstract exercises.

1. Written addition problems might look like this: $\square + 10 = \square$, where dice can be used to provide random numbers to go in either the first, or sometimes the second, box. An activity sheet to practise addition problems like these can be found on the CW.

2. Written subtraction problems might look like this: $\square - 10 = \square$. Again, vary the exercise by sometimes giving a number to be put in the first box and sometimes in the second box. An activity sheet to practise subtraction problems like these can be found on the CW.

3. Later, extend this abstract work to adding and subtracting tens and hundreds from 3-digit numbers.

Game

Steer the Number

This is another Ian Sugarman game from *Teaching and Learning Early Number*, for two or three players.

Teaching points:

▶ The game teaches place value.

▶ It teaches adding and subtracting multiples of 10 from 2-digit numbers.

▶ It shows how 2-digit mental calculations can be achieved in steps, one 'column' at a time.

▶ It gives practice in using a calculator.

Equipment needed:

▶ A tens-and-units place value mat.

▶ Base-10 materials, e.g. Cuisenaire orange and white rods, or Dienes blocks.

▶ A pack of cards with one each of the numbers 1–99 (or a list of ten unique 2-digit numbers for each player).

▶ A calculator.

Rules:

Each player takes ten cards from the shuffled pack, or is given a list of ten random 2-digit numbers (numbers that no other player is given). Players win a point when one of these numbers is created during the course of the game. A random number (that no player has been given) is chosen as a starting number and is built from concrete materials on the place value mat.

On your turn you must make one change to the quantity on the mat, by either adding or subtracting any number of 10-rods *or* unit-cubes, and announcing what you are doing. For example: *I'm taking away two tens, so now there is … left.* After the action and the verbal commentary, use the calculator to record the addition/subtraction. You may not add or subtract an amount that would require adjustments to both sides of the mat (e.g. you may not

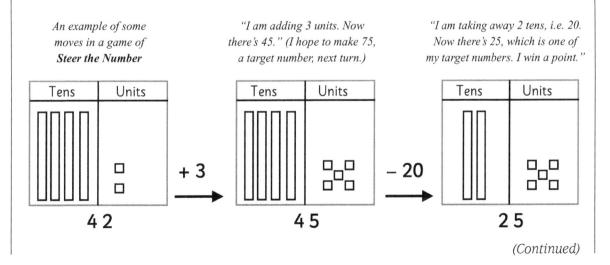

An example of some moves in a game of Steer the Number

"I am adding 3 units. Now there's 45." (I hope to make 75, a target number, next turn.)

"I am taking away 2 tens, i.e. 20. Now there's 25, which is one of my target numbers. I win a point."

(Continued)

(Continued)

add more than 7 to 2, or subtract more than 2 from 2); nor are you allowed to miss a turn. At any time that the mat contains the exact number on a player's list, whether by their own actions or their opponents' actions, the player crosses the number off the list and wins a point. The winner is the first player to have made all ten numbers and won 10 points.

Tips:

There is more luck involved when each player keeps their list of target numbers hidden from the others. On the other hand, it can be more fun for players to see all the target numbers and to try to think up what strategy will maximise their own chances of winning.

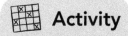 **Activity**

Transform a 2-digit number in two steps

Pupils will find this abstract activity more meaningful if they have previously played the Steer the Number game above.

Pupils make a starting number by taking two digit cards and arranging them in whichever order they prefer. A second 2-digit number is made by throwing tens and units dice, i.e. no choice is given about the order of the digits of this second number. The pupils must say, and then record on paper, how to change the first number into the second, in two steps: the first step will alter the tens and the second step will alter the digits. For example, to change 28 to 76:

28 ➔ 76   *Add fifty, subtract two.*   28 + 50 = 78   78 − 2 = 76

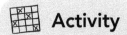 **Activity**

Teach the threefold repeating pattern: units, tens and hundreds

Make explicit to pupils that numbers are written in groups of three: first units, tens and hundreds of *ones*, then units, tens and hundreds of *thousands*, then units, tens and hundreds of *millions*, etc. (See the introduction to this section.)

Teach pupils to make and label place value columns in sets of three, like those illustrated below. Use thick lines to emphasise the threefold grouping. After writing the labels as shown, pupils might like to put into brackets the final 's' of the 'millions' and 'thousands' labels and the word 'ones' (and half of the word 'tens', leaving just the contraction '-ty') since these do not form part of the spoken labels.

Reassure pupils that, once they can read and write 3-digit numbers, they can read and write any number.

Millions			Thousands			Ones		
Hundreds	Tens	Units	Hundreds	Tens	Units	Hundreds	Tens	Units

Millions			Thousands			Ones		
H	T	U	H	T	U	H	T	U

⊞ Activities

Explore place value as a shorthand

1. Dictate any 4-digit number whose digits range from 1 to 9 (but not zero) for the pupils to write down as follows: numerals are to be used for the digits but words (or letters for the contraction 'ty' for the word 'ten') are to be used for the values. For example, for the dictated number '2375', the pupils must write:

   2 thousand 3 hundred and 7-ty 5

Pupils should turn the page sideways – landscape format – so that the whole number can be written on a single line. Pupils now use a highlighter to write over the digits, and at the end of the line write the whole number in digits, which they copy from the board.

   2 thousand **3** hundred and **7**-ty **5** = **2375**

Continue to dictate other 4-digit numbers in the same way. After a while, ask pupils what they notice. If necessary, draw their attention to the fact that the digits are always in the same order, and that therefore the words 'hundreds' or 'thousands' are implied even when they are not written out, just as the word 'units' is implied but not spoken in the numbers below 10.

2. Have pupils write a 4-digit number using only digits but with all the values shown as multiplications of powers of ten. For example, the number 2375 is written:

   $(2 \times 1000) + (3 \times 100) + (7 \times 10) + (5 \times 1)$

Even without the brackets, this is an unnecessarily long way of writing a 4-digit number, even though it is mathematically correct. The convention of having columns denoting the value of digits is therefore revealed as a useful shorthand.

Activities

Read and write multi-digit numbers

1. Show pupils how the place value columns work, starting with 3-digit numbers that contain no zeros at first, e.g. 365. Repeat the same digits in the thousands columns, e.g. 365 365, and explain how to read this new number, pointing to the column headings as you do so. Repeat the same digits in the millions columns and explain how to read this new number: 365 365 365. Give lots of practice in reading a variety of 3-digit, 6-digit and 9-digit numbers, before introducing numbers with zeros and numbers of other amounts of digits.

2. Invite a pupil to label nine columns and to write a 9-digit number with one digit in each column. The number is hidden under a sheet of paper. Other pupils in the group must read the number aloud, while the sheet of paper is moved to the right in stages, so that three new digits are revealed at each stage.

3. Show pupils how to insert commas between each triple-column grouping of H, T, and U. Emphasise that the groups of three must be counted from the right, or from the decimal point, and only then can the number be read, starting from the left. Commas should not be too large, must always sit on the line, and should never be able to be confused with a decimal point.

4. Give pupils practice in adding and subtracting 10 or 100, from 4-digit, 5-digit and 6-digit numbers.

⊞ Activities

Build up large numbers, one column at a time

1. Use a page with clearly marked column headings as a base sheet, and some transparent overlays. Deconstruct a 3-digit number onto three separate transparent overlays, and then put the overlays one over the other, on top of the headed columns, to reconstruct the number. For example, for the number 825, make one overlay showing 800, another showing 20 and a third showing 5. While you do this, remind pupils of the work they have already done in building 3-digit numbers from concrete materials. When the number is reconstructed, by putting the overlays on top of each other, the last two digits seem to be superimposed onto zeros (the number will be easier to read if you exaggerate the size of the zeros slightly). Eva Grauberg, from whose book *Elementary Mathematics and Language Difficulties* this activity is taken, suggests that pupils can find it helpful to see numerals superimposed onto zeros in this way.

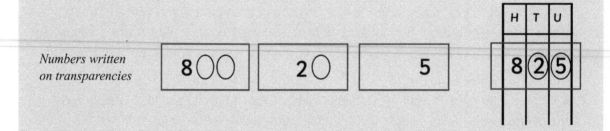

Numbers written on transparencies

2. Repeat the activity with numbers that include zero as a place-holder.

3. Repeat the activity with numbers larger than three digits.

4. Repeat the activity without the overlays, but simply writing a number on paper, by starting with the largest value and writing new digits inside the zeros as lesser values are added to complete the number. Pupils should be encouraged to copy this procedure themselves. Later, pupils can write 'invisible' zeros, without actually marking the paper, to remind themselves of the real value of each digit as they combine digits to build a multi-digit number.

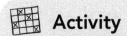 **Activity**

What is the value of ...?

Step 1

Build a 3-digit number out of base-10 materials – for example, the number 241.

Step 2

Write the number so that each digit is in a separate, labelled, column.

Step 3

Use both the concrete and the written representations to answer such questions as:

What is the value of the 2? [Answer: 200.]

What value has the 4 in the number 241? [Answer: 40.]

How many tens are shown in the tens position? [Answer: 4 tens.]

Note that these questions are place value questions.

Step 4

Contrast the above place value questions with the following, and demonstrate the difference with concrete materials:

How many tens are there in 241? [Answer: 24.]

How many hundreds are needed to build 241? [Answer: 2.]

How many units are in 241? [Answer: 241.]

Note that these questions are really division questions, but of a kind that can be easily answered by simply looking at the digits and their positions. This happens because the division required to answer these types of questions is division by a power of 10, and our place value system is a decimal one, i.e. it is based on powers of 10.

Step 5

Repeat this exercise without the concrete materials, using written notation alone. At first, have pupils always label the place value columns; later do without the labels. Give plenty of practice in answering both types of questions, and – crucially – in distinguishing between the two types.

Step 6

Ask both types of questions about numbers larger than three digits.

Game

Two-Digit Sequences

This game, based on one devised by Professor Sharma, is for two players (see his 1993 articles on the *Place Value Concept*).

Teaching points:

▶ The game focuses on place value.

▶ It teaches that the leftmost digit (the one in the tens position in a 2-digit number) is the most important signifier of value.

▶ It gives practice in ordering (putting into sequence) 2-digit numbers.

▶ It makes explicit how many whole tens are contained within a 2-digit number.

▶ It helps connect the spoken words we use for 2-digit numbers with their written notation.

Equipment needed:

▶ A pack of digit cards, including zeros. Use four cards each of the numbers 0–9.

▶ Paper and pencil for each player.

Rules:

Take turns to take two cards from the top of the shuffled pack, and arrange the two cards on the table in whichever order you choose. Write down the number as a simple tens and units statement. For example, if your cards are 2 and 4, you might choose to position the card showing 4 to the left of the 2, and write *4 tens + 2 units = 42*. Repeat this four more times with new cards, until each player has made five 2-digit numbers and written five number statements.

Players now rearrange their 2-digit numbers so that the digit cards are lined up in two columns, and the five numbers are sorted into a sequence, in descending order. Each player checks the other's sequence. If the cards are not correctly sequenced, the opponent is allowed to remove any cards in the wrong order, taking care to remove the minimum number of cards necessary to leave a descending sequence. Players score one point for each ten contained in the correctly ordered numbers.

Tips:

The writing is an important part of this game, because it reinforces the fact that position determines value. It also provides a handy memo of what the numbers were, in case the cards get mixed up during the sequencing activity.

Variation:

Play with three cards to make 3-digit numbers. Score one point for each hundred.

Game

Three-Digit Sequences (Focus on Tens)

This game, for two players, is a version of the one above, but focuses on tens within a 3-digit number.

Teaching points:

▶ The game teaches place value.

▶ It teaches that to determine value one must examine the digits from left to right.

▶ It gives practice in sequencing 3-digit numbers.

▶ It makes explicit how many whole tens are contained within a 3-digit number, as opposed to just identifying what digit lies in the tens place (two questions that are very often confused).

Equipment needed:

▶ A pack of digit cards, including zeros. Use four cards each of the numbers 0–9.

▶ Paper and pencil for each player.

Rules:

Take turns to take three cards from the top of the shuffled pack, and arrange them on the table in whichever order you choose. Write down the number as a simple hundreds, tens and units statement. For example, if your cards are 2, 5 and 4, you might choose to position the card showing 5 to the left of the 4 which in turn is to the left of the 2, and write *5 hundreds + 4 tens + 2 units = 542*. Repeat this twice more with new cards, until each player has made three 3-digit numbers and written three number statements.

Players rearrange their 3-digit numbers so that the digit cards are lined up in three columns, and the three numbers are sequenced in descending order. The score is calculated as one point for each ten that goes to build up each number, e.g. in the example above the score is 54, because there are 54 tens in 542.

Tips:

One of the most important teaching points of this game is to get children to understand the difference between looking to see what digit is in the tens place in a multi-digit number (i.e. 4 in 542), and understanding how many whole tens are contained within a multi-digit number, or how many tens would be needed to build the number out of tens and units (i.e. 54 in 542). This is often a major source of confusion, and is best explained by using base-10 concrete materials at first, as described in an earlier activity, followed by games such as this.

Game

Place Value Boxes

A game for two or more players.

Teaching points:

▶ The game teaches place value in large numbers.

▶ It gives practice in making connections between column value (e.g. three tens) and quantity value (30).

Equipment needed:

▶ A pack of digit cards made of four each of the digits 0–9.

▶ Paper and pencil for each player.

Rules:

Each player draws six boxes with a very small gap between each set of three. Each box represents one place value column. One card is dealt to each player on each round. On your turn, you must choose which box to copy the digit into. After six rounds, each player will have a 6-digit number, which they must read aloud. Decide before the game starts, whether the winner will have the largest or the smallest number.

Variation 1:

Give each player one set of the digits 0–9, shuffled and face down. Players turn over the top six cards from this pack, one at a time, as above. This variation involves rather more strategy than the basic game.

Variation 2:

At the start of the game, agree on a target number for all players to aim for. A 6-digit round number is best. The winner is the player who comes closest to the target.

Variation 3:

Players draw nine boxes with a very small gap between each set of three and aim to create the largest (or smallest) 9-digit number.

Tips:

You can see from the illustration what a 6-digit game will look like. For the sake of completeness, game boards are provided on the CW but I would recommend that you resist the temptation to photocopy the box format. Pupils will learn much more by having to sketch their own boxes each time they play.

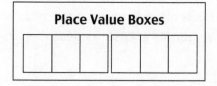

Place Value Boxes

Game

Calculator Skittles

A game for any number of players.

Teaching points:

▶ The game teaches place value in large numbers.

▶ It also teaches how to use a calculator for subtraction.

Equipment needed:

▶ A calculator for each player.

Rules:

Choose any 4-digit number that does not include a zero, and enter it into your calculator. You may repeat digits within your chosen number if you like. The teacher calls out any number between 1 and 9 for the players to 'knock down'. Each player who has that digit on their calculator screen is now allowed to perform one, and only one, subtraction on the calculator, the aim being to replace that digit with a zero. Any pupils who mistake the place value of the digit and do not manage to 'knock it down' to zero must live with their mistake and continue with whatever number their calculator now shows. The teacher continues calling out random digits until one or more of the players achieves a zero display on their calculator and is awarded a point. Players then choose new numbers and a new round begins. The winner is the player with the most points after a certain period of time.

Variation 1:

Instead of letting children choose, players get allocated a 4-digit number by dealing digit cards or throwing dice.

Variation 2:

Use numbers that have more than 4 digits.

Tips:

The teacher can use a die, or a pack of digit cards, to generate the random numbers between 1 and 9. If pupils write down the number they started with, they can demonstrate at the end exactly how they arrived at zero.

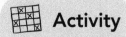 **Activity**

Partition numbers into tens and units in various ways

Make a 2-digit number out of Cuisenaire rods or base-10 materials, e.g. 52 made of five longs and two cubes. Earlier activities have shown pupils that this number can be split into tens and units and read as five tens and two units, or as 50 + 2. The focus of this activity is to show that other splits are also possible.

Place the tens on one small piece of paper and the units on an adjacent piece, so that you are creating two visual groups. One at a time, move one 10-rod from one group to the other, to show that just as 52 can be made of 50 and 2, it can also be made of 40 + 12, or 30 + 22, or 20 + 32, or 10 + 42, as illustrated.

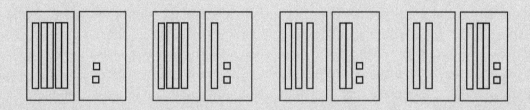

This concept of partitioning the tens in different ways, while keeping ideas of place value firmly in mind, is a necessary step before pupils can really understand decomposition in subtraction. It will also prove very useful for short division.

When pupils are ready, repeat the activity for 3-digit numbers.

Finally, practise partitioning numbers in various ways without the concrete materials.

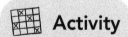 **Activity**

Split off the 'teen' numbers

This is an extension of the activity above, but with the focus on splitting off the numbers between 10 and 19, which is what needs to happen during decomposition for subtraction.

Make 2-digit, and later 3-digit, numbers, by throwing dice or dealing digit cards. Pupils must split this number into the 'teen' number, and whatever is left. The process can be written down either as a standard addition sum, or using an informal triad notation, as illustrated here.

79 = 19 + 60

or 79 = 60 + 19

$$79 \quad\quad 79$$

19 + 60   or   60 + 19

Game

Jump 10

A game for two or more players.

Teaching points:

▸ The game teaches how to use number lines to record simple additions.

▸ It shows that numbers that are ten apart share the same digit in the unit position.

▸ It teaches how to relate vertical place value thinking to horizontal mental calculation processes.

Equipment needed:

▸ Paper and pencil for each player.

▸ A die with half the faces labelled '+1' and the other half labelled 'Jump 10', or a coin to be spun with one of these labels stuck to each side.

Rules:

Each player draws their own number line. Take turns to throw the die and record the instructions on your number line as a single jump above the line. Announce the running total and record it under the line at the end of your turn. Players race to have the highest score after a certain number of turns, or a certain period of time.

Variation 1:

Race to be the first to hit a pre-agreed target number.

Variation 2:

Play this as a solitaire game. First determine a target number, perhaps by throwing dice, and then try to predict how many throws it will take to reach the target.

Variation 3:

Change the instructions on the die to read 'Jump 10' and 'Jump 100'.

Variation 4:

Start at an agreed number and work backwards. In this case the die must be labelled '−1' and 'Jump back 10'. Players must start their recording at the rightmost end of the number line and draw the jumps backwards, towards the left, including arrows on the jumps to show the direction of play.

Tips:

Turn the paper sideways, landscape fashion, so that more jumps can be fitted onto a single line. Do not allow players to 'jump 10' by counting up in ones or by bridging though 10.

(Continued)

(Continued)

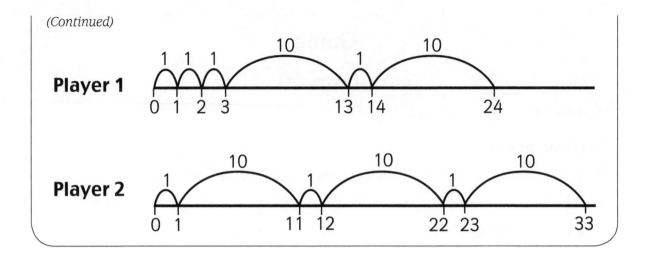

Player 1

Player 2

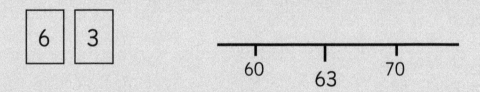

Activities

Locate any number on a number line

1. This activity can also be found in Section 2. Here, pupils are focusing on how the tens-and-units structure of a 2-digit number relates to the sequential number line concept. Pupils take a 2-digit number and mark it anywhere on an empty number line. Pupils should mark on the number line the two round numbers (multiples of 10) on either side of the number.

6 3

60   63   70

2. Repeat the activity for 3-digit numbers. Pupils must now mark the multiples of 10 on either side, and also the multiples of 100 on either side. Sometimes include numbers where the adjacent multiple of 10 is also the adjacent multiple of 100, e.g. 295 or 603.

These activities could lead into teaching about how to round numbers to the nearest 10 or 100.

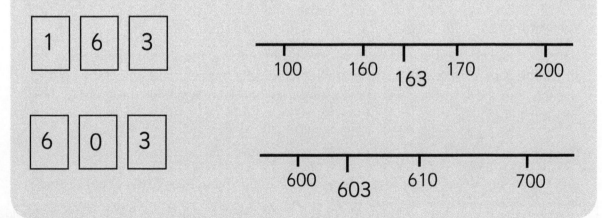

1 6 3

100   160 163 170   200

6 0 3

600 603   610   700

Game

The Six-Card Rounding Game

A game for two, three or more players. You can find a short demonstration video of this game on the CW. ⌖

Teaching points:

▶ The game teaches place value.

▶ It focuses on rounding 2-digit numbers to the nearest 10.

▶ It gives practice in rearranging and reading different combinations of digits.

Equipment needed:

▶ A pack of digit cards made of four cards of each of the numbers 0–9.

Rules:

Players are dealt six cards each, which they turn face up and rearrange as three 2-digit numbers. The aim is to make numbers which, when rounded to the nearest 10, are consecutive multiples of 10. Two consecutive round numbers score 2 points; three consecutive round numbers score 5 points. For example, a player dealt 1, 1, 5, 6, 7 and 7 could make 56 (rounding to 60) and 71 (rounding to 70) for 2 points, or 51 and 61 (rounding to 50 and 60) for 2 points, or 71 and 76 for 2 points. However, the same player could score 5 points for making 61, 71 and 75. The winner is the player with the highest score after five rounds.

Game

The Rounding Challenge

A game for two, three or more players.

Teaching points:

▶ The game teaches place value and gives practice in rearranging and reading different combinations of digits.

▶ The game focuses on rounding 2-digit numbers to the nearest 10.

Equipment needed:

▶ A pack of digit cards made of four cards of each of the numbers 0–9.

Rules:

As in the game above, players are dealt six cards each, which they turn face up and rearrange as three 2-digit numbers. The aim, as above, is to make numbers that, when rounded to the nearest 10, are consecutive multiples of 10. A player who succeeds with the six dealt cards will score 5 points. A player who cannot manage this may take another card from the top of the pack, and tries again to make three 2-digit numbers that round to consecutive round numbers (leaving one card unused), to score 3 points. If an eighth card is needed to succeed, the score is 1 point. The winner is the player with the highest score after five rounds.

Variation:

Players are dealt nine cards to create three 3-digit numbers that are each rounded to the nearest 100, aiming for three consecutive multiples of 100.

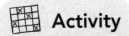 **Activity**

Teach × 10 and ÷ 10 as a shift between columns

Use base-10 concrete materials on place value mats to show multiplication and division by 10. For example, if you start with three units, and multiply by 10, each of the three units becomes a ten, so the result is three tens, whose proper place is in the next section to the left, the tens column.

When these multiplications are recorded, make explicit to pupils how the digits have moved one column to the left. It is not true that you 'add a zero', because adding zero leaves numbers unaltered. What actually happens on paper is that the digit shifts into the next column, and a zero is needed to hold the place (in this example the units place), to record the fact that a column shift has occurred and to indicate the new value of the digits.

Before recording each multiplication on paper, use a transparent overlay on a place value recording sheet with labelled columns, and slide the overlay so that the digits visibly move from one column to the next. Have pupils articulate what is happening to the base-10 materials on the place value mat, and how this connects to what is happening to the digit(s) on the plastic overlay.

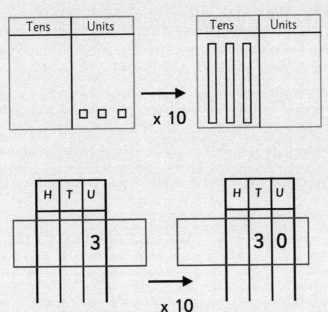

Alongside examples of multiplication, use the same activity to explore division by 10. Create a quantity from concrete materials on a place value mat. Pick up one of the tens and mime the action of cutting it into ten cubes before making the exchange concretely and showing that a ten will become [a] one. Point out that this is what will happen to each of the tens. Pick up a hundred and mime how it can be sliced into ten long rods, before making the exchange concretely and explaining that this is what will happen to each one of the hundreds. Therefore, after dividing by 10, we retain exactly the same number of blocks but each block now has a value that is 10 times smaller, or a tenth of what it used to be. The designated place for the scaled-down blocks is in the next column to the right. Have the child write the number on a transparent overlay on top of a set of labelled place value columns, before sliding the overlay to model the shift between columns.

Take care when practising division not to create numbers with decimals before the pupils are ready for them.

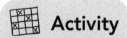 **Activity**

Extend place value thinking to decimals

Introduce decimals as an extension of the place value system.

Demonstrate with concrete materials how the value of the units changes tenfold with each column: moving from right to left the values increase by 10 times the amount, or moving from left to right the values become a tenth of what they were. Remind pupils of the three-fold recurring pattern of place value headings. Demonstrate how the shapes of the base-10 materials also have a threefold recurring pattern: cube, long and flat. Point out that the same repeating patterns continue to the left into the columns for larger powers of 10 and to the right into the decimal columns.

The conversation about the repeating shapes of the base-10 blocks – cube, long, flat – has more impact, and will therefore be more memorable, if you have a 1000 cube to show. These are available to buy as part of a base-10 set of blocks, but a good alternative is to stack ten flat 100-squares on top of each other to create a cube of the right size (i.e. 10 cm by 10 cm by 10 cm). A cube in which the 100s are distinct makes it even easier for children to realise, by hands-on experience of building the cube and taking it apart again, that one-tenth of 1000 is 100 and that ten hundreds are a thousand. You can extrapolate from the same equipment to show that 1 (which is also a cube) could be split into tenths in just the same way (each slice of which would be a flat shape) which in turn could be cut into ten strips (each of which would be a long). There is no equipment available on sale to show these fractions at the correct scale, but you can cut out ten 1 cm squares from 1 cm thick card and stack them on top of each other to create a cube the same size as a white Cuisenaire cube or a single base-10 unit. This is fiddly to do, but most children are delighted when they first see for themselves how 1 can be split into ten tenths.

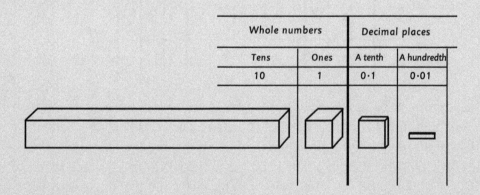

Whole numbers		Decimal places	
Tens	Ones	A tenth	A hundredth
10	1	0·1	0·01

When talking about decimals, enunciate very clearly so that pupils can hear the difference between tenths and tens, and between hundredths and hundreds. Use fraction notation, rather than lower-case letters, to label the decimal columns, as shown below.

Use headed columns like these to practise reading, writing and ordering decimal numbers. On top of the thick line separating the whole numbers from the fractional parts of the number, encourage pupils to mark an exaggeratedly large, or brightly coloured, decimal point.

Thousands			Ones			Decimals	
H	T	U	H	T	U	$\frac{1}{10}$	$\frac{1}{100}$
					4 • 5		
			1	0	6 • 2	5	

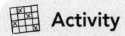 **Activity**

Connect decimal place value notation to money

Remember that most children first meet decimal notation in relation to money and prices.

Use labelled columns to read and write amounts of money. Have pupils put various prices that include both pounds and pence in ascending or descending order. Pupils should first read the amounts as money and then reread them as plain decimal numbers.

Make explicit to children that money is always written with two decimal places, even when the second decimal place is a zero. By contrast, in all other quantities, only zeros that act as place-holders need be written, i.e. the zero at the end of 9.0 is as superfluous as the zero at the start of 09.

Another important difference to teach children is that only in money may we express the digits beyond the decimal point as if they were tens and units, e.g. six pounds *twenty-five*, but six point *two five*.

SECTION 4

Times tables, multiplication and division

Overview

Trying to learn times tables can be a nightmare for dyscalculic pupils. They have to expend an enormous amount of time and effort to memorise what, for them, is one meaningless string of words after another, only to find that they cannot access any fact from the middle of the sequence on its own but must recite the whole chant again from the very beginning to reach an answer. Even worse, they often find that the act of learning a new table seems to wipe clean all memory of a previously learned table.

Learning tables by heart is so difficult for dyscalculic learners that I believe it should not even be attempted. Pupils are much better off learning to understand what multiplication and division mean and how tables are constructed, so that they can derive any multiplication or division fact by logic and reasoning. Pupils should either be given enough time to find an answer by working from first principles, or should be given a tables square from which they can copy any answers they need immediately.

Pupils can be helped to see how numbers are built up out of equal-sized groups by using appropriate visual models, the best of which is the area model of multiplication and division. In the early stages of teaching multiplication and division, the area model should be constructed concretely from Cuisenaire rods arranged into a rectangular array. At a later stage, the same concept is represented by diagrams or sketches of rectangles to help support the pupils' mental calculations. After plenty of practice, pupils learn to visualise a rectangular area and manipulate it in their mind's eye. To be successful at the abstract stage, pupils will need to be reasonably proficient in step-counting and bridging techniques, both of which have been covered in the first two sections of this book.

Those multiplication facts that produce the most regular patterns, namely the 2×, 5× and 10× facts, are the easiest to learn and can therefore be treated as 'key' tables facts. The idea of teaching key facts (as discussed previously, with reference to key component facts) is to minimise the burden on the learner's memory and to provide a secure starting point from which to derive related numerical facts. In this section, the earlier activities are designed to help learners develop a good understanding of what multiplication and division actually mean. Once this is established, the focus can turn to the key tables facts: the 2×, 5× and 10× steps. Next, pupils are taught to derive the multiplication facts that are a single step away from one of the key facts. Finally, pupils learn to derive the harder facts that are more than one step of logic away from a key fact.

The idea of teaching children to reason from a key tables fact is widespread and is, of course, the only sensible route for learners who are unable to memorise number facts reliably. Where my approach differs from most other practitioners, is:

▶ A firm belief in the importance of developing a learner's conceptual understanding through engaging in plenty of concrete activities, before any abstract work on multiplication or division begins. During this crucial learning stage at the concrete level the pupil is guided, and given time, to model and rehearse every step of reasoning by exploring, arranging and manipulating Cuisenaire rods on rectangular areas.

▶ Careful planning and management of the transition between concrete and abstract work. After a solid grounding based on the area model, which is a strongly visual approach to multiplication and division, I encourage my pupils to use diagrams and sketches to support and clarify their thinking.

▶ Instead of having children learn one multiplication table at a time, my approach is to focus on finding the individual *steps* of multiplication tables, one step at a time. The individual steps apply to any multiplication table, up to 10 and beyond. Working in this way requires patience because the progress appears to be slow until, all at once, children reach the point at which they have all the necessary knowledge and understanding to find any multiplication table fact.

You can find a video about this section of *The Dyscalculia Toolkit* on the CW.

What are the main problems?

▶ Being unable to memorise and recall the multiplication tables facts by heart.

▶ Having such a hazy or muddled understanding of the concepts of multiplication and division that, when their memory fails, pupils have no idea how to work from first principles towards a solution.

▶ Finding it difficult to grasp the idea of working with equal-sized sets, possibly due to a persistence in seeing numbers as collections of single units, rather than as a group bonding to form one larger unit.

▶ Not understanding exactly how division relates to multiplication.

▶ Being unlikely to notice patterns until they are explicitly pointed out.

▶ Having such a weak number sense that there is no realistic possibility of estimating whether any multiplication or division answer is reasonable.

▶ Not yet having mastered some of the necessary mathematical pre-skills, such as efficient mental addition or a basic understanding of place value. (The required foundation skills are listed in more detail in the section below on 'How to help'.)

How to help

▶ Give pupils practice in step-counting.

▶ Give pupils practice in simple grouping of small quantities.

▶ Use appropriate concrete materials that will help build cognitive models. Discrete material, such as counters, should give way very quickly to continuous materials, such as Cuisenaire rods.

▶ Let the pupils manipulate the concrete material themselves. Continue to offer concrete materials until pupils are ready to work with drawings and sketches instead, during their progression towards purely abstract work.

▶ Teach the area model of multiplication and division.

▶ Show pupils how diagrams, particularly sketches of rectangles, can clarify thinking about multiplication and division.

▶ Encourage pupils to talk aloud about what they are doing and to use their own words to articulate what a multiplication or division problem means and how it might be solved.

▶ Make sure all the foundation techniques are understood and have been thoroughly practised. They include:

　○ Knowing (without resorting to counting) how single-digit numbers can be built from, or partitioned into, component parts;

　○ basic mental addition techniques, including bridging through 10;

　○ complementary addition to solve subtractions;

　○ a basic understanding of place value and columns;

　○ place value multiplication and division by 10.

The idea of identifying and putting all the necessary pre-skills in place as part of a systematic approach to teaching multiplication and division is further developed, and explored in very great detail, in Part III of *Overcoming Difficulties with Number*.

▶ Teach division at the same time and alongside multiplication, from the very beginning. Teach in a way that reinforces, again and again, the connection between multiplication and division.

▶ Teach division as the inverse of multiplication, but do not present division as repeated subtraction. Instead, present both multiplication and division as repeated addition of equal-sized groups. Only the point of view is different: division focuses on the groups (how many groups, or how many in each group) that build up to a certain number, while multiplication focuses on the total quantity that is built from groups.

▶ Point out to pupils the patterns that multiples create. Encourage pupils to explore the patterns using concrete materials as well as using pictorial representations.

▶ Play games that teach and practise multiplication and division facts. Send games home to be played with an adult, as an alternative to written homework.

▶ Explore the language of multiplication and division. For example: What does 'times' mean? What is the difference between 'divide' and 'divided by'? etc.

▶ Limit the amount of memorising to a minimum number of key facts.

▶ Teach explicitly how to derive new facts by logic and reasoning from known facts.

▶ Minimise the number of strategies and procedures that a pupil is expected to know. When there are several possible strategies, allow pupils to make individual choices about which one they would prefer to learn and to practise.

▶ Give children the opportunity to discover, through hands-on practical experience, that multiplication is commutative, and that division is not.

▶ As soon as children understand that multiplication is commutative, encourage them to switch the position of the numbers in the question whenever that would simplify the calculation. For example, any child who has had plenty of experience of doubling (which all my pupils have, because the 2× step is one of the much-practised key facts) should find it quicker to double a number than to step-count in 2s: to calculate either 7×2 or 2×7, it is easier to double 7 than to step-count seven steps of 2.

▶ Allow dyscalculic pupils to use a tables square for all work that is not directly testing their knowledge of multiplication facts.

▶ Make word problems an integral part of the teaching. Encourage pupils to make up their own problems, located in real and everyday situations.

▶ When taking pupils beyond the basic tables facts, e.g. to multiplying 2-digit numbers together or to short division (both of which are beyond the scope of this book), teach the boxes method, which is based on the area model of multiplication and division.

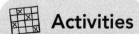 **Activities**

Build small numbers out of equal-sized groups

As a preliminary to these activities, ask your pupils to use counters or glass nuggets to show 'two threes' or 'three fours'. Pupils who do not understand the vocabulary of multiplication will demonstrate their lack of understanding by showing you five objects (2 and 3) in response to the first request and seven (3 and 4) in response to the second.

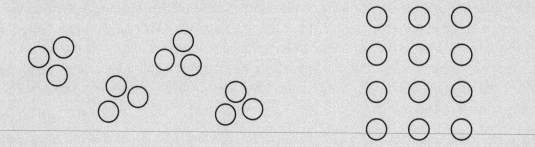

Four groups of 3   *An array of four 3s, or three 4s*

1. Build up pupils' understanding gradually, for example by making groups of three objects and saying: *Here's 3. Here's another 3, so that's two 3s all together. This is another group of 3, so now we've got three 3s. What must I do to have four 3s?* etc.

2. Focus on the grouping. Let pupils start by simply making the groups distinct, without any special pattern. After a while, if children do not do it for themselves, show pupils how to arrange the objects into rectangular arrays, with rows and columns lined up.

3. Focus on the total amount. Ask how many counters are in each array. Insist that pupils count in steps, not in ones, to find the total.

Later, ask pupils to predict, or guess, how many counters will be needed to make a particular array, say four 3s or six 2s. Pupils make the array only after they have committed themselves to a guess, and check their answer by counting in steps, not in ones.

4. Make up little scenarios to turn the arrays into a story or word problem. For example, for the illustrated array, you could pretend that each counter represents the plate you eat off at a meal, so the top row shows breakfast, lunch and supper on one day, and the next row represents breakfast, lunch and supper on the next day, etc., so the whole array gives the answer to the question *How many plates are used in four days?* or *How many meals do you eat in four days?* Or you might pretend that each nugget is a sweet from a packet of three, or a pupil in a team, or a wheel on a tricycle, etc. Model a few story word problems, then have the pupils make up their own about everyday situations involving small numbers. Some children may need a scribe to record their stories.

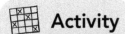 **Activity**

Connect division to multiplication from the very beginning

In the activities above, the pupils have been introduced to vocabulary such as 'four 3s' without necessarily being told that this is the vocabulary of multiplication. In the same way, introduce division questions without telling the pupils that this is what they are doing.

For example, ask pupils questions such as *If we want to sort 12 counters into groups of three, how many groups will there be?* or, *Let's pretend that these nuggets are balloons and that we're preparing party bags and putting two balloons in each bag. How many bags can we fill with these eight balloons? What if we had 16 balloons?* Or, using the very common sharing model of division, *Say these buttons were made of chocolate and we want to share this chocolate fairly between X people*, etc. When pupils use concrete materials to illustrate these problems, or to help themselves solve these problems, encourage them to organise the materials into rectangular arrays.

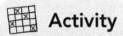 **Activity**

Illustrate simple word problems

Both the previous activities involve pupils inventing stories, or word problems, to match arrays that have been built out of concrete materials. Write some of the stories down, including both multiplication problems and division problems, and bring them out at a later lesson without the concrete material.

Read a batch of problems to a group of pupils. Encourage each pupil to illustrate the word problems with sketches or simple drawings, i.e. drawings that do not include any unnecessary detail or decoration. Pupils are often surprised to see that their drawings not only illustrate the question but also provide the answer.

This activity highlights the relationship between multiplication and division because pupils find that there is no difference between the type of sketches that illustrate multiplication and those that illustrate division scenarios.

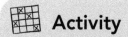 **Activity**

Use Cuisenaire rods to show that multiplication is commutative

This activity is suggested by Professor Sharma, who writes about it in detail in two of his 1980 *Math Notebook* articles and also demonstrates it in his teaching videos and DVDs. The activity promotes the area model of multiplication.

Step 1

Start with small groups of small numbers, echoing the earlier activities where pupils organised nuggets into arrays, e.g. four 3s or two 5s. Ask pupils now to make these quantities out of Cuisenaire rods. Have pupils arrange the rods into rectangles in which the rods are set out horizontally, one above the other, as shown here. The colour of the rods identifies the times table from which a fact is taken, so that a rectangle made of any number of light green rods is recognised as part of the 3× table and a rectangle of yellow rods models a fact from the 5× table. Show pupils how to 'read' the dimensions of the rectangular arrays, e.g. *Here are four threes, in a rectangle that measures 4 along this side and 3 along that side*, or *This is a 3 by 4 rectangle*.

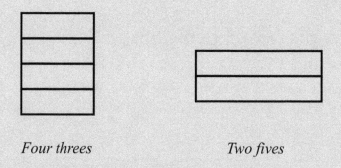

Four threes   *Two fives*

Pupils should repeat the activity with other small rectangles of various numbers of rods.

Step 2

After making a rectangle such as 4 × 3 out of light green Cuisenaire rods, tell pupils that the answer to the multiplication question 4 × 3 lies in the surface area of the rectangle. If necessary, make another rectangle of the same dimensions out of separate unit cubes that the pupils can count to prove this fact. Now demonstrate how to read rectangles as multiplication: point to the relevant sides when saying the numbers *4 times 3*, and then stroke the surface as you say the solution, *12*. Next have pupils make 3 × 4. This new rectangle is made of three purple rods. Rotate the rectangle one-quarter turn in either direction and place it on top of the light green rectangle. It is, of course, an exact fit. Have pupils read this new rectangle, while pointing to the relevant sides during the question *3 times 4*, and using the palm of their hand on the surface area while giving the answer *12*.

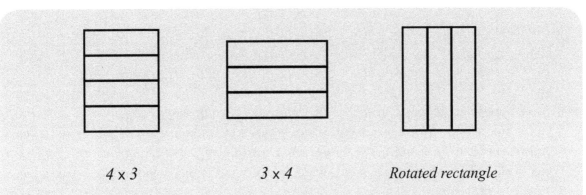

| *4 x 3* | *3 x 4* | *Rotated rectangle* |

Pupils should repeat the activity with other small rectangles of various numbers of rods.

Once pupils understand about commutativity, they should be encouraged to switch the order of the numbers in a multiplication question whenever it would make for an easier or quicker calculation.

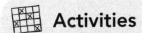 **Activities**

Use Cuisenaire rods to connect multiplication and division

1. Have pupils make the same kinds of rectangular arrays out of rods as in the previous activity. Demonstrate how to read the rectangle as a division problem. For example, in the 4 × 3 rectangle, use the flat of your hand on the surface while saying *12 can be built from 4* (on the word 'four' point to the vertical side of the rectangle) *3s* (point horizontally along the top of the rectangle), *so 12 divided by 4 is 3, and 12 divided by 3 is 4*. Give pupils lots of practice in making pairs of equivalent rectangles and in reading each rectangle aloud both as a multiplication and as a division.

2. Pupils record multiplication or division facts as rectangles drawn or shaded on squared paper. Squares of 1 cm are best, to match the dimensions of the Cuisenaire rods. Either of the examples below can be used to record either of the multiplication expressions 3 × 4 or 4 × 3, or either of the division expressions 12 ÷ 4 or 12 ÷ 3.

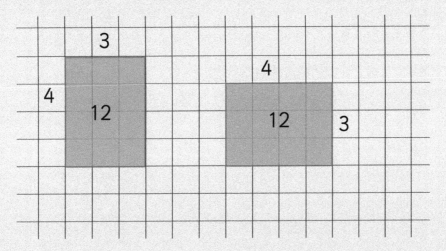

(Continued)

(Continued)

3. Pupils can record the same family of facts as equations in digits:

$$3 \times 4 = 12 \qquad 4 \times 3 = 12 \qquad 12 \div 3 = 4 \qquad 12 \div 4 = 3$$

4. Give pupils enough practice so that they can 'see' both possible rectangles whatever the orientation, and will accept that a rectangle made of three black rods, for example, can represent both 3×7 and 7×3. If they see 3 columns of 7 (with the black rods arranged vertically) they can, with practice, switch in their minds to imagining 7 rows of 3 (with the 3s arranged horizontally).

5. In terms of Cuisenaire rods, division problems can be 'translated' like this: $12 \div 3$ means that you have to make a rectangle with an area of 12. One side of the rectangle must be 3. The answer will be the other side of the rectangle, along the top. Having the answer along the top of the rectangle will connect it, later, with the short-division written notation.

Once the pupils have solved this problem, dismantle the rectangle and lay the rods end to end, against rods that measure 12 units in length (i.e. an orange and a red). Tell pupils that another way of 'translating' the problem is: *How many 3s are there in 12?*

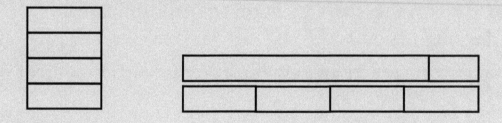

This might be a good time to explore with pupils the idea that, although multiplication is commutative, division is not: for example, four 2s are the same as two 4s, but 4 divided by 2 is not the same as 2 divided by 4.

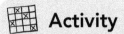 **Activity**

Diagrammatic recording of multiplication and division

After making various rectangles with Cuisenaire rods and reading them in terms of both multiplication and division (as described in the previous activity), have the child record some of the facts on sketches of rectangles. At first you can do this with the rods still in view but, once the pupil is familiar with the idea, start asking for some facts to be sketched and recorded from memory.

Recording the facts on a diagram is a way of practising the area model of multiplication and division at a more abstract level, while reinforcing the connection between the two operations. It is also a good way of helping learners develop visualisation skills. Explain to pupils that there is no need to try to keep the diagrams to scale: a rectangle of any shape and size is a useful representation of multiplication or division.

An extension of this activity is to provide rectangle sketches on which either the dimensions of the two sides, or the area of the whole, is given, the challenge being for the pupil to supply the missing pieces of information. In the example illustrated, there is only one correct answer for the rectangle at the left but more than one possible correct answer for the rectangle at the right (see also the later activities on changing the shape of the multiplication rectangle).

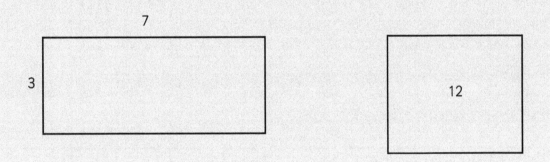

At this stage, you must take care to include only facts that the child already knows, or has been given. Later, as pupils learn how to find more and more multiplication facts for themselves, you can return to this activity, at which point you can use a blank template (see CW) to create multiplication and division problems for a pupil to solve, or for pupils to make up for each other to solve.

A bonus of using the area model of multiplication, and of using the term explicitly with pupils, is that it eliminates later confusion between the terms *area* and *perimeter*.

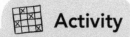 **Activity**

Connect step-counting (repeated addition) with multiplication

Step 1

Set out ten bases in a row, for example ten squares of paper, or saucers, or shallow trays. Leave a larger gap between the fifth and sixth base.

Step 2

Put two objects on each, for example two glass nuggets or beads, saying: *one two, two twos, three twos, four twos*, etc.

Step 3

Go back to the beginning and announce that now you are finding out how many there are in total, or *How much is ten twos?* Step-count aloud as you point to each group: *two, four, six, eight*, etc.

Pupils should copy your actions and words, until they can carry out all three steps of the activity for themselves.

Instead of the language 'three twos' or 'four twos', you can sometimes substitute 'three groups of two', 'four sets of two', etc. But never use the words 'lots of two', because most children interpret 'lots' as 'a large amount' (as in 'lots and lots of …'). Similarly, the word 'times' has no meaning for young children and must be introduced with care.

Repeat the activity for the 5× table. Arrange the five objects in the familiar spot pattern, to minimise counting and recounting, and to emphasise at the step-counting stage exactly how much is being added at each step.

On another occasion, repeat the activity with a red Cuisenaire rod on each base for the 2× table and a yellow rod on each base for the 5× table. Step-counting in twos and fives must be done without using fingers or counting in ones.

Repeat the activity with an orange Cuisenaire rod on each base for the 10× table.

Once or twice, have pupils set out 20 bases, with a gap after every five, and step-count in twos, fives or tens. It is important to let pupils set up and complete the whole activity themselves, so that they can internalise the connection between the counting out of the bases and step-counting the total amounts.

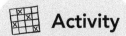 **Activity**

Step-count one or two steps from various tables facts

Step 1

Set out ten bases, as for the previous activity. Put a red, yellow or orange Cuisenaire rod on each base, depending on which multiplication table you are examining. The aim of this activity is not to learn any particular set of facts, but to develop an understanding of the structure of a multiplication table and how each step relates to other steps. This is why I recommend using red, yellow or orange rods for this activity, so that pupils are not distracted by having to think too much about the numerical answers.

Step 2

Take a large sheet of paper and cover some of the bases from the right. For example, cover all the bases except the four at the left. Ask the pupil the value of all the rods they see. Pupils are allowed to step-count to find the answer, e.g. *five, ten, fifteen, twenty*, but may not count in ones.

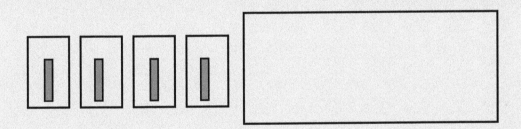

Step 3

Move the paper one position in either direction. Pupils must use their previous answer to tell you the new total; they may not start the step-count from the beginning again. Move the paper back, and ask the pupils to remind themselves of that total, before moving the paper one step in the other direction. Again, the aim of the activity is that pupils use their previous answer to find the new total.

Step 4

After practising this activity a few times, it should be possible to use empty bases, with the pupils imagining an amount on each base, at which point you can extend the activity to numbers other than 2, 5 and 10. You can photocopy and laminate a page like the example illustrated. If you wish to add two more bases so that a table is practised up to the twelfth step, leave a slightly larger gap after the tenth base, as well as after the fifth base, to create visual groupings of two fives plus two more. Choose any base and write down what multiplication fact it represents. Use a cover sheet to hide the rest of the bases to the right, moving

(Continued)

(Continued)

the sheet one base to the left or to the right, as described above, to give pupils practice in working out one step more or one step less than the written product.

For example, working in the 4 times table, write 32 in or above the eighth box and say: *Imagine groups of four. These eight bases would total 32, because I know that 8 × 4 = 32.* Move the cover sheet to the left and ask pupils to calculate *Seven fours, which is one four less than 8 × 4.*

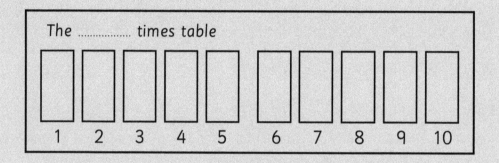

Remember that the object of this activity is not to get pupils to learn their tables, but to step-count one or two steps, up or down, from a given or known multiplication fact.

Activity

Practise mental step-counting from given tables facts

Activities in the earlier sections of this book recommend that pupils count up and down, at first with the support of concrete materials in ones and later in larger regular steps. Multiplication requires pupils to step-count in groups of various sizes. However, pupils who have difficulties with arithmetic cannot be expected to learn the steps of every multiplication table by heart. Instead, pupils should understand that step-counting is really repeated addition, and many need reminding of how best to deal with addition: *not* by counting in ones, but by adding in chunks along a number line (either on paper or in their mind's eye) and bridging through 10 whenever necessary.

To practise step-counting in fives, allow pupils to use the number line method of addition, if necessary, until they notice the strong pattern that allows them to step-count mentally, from any starting point that is a multiple of 5. Pupils can be asked to practise quite long sequences of step-counts, both up and down, in ones, twos, fives, and tens, without any concrete or visual supporting materials.

The larger numbers, 9, 8, 7 and 6, are hard, because they require additions that often include bridging through 10. Step-counting in 3s, 4s or 12s may also be difficult for some pupils. To practise these additions, remind pupils of how to use a number line for addition and for bridging through 10, and set them problems that require only one step to be added to a tables product. For example, 18 + 3, 28 + 4, 12 + 6, 18 + 9, 36 + 6, 16 + 8, 35 + 7. Pupils may choose to record the bridging through 10 in either of the ways shown here, i.e. as two cumulative jumps, or as one jump subdivided into two.

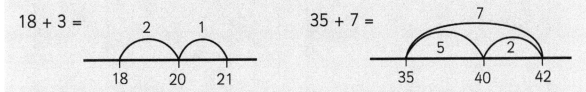

After pupils have done a few additions of this sort on paper, hide their work and have them repeat the steps to the solution on an imaginary number line in their mind's eye. On later occasions, challenge pupils to try two consecutive tables steps on an imaginary number line.

The aim of this activity is to get pupils to the stage of being able to add one or two steps of a tables sequence mentally, even when it involves bridging through 10.

Activities

Make times tables patterns on a 100-square

1. Use a shallow cardboard tray measuring 10cm × 10cm (see CW) or a frame with a hole of the same size cut out of craft foam or kitchen sponge. From left to right, and from the top down, have pupils make the pattern of the 2 times table in the tray. The result will be neat but boring: the whole tray will be filled with red rods (you will need more than one box of Cuisenaire rods). The same exercise for the 5 times table and the 10 times table will, of course, produce similarly dull and uniformly coloured results, because 2, 5 and 10 are all factors of 10.

Try the same exercise for the pattern of the 3 times table. Pupils will be able to fit three light green rods along the top, but will have to split the next rod into 1 + 2 in order to fit it into the tray. At the end of the next row, a rod will have to be split again, but this time the same two components will be used in the reverse order. As pupils fill more and more space, the pattern begins to emerge and pupils can predict what will happen. Pupils also get to see that the number 3 can be split in only one way: 1 + 2 or 2 + 1. Once it fills the tray, the pattern is striking and memorable.

Pupils will benefit from repeating the activity for other numbers. The times table pattern for 6, for example, reveals that the number 6 is only ever split in one way: 2 + 4 or 4 + 2. Knowing this will make pupils more confident when trying to derive new tables facts from known facts, which is what dyscalculic pupils need to learn to do. (See also the following activity on making times tables patterns on number lines.)

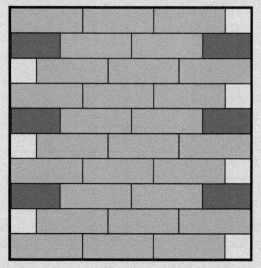

The 3 times table made of Cuisenaire rods in a 10 cm × 10 cm tray

The pattern of the 3 times table shown by shading on a 100 square

2. A slightly different way of seeing the times tables patterns is to get pupils to shade squares on a numbered paper 100-square. For example, shading every third or ninth number reveals a strong diagonal, while shading every second, fifth or tenth produces unbroken vertical lines.

Encourage pupils to make connections between the patterns made by the 2 and 4 times tables, the patterns made by the 3 and 6 times tables, and between the patterns of the 3, 6 and 9 times tables. Point out to your pupils that the 7 times table does not make a strong pattern, which is precisely what makes it such a difficult times table to learn.

 🔲 **Activities**

Make times tables patterns on number lines

These activities target the multiplication tables of the numbers above 5 and look at the first 10 steps of various tables.

1. Give pupils a 'skeleton' of a multiplication table on a number line (see the illustration and CW👆). A skeleton is nothing more than a line starting at zero on which ten equal jumps are drawn. Show clearly where the half-way point lies.

Have pupils fill in all the appropriate numbers for a chosen times table, e.g. 6×. Discuss with pupils what they have noticed. We want them to notice that there are only four occasions where bridging through 10 is necessary, and that on each of those occasions the 6 is split in the same way: 4 + 2 (or 2 + 4). We also want them to notice that because 6 is an even number, all the numbers they have labelled on the number line are also even numbers. We can connect this fact to the way 6 is split and labelled on the jumps, since any other way of splitting 6 into components requires odd numbers to be used. (See also the previous activity on making times tables patterns with Cuisenaire rods.)

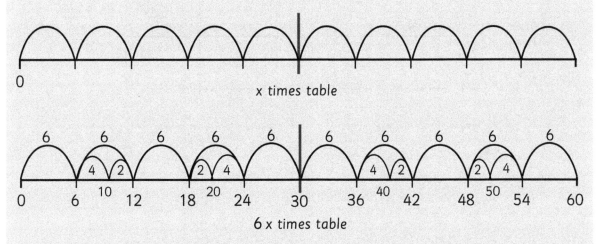

2. Repeat the activity for other multiplication tables. Point out to pupils that the pattern is symmetrical for all multiplication tables at the half-way point of the 10-step table: folding the number line in the middle highlights the fact that the pattern of whole jumps and bridging jumps in the first half of the table is a mirror image of those in the second half of the multiplication table.

The page of skeleton tables on the CW 👆 can be laminated and used for pupils to explore the number line patterns of any multiplication table and are particularly recommended for the 6, 7, 8 and 12 times tables.

▦ Activities

Key fact: Double means 'multiply by 2'

1. Pupils have already done lots of work on doubling (see activities in earlier sections), but now need to connect that knowledge to times table and multiplication work. Give plenty of practice in doubling and halving, making a point of using the terms 'multiply' and 'divide' when asking the questions and the signs '×' and '÷' when recording the work.

Using a mirror can help pupils understand that doubling is not the same as adding, even though the solution to a doubling question can be achieved by adding. Use the vocabulary 'twice as much' and 'twice as many' alongside 'multiply by 2'.

2. Use mirrors together with counters or rods, or drawings with clear mirror lines of symmetry, to show pupils that 'double and double again' is the same as '4 times' a number. This second activity reinforces the idea that doubling means multiplication, not addition.

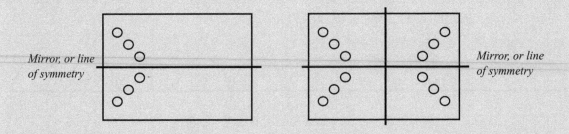

Mirror, or line of symmetry · *Mirror, or line of symmetry*

'Double' means 'twice as much'
2 × 3

'Double and double again' means 'four times as much'
4 × 3

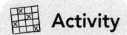 **Activity**

Key facts: ×5 is half of ×10

Step 1

Pupils should know the answer to 10 times any number, and they should also know how to make the appropriate rectangle out of Cuisenaire rods to illustrate the area model of multiplication (see Section 3 and earlier activities in this section).

Show pupils how halving any array or rectangle that is made of 10 times a number, would create two new rectangles in which one side is 5 units, i.e. each new rectangular array illustrates a fact from the 5 times table. If pupils choose to make their rectangle out of orange rods, they can either imagine a saw slicing each orange rod in half, or physically remake the rectangle by substituting two yellow rods for every orange one.

Have pupils repeat this activity with other numbers, until they have entirely convinced themselves that 5 times a number is always half of 10 times the number.

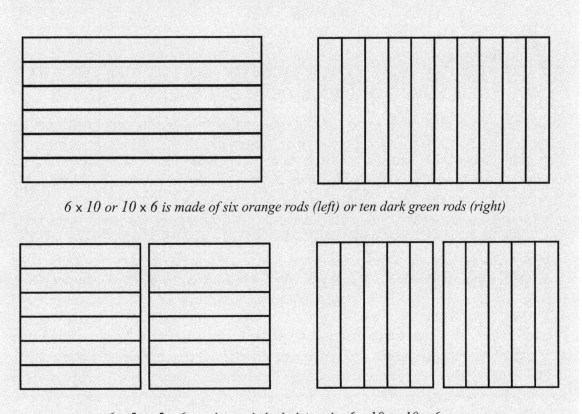

6 x 10 or 10 x 6 is made of six orange rods (left) or ten dark green rods (right)

6 x 5 or 5 x 6 can be made by halving the 6 x 10 or 10 x 6 arrays

Step 2

Give pupils written practice of finding 5 times a number. At first, ask pupils to write the intermediate step, as in the example below. Noting the intermediate fact helps pupils focus on which number needs manipulating, which is especially useful in situations where the 5 sometimes appears before and sometimes after the multiplication sign:

(Continued)

(Continued)

$8 \times 5 = $ half of $\underline{80} = $ ___

$5 \times 6 = $ half of __ $ = $ ___

$12 \times 5 = $ half of __ $ = $ ___

$5 \times 20 = $ half of __ $ = $ ___ etc.

Step 3

Show pupils how to reduce the amount of writing by substituting the fraction '½' for the word 'half' and the multiplication sign '×' for the word 'of'. Pupils will find this knowledge (i.e. half of … = ½ × …) very useful later, both when solving word problems and when working with fractions.

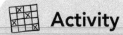 **Activity**

How many 10s? So, twice as many 5s

Following on from the activity above, this activity applies the same concept to division.

Start with multiples of 10 and ask children how many tens there are in each number. Remind children of the Three-Digit Sequences game and the activity in which they shifted digits between place value columns in order to multiply or divide by 10 (both from Section 3). If necessary, use Cuisenaire rods or Dienes blocks to discover how many tens there are in some random 2-digit and 3-digit multiples of 10. Either by looking at rods in front of them, or by reasoning abstractly, children should be able to see that however many 10s there are in a number, there will be twice as many 5s. Therefore, in order to divide any number by 5, we can first divide by 10 and then double the answer.

After practising this reasoning on multiples of 10, here is how to extend the idea to multiples of 5: partition off the five 'extra' units in any multiple of 5 that is not also a multiple of 10, then deal with the two components separately. For example, to divide 85 by 5, partition the 85 into 80 + 5. We can see that there are 8 tens in 80, which means there must be twice as many (i.e. 16) fives in the same number, plus one more five in the units that were separated off, so the answer to 85 ÷ 5 is 17.

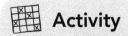 **Activity**

×9 is almost ×10

The 9× step of any table, or the 9 times table itself, is an easy one to learn for children who are familiar with Cuisenaire rods and with the area model of multiplication. For example, for 9 × 4, or 4 × 9, make a rectangle for 10 × 4 out of four 10s and show where an imaginary saw could chop off one unit from the end of every 10-rod. Use a single rod to model the quantity that needs to be removed to turn 10 × 4 into 9 × 4. Put the purple rod on top of the orange rectangle to show that the solution to 9 × 4 is 40 − 4. Move the purple rod so that it sits on top of only one orange rod, instead of straddling them all. This repositioning makes it clear that all but one of the tens can remain untouched and that complement facts can quickly help us find the answer: the complement of 4 is 6, so 40 − 4 = 36.

Ask the child to use Cuisenaire rods for the 9× step of all the tables, in a random order, to demonstrate that 9 × 6 is 6 less than 60, that 9 × 9 is 9 less than 90, that 9 × 7 is 7 less than 70, etc., before asking the child to answer the same questions without rods being present.

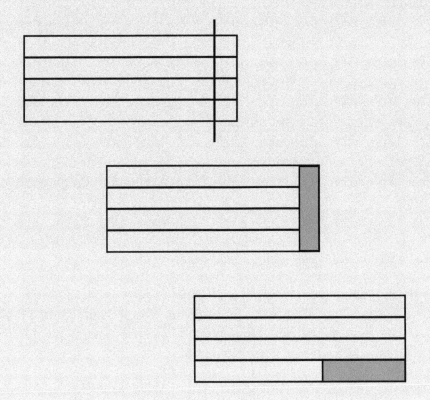

⊞ Activity

Find all the steps of any times table by reasoning from key facts

As children will have already discovered, some tables facts produce patterns that are much more regular than others. The 2×, 5× and 10× facts are the easiest to learn, because ours is a decimal number system and 10 is divisible by 2, 5 and 10. Many teachers, myself included, take advantage of the obvious regularity of these number patterns to encourage children to use these particular facts as starting points from which to derive other multiplication and division facts. Dorian Yeo, in her book *Dyslexia, Dyspraxia & Mathematics*, calls this the 'universal strategy' for all times tables. I, and many other practitioners, describe this approach loosely as 'reasoning from key facts'. The main benefit of teaching this approach is that pupils feel reassured to know that the demands on their memory will be limited to a few key facts, and that they will not have to remember different strategies for each different multiplication table.

The progression described here as a single activity will, in practice, need to be spread across many different sessions, with as much revision and repetition at every stage as the individual learner needs. The preliminary stage is to make sure that the necessary pre-skills are secure (see the earlier activities in this section). Once children have developed some conceptual understanding about multiplication and division, and when they either know the key facts or know how to derive them, pupils are ready to be taught how to find those steps of any times table that are only a single step of calculation away from one of the key facts. Later, pupils will learn to calculate the facts that lie more than one step away from a key fact. As already mentioned in the overview to this section, I do not advocate children learning one table at a time. Instead, I recommend that children focus on one step at a time.

This approach is explored in very great detail in my ebook *Understanding Times Tables*, in which demonstration videos are embedded into every chapter.

Start by showing pupils that a multiplication table is nothing but a string of ten number facts: set out a rectangle of ten matching Cuisenaire rods. I recommend a tables structure of ten steps. Whenever children are required to find facts beyond the first ten multiples, the basic tables format can be temporarily extended.

Place the rectangle of rods onto 1 cm squared paper. Have pupils highlight the labels for the 2×, 5× and 10× steps, or draw thick lines at the bottom and the halfway point of the outlined area to show the positions of the 5× and 10× key facts. Remind pupils of the previous activities in which they learned and practised how to find the key facts. Later, use the same marked-up and labelled outline as a base for rectangles built from other colours of rods, to model times tables of other numbers, so as to emphasise the fact that the underlying structure is common to all times tables.

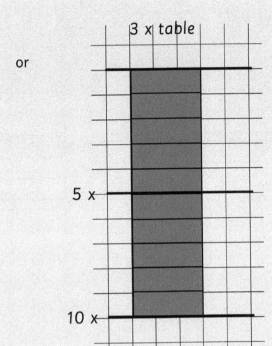

Work through all the easier steps in turn, namely the 3×, 4×, 6×, 9× and 11× steps of all the tables. The usefulness of the earlier step-counting activities now becomes evident, in that the pupil should be free to focus on the reasoning process without having to think too hard about the actual numerical answers. Whenever you wish to show the 11× step, temporarily add one more rod to the bottom of the rectangle. Keep moving the rods, in rectangular blocks, to match each step of the logical reasoning. For example, with 10 rods set out as a rectangle, pick up the top five rods when announcing the key 5× fact, return them as a block and immediately pick them up again with an extra rod, to show 6× the number, while saying, *Here are five 6s, a key fact that we know is 30, so six 6s are … one 6 more than 30, which is 36.*

After a while, use sketches of rectangles, instead of rods. A small whiteboard is ideal for this as the sketched rectangles need constant alteration to keep up with the reasoning process. This pictorial stage is a transitional stage, its aim being to model the processes that children need to learn to visualise in order to be able to succeed with mental calculation methods.

Here is a summary of the reasoning route for the easier steps: 3× any number is just one more step than the key 2× fact, just as 6× is one more step than the key 5× fact and 11× is one more step than the key 10× fact. The 4× step is also a single step away from a key fact when it is found not by step-counting, but instead by doubling the 2× key fact. The 9× step is one step back from 10×.

(Continued)

(Continued)

Easier tables steps are only one step away from a key fact: Cuisenaire rods (top), sketches (below)

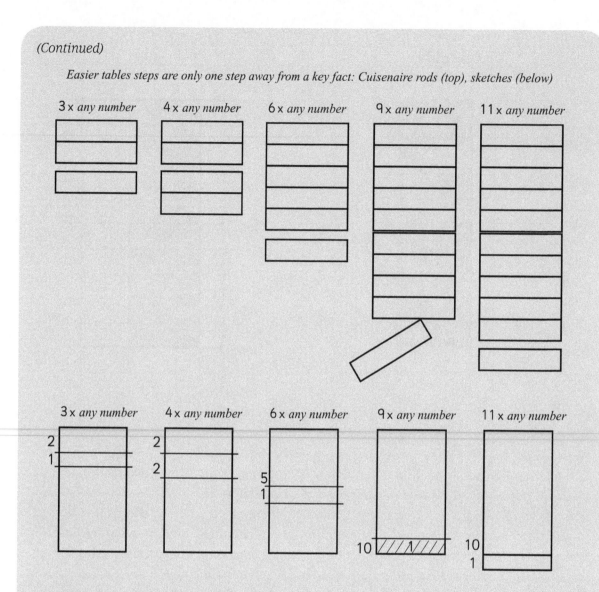

When the method for finding all the easier steps is well established, children can start working on the harder steps. The 7× and 8× steps are invariably the hardest steps of any table but you can reassure pupils that very few facts remain to be learned (only 7 × 7, 7 × 8 and 8 × 8 will be new facts for a learner who realises that multiplication is commutative). Nevertheless, I would recommend working systematically through the 7× and 8× steps of all the tables, discussing how to calculate these steps with the maximum chance of accuracy and the minimum amount of effort. The best way to find the 7× step is to see it as two steps further than 5×. It is possible to add these two steps separately, but a more efficient way would be to add the two extra steps – remember that double any number is a well-practised key fact – as a single chunk. Similarly, 12× any number can be found by adding two key facts together. There are three choices for 8×: three steps up from 5×, or two steps back from 10× (the least popular and often the least accurate choice), or double the 4× fact (i.e. double and double again to get the 4× fact, then double yet again). Pupils should be allowed to choose their favourite strategy for 8×, and should be encouraged to stick to the same chosen strategy for the 8× step whatever the table.

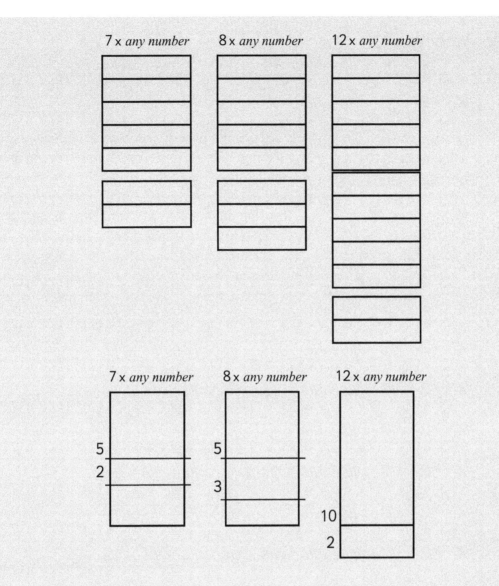

You can now begin to look ahead in this section (Section 4) and start playing the games provided. They have been designed to practise the reasoning strategies and to reinforce the players' understanding of the connection between multiplication and division.

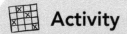 **Activity**

Practise all the steps of any times table by reasoning from key facts

This activity follows on from the previous activity and is designed to provide the necessary practice for children to try out the newly learned reasoning methods. Work though all the times tables in turn, starting with the 3s and 4s (because they contain smaller numbers) and ending with the 7s and 8s (because they are generally accepted to contain the hardest facts). Where, previously, children were focusing on one step at a time, this activity helps them to consolidate what they know about tables and challenges them to develop the mental flexibility to be able to switch from one reasoning path to another. Use Cuisenaire rods arranged as rectangles to help support the mental reasoning process whenever necessary. Move on to using sketches alone, or pure visualisation skills, as soon as the pupil is ready.

For abstract practice of a single times table, you can use a simple vertical list of the first 10 tables steps, like this:

1 ×

2 ×

3 ×

4 ×

5 ×

6 ×

7 ×

8 ×

9 ×

10 ×

One benefit of using a blank outline list such as this is so that you can ask for answers to be given orally only and in any order, marking each correct answer with a simple tick. The idea is not to let pupils get into the habit of finding the answers in sequence every time they practise a table. By this stage, pupils should not need practice in adding one step at a time to the previous answer; instead what they need is practice in finding new tables facts from known key facts. Encourage pupils to talk aloud through their reasoning. For example, if asked 7 × 6, a pupil might say: *5 times 6 is half of 60, that's 30, plus two more 6s, is 30 plus 12, which is 42* or (after having played some of the games that highlight connections between pairs of tables) a pupil might say: *I know 7 × 3 is 21, so 7 × 6 must be twice as much, which is 42.*

Another advantage of using a simple blank list of tables steps is that the same list can be used to practise all the tables, one at a time. It can be sent home for extra practice, instead of written homework, to allow pupils to do all their thinking aloud without embarrassment and without disturbing other pupils. However, parents must be told that the aim of the homework is for pupils to practise reasoning efficiently from key facts. The actual answers are only of secondary importance, so working out the sequence in order, or calculating by counting in ones, would defeat the purpose of the exercise.

Note that pupils with dyscalculia will probably never be able to remember their times tables facts, however many times they practise them. The aim of these activities, therefore, is for pupils to realise that only a few crucial facts have to be known, and that new facts can be derived by logic.

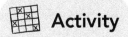 **Activity**

Find division facts by reasoning from key facts

Children who have been given enough practice at the concrete level with Cuisenaire rods will already have a good sense of how multiplication is related to division. The purpose of this activity is to reinforce the idea that the same facts can be seen from both points of view and, in particular, that the calculations we engage in, for either operation, are about building *up* quantities and do not need to involve subtraction or working backwards.

In order to work towards a division answer, we need to think about the number to be divided, in relation to the key facts of the relevant table. For example, to find 42 ÷ 6, encourage the child to arrange ten dark-green rods into a rectangle and to show on the surface of the rods the areas that correspond to the three key multiples of the 6× table, namely 12, 30 and 60. Alternatively, the pupil can just sketch the relevant rectangles, or use a list of tables questions from 1 to 10, like the simple vertical list described in the previous activity, and fill in the answers for the key facts. With the visual support of the rods, or the sketched areas, or the outline list, the child is now able to make a sensible guess about where 42 lies, in relation to 30 or 60. Paying attention to the relative positions of the numbers in question reveals the fact that 42 is nearer to 30, in fact it is exactly 12 more than 30. We know very well that 12 is double 6, which is how we can work out that 42 is two more steps further along the 6 times table than the key 5× fact. Therefore 42 ÷ 6 is 7.

6x table

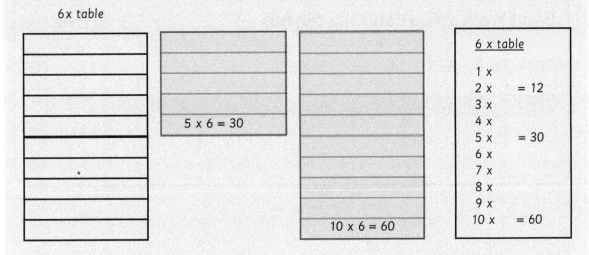

Use key facts to find division answers: e.g. to find 42 ÷ 6, think about where 42 lies, in relation to 30 and 60.

There will be more opportunities to practise this kind of reasoning, as it applies to both multiplication and division, while playing the many games provided in this section.

Game

Don't Walk if You Can Take the Bus

This is a game for two or more players. Players need to prepare the game board before play starts.

Teaching points:

▶ The game practises any desired multiplication table.

▶ It teaches players to derive new facts by step-counting from the key tables facts of 2×, 5× and 10×.

Equipment needed:

▶ Cuisenaire rods and 1 cm squared paper to use as a game board, for the basic game.

▶ A plain paper game board for the variation (see CW, or sketch your own game board).

▶ A single pawn or token, shared by both players.

▶ Five 'bus stops' (e.g. lolly sticks or toothpicks stuck in Blu-Tack).

▶ A 1–10 die.

Rules:

Take ten rods to match the multiplication table you wish to practise. Arrange the rods end to end on the squared paper. Draw an arrow pointing to the end of each rod, and label each arrow with the relevant question from the multiplication table sequence, but not the answer. The example illustrated, for the 6 times table, would be made of dark-green rods and labelled as shown. Erect the 'bus stops' at the start of the track and at the end of the first, second, fifth and tenth rods.

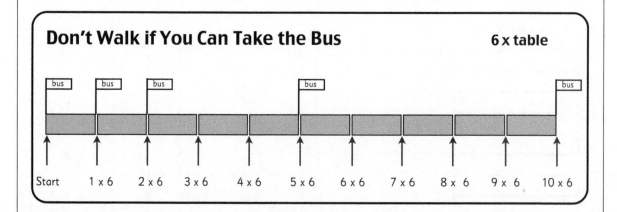

Don't Walk if You Can Take the Bus   **6 x table**

Start   1 x 6   2 x 6   3 x 6   4 x 6   5 x 6   6 x 6   7 x 6   8 x 6   9 x 6   10 x 6

Place the pawn on the start arrow at the beginning of each player's turn. On your turn, throw the die and work out how best to move the pawn to the arrow that matches the throw. Note that the pawn moves from arrow to arrow. On your turn, you may take one bus journey of any length (i.e. a journey of 1, 2, 3 or 4 stops), and may then need to 'walk' the pawn a little further, in either direction, to reach the required spot. On arrival, you must answer the times tables question correctly. If the answer is wrong, the pawn has to go back to the nearest 'bus stop' and be 'walked' again, while you try again to find the right answer.

A scorer keeps a tally score of the number of rods, i.e. the number of times table steps, that the pawn 'walks' on each turn. The scoring, in which the lowest score wins, is designed to give players an incentive to minimise the number of steps of reasoning, and to step-count carefully from the nearest key fact.

For example, a player who throws 9 on the die and chooses to take the bus to 10 and walk back will score an excellent 1, whereas a player who chooses to take the bus to 5 and walk forwards will score 4, and if the answer is not correct until after a second try the score will go up to 8.

The winner is the player with the lowest score after, say, 5 minutes. An alternative way to score the game is to give each player the same number of coins at the start of a game, with a charge of one coin for each step the pawn is walked, the loser being the first player to run out of money.

Variation:

For younger players working on the early tables (3×, 4× and 5×), the board can be made to show dot patterns instead of rods. In this case, use a game board with a wide 'road' on plain paper, divided into ten equal stretches (see CW), and draw one dot pattern in each space. The pawn moves between the lines that the arrows point to (rather than from space to space). The illustration shows what a game for the 4× table would look like.

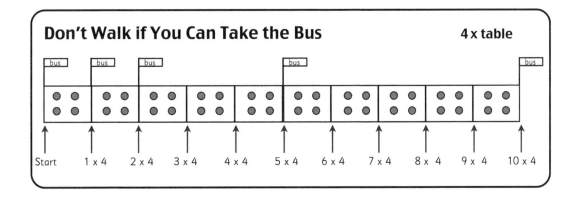

Tip:

Whichever variation you choose, the scorer should be someone who knows the correct answers and who will insist that the reasoning from the key fact is achieved by step-counting and bridging, not by counting in ones.

Game

Mouse Tables

This lovely game, for two players (and a mouse), was taught to me by Laura Thompson.

Teaching points:

▶ The game gives practice in any desired multiplication table.

▶ It gives practice in step-counting and in matching answers to multiplication questions.

▶ It does not put any time pressure on players, and therefore encourages logical thinking.

▶ It extends the reasoning technique beyond the basic 10 steps to the 12th step of the chosen table.

Equipment needed:

▶ A game board (see CW, or sketch your own game board).

▶ Twelve laminated cards small enough for all of them to fit onto the board.

▶ A dry-wipe pen.

▶ A small finger puppet in the shape of a mouse, of just the right size to contain one card (or an envelope with a picture of a mouse on it).

Rules:

Both players share the same board and prepare it by writing in each box, after the multiplication sign, the number of the table that is being targeted. Prepare cards for the game by step-counting aloud and writing one product on each of the 12 laminated answer cards, using the dry-wipe pen. Turn the cards face down and mix them up. Take one card at random and put it, still face down, inside the mouse finger-puppet. Now take turns to pick up any card, read the number and match it to the question. After checking with your opponent that your answer is correct, place the card on top of the appropriate box. For example, if you are practising the 6× table and you pick up the card for 42, you must read the number 42 aloud, say *42 is 7 times 6*, check that your opponent agrees, and then place the card on top of the question 7 × 6 on the board.

Continue until nine boxes have been covered and only two cards remain to be placed (remember, there is another card in the mouse). Both players must now pause and guess what number the mouse is hiding. You have a one in three chance of guessing correctly, assuming you can work out the right answers to the three remaining questions. Record the guesses on a piece of scrap paper, and play on. The game can end in a draw if players do not consult when writing their prediction, so I tend to give the person whose turn is next the first choice of the three remaining numbers, leaving the other player a choice between only two numbers. If neither player guesses correctly, the mouse is deemed to have won.

Tips:

Do not rush pupils: the scoring system of this game is deliberately designed to take the focus off the speed with which pupils must find a tables fact, in order to encourage reasoning and also in order to promote the idea that accuracy is more important than speed.

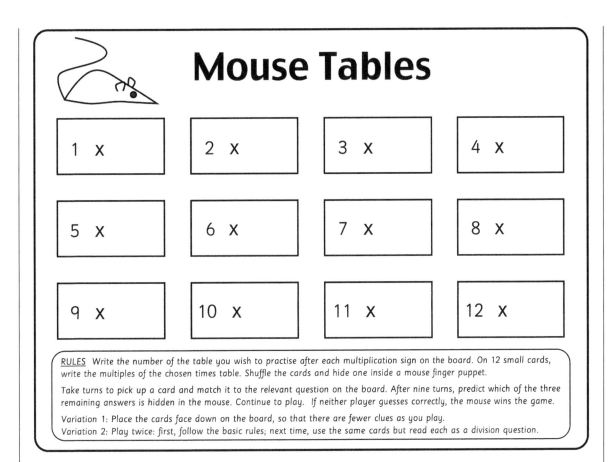

Mouse Tables

1 X	2 X	3 X	4 X
5 X	6 X	7 X	8 X
9 X	10 X	11 X	12 X

RULES Write the number of the table you wish to practise after each multiplication sign on the board. On 12 small cards, write the multiples of the chosen times table. Shuffle the cards and hide one inside a mouse finger puppet.

Take turns to pick up a card and match it to the relevant question on the board. After nine turns, predict which of the three remaining answers is hidden in the mouse. Continue to play. If neither player guesses correctly, the mouse wins the game.

Variation 1: Place the cards face down on the board, so that there are fewer clues as you play.

Variation 2: Play twice: first, follow the basic rules; next time, use the same cards but read each as a division question.

Do not be tempted to provide the pupils with ready-prepared answer cards: the act of step-counting and physically writing the multiples before the game can start is an important part of the learning experience. If you copy and laminate a board like the one illustrated, it can be used and reused for any table.

Variation 1:

Instead of placing the cards that cover the boxes face up, place the cards face down on the board so that neither the question nor the answer can be seen. This makes the game harder since fewer clues are visible during play.

Variation 2:

Adapt the game for division in order to reinforce the connection between the operations. Play on exactly the same board and in exactly the same way as described above, until it comes to reading the cards aloud. At that point, if, for example, you are practising the 6× table and you pick up the card for 42, you must say *42 divided by 6 is … 7*, before placing the card on top of the 7 × 6 question. The purpose of playing the game in this way is to show children that treating each fact as division is no more difficult than treating it as multiplication.

Variation 3:

A different way of adapting the game for division is to use a board (see CW) consisting of 12 empty rectangles, and a set of 12 answer cards each showing a number from 1 to 12. Before play, pupils start by step-counting aloud and writing the first 12 steps of the count on

(Continued)

(Continued)

the board (not on the cards, as they did for the basic game), with one multiple written in each rectangle, to the left of a division sign. The multiples can sometimes be written in ascending and sometimes in descending order on the board. The number of the times table that is being practised should be written after each division sign on the game board. The illustration shows a game board prepared for practising the 8× table. The purpose of playing both the multiplication version and the division variation of the game on the same multiplication table is to make children notice the relationship between the two operations.

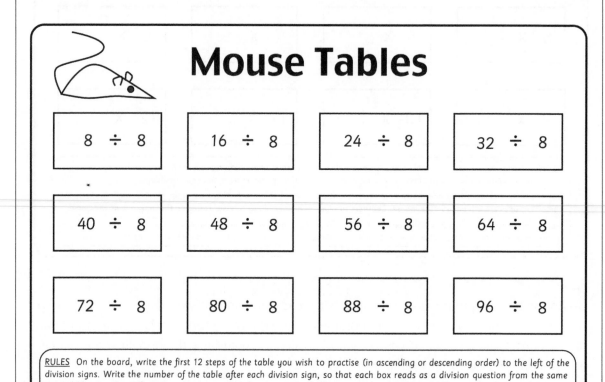

Mouse Tables

8 ÷ 8	16 ÷ 8	24 ÷ 8	32 ÷ 8
40 ÷ 8	48 ÷ 8	56 ÷ 8	64 ÷ 8
72 ÷ 8	80 ÷ 8	88 ÷ 8	96 ÷ 8

RULES On the board, write the first 12 steps of the table you wish to practise (in ascending or descending order) to the left of the division signs. Write the number of the table after each division sign, so that each box reads as a division question from the same times table. On 12 small cards, write the numbers from 1 to 12. Shuffle the cards and hide one inside a mouse finger puppet.

Take turns to take a card and place it, face down, on the relevant division question. After nine turns, predict which of the three remaining numbers is hidden by the mouse. Continue to play. If neither player guesses correctly, the mouse wins the game.

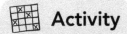 **Activity**

Construct a multiplication grid

Tables squares can be bought commercially, and there is a particularly useful version available in foldable plastic. All dyscalculic pupils should be allowed to use tables squares when the problems they are working on are not primarily designed to practise multiplication facts.

In this activity, pupils make their own multiplication grid from 1 × 1 up to 10 × 10, so that they really understand what the numbers represent and how they relate to each other. I recommend that any pupil who intends to use a tables square should spend some time on this activity first.

Step 1

Make an empty grid on paper with 1 cm squares, by marking out a 10 cm × 10 cm square and labelling each column and each row from 1 to 10.

Step 2

Start with any easy multiplication fact with which the pupils are already familiar, e.g. 2 × 3. Use Cuisenaire rods to build the multiplication as a rectangle (using the area model of multiplication, as in earlier activities). Place the light green rectangle on the multiplication grid at the top left-hand corner. Use a large L-shaped piece of card, as illustrated, to isolate the rectangle. Show pupils how to use the grid labelling to 'read' the multiplication as both 3 × 2 and 2 × 3. Remove the rods, but leave the L-shaped guide in place. The answer to the multiplication, which the pupil already knows to be 6, can be clearly seen in the six empty squares that the L-shape has isolated. Pupils write the number 6 in the 6th square reading from left to right and top to bottom, which is also, of course, the square where the column and row labelled 3 and 2 intersect.

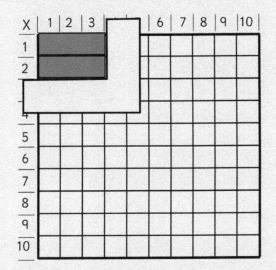
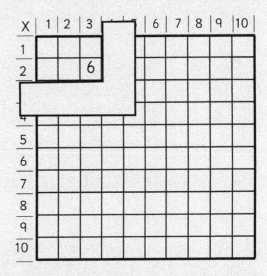

(Continued)

(Continued)

Step 3

Rotate the rods rectangle and repeat the procedure with the rectangle and the L-shaped guide to find the second position on the grid for the answer 6.

Step 4

Repeat the procedure with rods on the grid for other familiar multiplications. After a while, it should not be necessary for pupils to physically rotate the rectangle in order to find the second position of the multiple. Remind pupils of their earlier work with rods when they explored the commutative property of multiplication. This means that if they know the answer to, say 4 × 7, they also know the answer to 7 × 4.

Step 5

Have pupils make all the square numbers out of rods and write the answers on the grid. Pupils should notice the diagonal line produced by these answers, and should also notice that these answers appear only once on the grid, in contrast to all the other numbers which appear in two places, on either side of the newly created diagonal.

Step 6

As soon as they are ready, pupils can dispense with physically making the rectangles out of rods. At this stage, pupils can abandon the 10 cm square, in favour of one on a larger scale that will be much easier to read clearly when filled with numbers. This may also be the right time to extend the size of the tables square for pupils who need to know how to find and use products up to 12 × 12. Many pupils will still find the L-shaped guide useful, especially those with dyspraxia who cannot easily track a straight line by sight alone.

Step 7

Teach pupils how to use the grid for division as well as for multiplication.

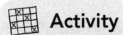 **Activity**

Complete a partially filled multiplication grid

Although it is a good idea for pupils to fill in a whole multiplication grid once or twice, it is also very time-consuming. In order to target particular tables, or the hardest multiplication facts, provide pupils with partially numbered grids to complete. As you can see from the illustrations (and the CW), I prefer to focus on the 100 facts up to 10×10, but the same activity can be performed on grids extended to 12×12 if you prefer.

X	1	2	3	4	5	6	7	8	9	10
1	1	2	3	4	5		7	8	9	10
2	2	4	6	8	10		14	16	18	20
3	3	6	9	12	15		21	24	27	30
4	4	8	12	16	20		28	32	36	40
5	5	10	15	20	25		35	40	45	50
6										
7	7	14	21	28	35		49	56	63	70
8	8	16	24	32	40		56	64	72	80
9	9	18	27	36	45		63	72	81	90
10	10	20	30	40	50		70	80	90	100

Partially completed grid for practising the 6 x table

X	1	2	3	4	5	6	7	8	9	10
1	1	2	3	4	5	6	7	8	9	10
2	2	4	6	8	10	12	14	16	18	20
3	3	6	9	12	15				27	30
4	4	8	12	16	20				36	40
5	5	10	15	20	25	30	35	40	45	50
6	6	12			30				54	60
7	7	14			35				63	70
8	8	16			40				72	80
9	9	18	27	36	45	54	63	72	81	90
10	10	20	30	40	50	60	70	80	90	100

Partially completed grid for practising the hardest tables facts

Games using self-correcting cards to practise individual times tables

The cheapest and most versatile resource for practising individual times tables is a set of self-correcting cards, with the questions shown on one side and the corresponding answers on the back. Cards like this can be bought, or they can be made by pupils or teachers (in which case, use a different colour of card for different times tables). A good alternative, because it increases the amount of practice the children get, is to use blank laminated cards and a dry-wipe pen and have the children prepare a new set of cards every time they play one of these games.

Game 1

Use the cards for learning and revision. Try to answer all the questions, first in order, then shuffled, against the clock, or in a race with another pupil.

Game 2

As above, but with the cards arranged so that the answers are face up. Make sure you know which times table is being practised before picking up each card in turn and supplying the question. You can phrase the question in either of two ways (except for square numbers), e.g. for a card showing 15, both 3×5 and 5×3 would be correct, whether it is the 5× table or the 3× table that is being targeted.

Variation:

Express the table fact as a division, e.g. if you pick up the card showing 15, say: $15 \div 3 = 5$ or $15 \div 5 = 3$.

Game 3

Match the questions to the answer. Use one set of cards laid out on a table in an array with the questions face up, as shown at the left here. At first the cards are laid out in order, later in a random order. Play by using a second, shuffled, set of cards with the answers face up. Place each card in turn on the matching card as quickly as possible. You can play this against the clock, or race against other pupils with their own sets and arrays of cards.

Variation:

Play in reverse, matching the answers to the questions, as shown at the right here.

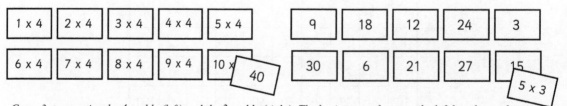

Game 3, to practise the 4x table (left) and the 3x table (right). The basic game shown at the left has the cards set out in sequence. The game shown at the right is the variation, as well as having cards set out in a random order.

Game 4

Two players have two or more sets of cards each, for the same times table. One player's cards are arranged with the multiplication questions face up and the other player's cards are arranged with the multiples, i.e. the answers to the questions, face up. Shuffle both sets of cards separately and play Snap.

Game

Multiples from the 1–6 Times Tables

A game for two players.

The Multiples Game
Multiples from the 1 – 6 times tables

1	2	3	4	5	6
7	8	9	10	11	12
13	14	15	16	17	18
19	20	21	22	23	24
25	26	27	28	29	30
31	32	33	34	35	36

RULES Two players use the same board and a 1–6 die. Players need counters in their own distinctive colour.

Take turns to throw the die and put one of your own counters on any number on the board that is a multiple of that number. But, neither player may cover a number in the top two rows on their first turn.

The winner is the first player with four counters in a row.

(Continued)

(Continued)

Teaching points:

▶ The game practises the multiplication tables facts up to 6 × 6.

▶ It provides a way of learning and remembering the meaning of the word 'multiple'.

▶ It reinforces the fact that all even numbers are in the 2× table (and vice versa).

▶ It helps pupils notice the connection between tables, especially between the 2× and the 4× tables, and between the 3× and the 6× tables.

▶ It reinforces the relationship between multiplication and division.

Equipment needed:

▶ A playing board with a 6 × 6 grid on which the numbers 1–36 are shown (see CW).

▶ A 6-sided die and counters in two colours, one colour for each player.

Rules:

Take turns to throw the die and put one of your own counters on any number on the board that is a multiple of the number on the die, provided it has not already been covered by a counter. But, neither player may place a counter anywhere in the top two rows, i.e. covering any number up to 12, during their first turn. The winner is the first player with four counters in a row.

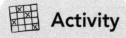 **Activity**

Harder mixed tables practice

Because the game above only practises the easier tables facts, this activity is designed to follow on from it and to give practice in the harder tables facts.

Put together two packs of digit cards, each containing only the numbers from 6 to 9. Each pack contains four cards for each of the four numbers. Shuffle both packs and turn them face down. For practice in the harder facts up to 12 × 12, add four cards for the number 12.

The pupil picks up one card from each pack and must multiply the numbers by each other, using previously learned reasoning techniques.

This activity can be set up in pairs, with one pupil using a multiplication square, or a calculator, to check the other's answers. Pupils swap roles when the packs have been used up once.

For pupils who find this activity too difficult, you could at first build one of the packs out of all the numbers from 1 to 9.

Game

Products in a Row

A game for two players.

Teaching points:

▶ The game practises two multiplication tables at a time.

▶ It highlights the connection between the multiplication tables of a number and the table of its double, e.g. that every other step of the 2× table is identical to a step from the 4× table. The same relationship exists between the 5× and 10× tables, between the 4× and 8× tables, between the 3× and 6× tables, and between the 6× and 12× tables.

▶ Both multiplication and division mental processes are used during play, but without mentioning the word 'division'.

▶ There is a strategic element to this game, by noticing which cards have been used.

Equipment needed:

▶ 24 blank cards (small laminated cards are ideal).

▶ A wide strip of paper for each player, on which there is space to set out 12 cards in a row.

Rules:

Decide which pair of related times tables to practise. On different occasions, play this game for the 2× and 4× tables, the 4× and 8× tables, the 3× and 6× tables (as in the illustration) and the 6× and 12× tables.

Write the answers to the first 12 steps of each of the chosen tables on the cards, one product to a card. Make sure the players notice which products appear in both tables, and understand why. Each player prepares a game board by writing the numbers from 1 to 12, in order, on a strip of paper. Space out the numbers so that one card, when placed on the game board, covers only one number. Players should note down on their board which pair of tables is being targeted.

Take turns to take one card from the top of the shuffled pack. Announce which multiplication question (relevant to this game) produces this answer. For example, if you pick up 36 during a game practising the 3× and 6× tables, you can say that 36 is produced by 6 × 6 or 12 × 3 (but not 9 × 4, because that fact is not relevant to this game). You now have the choice of placing the card on top of either the number 6 or the number 12 on your paper strip. Once a card has been placed, it cannot be moved. If you cannot place the card on your turn, or if your opponent correctly challenges a mistake on your part, return the card to the bottom of the pack.

(Continued)

(Continued)

The winner is the first player with three cards in a row, covering three consecutive numbers on the player's game board. Note that a winning hand of three cards in a row will not necessarily show three consecutive products, as you can see from the illustration.

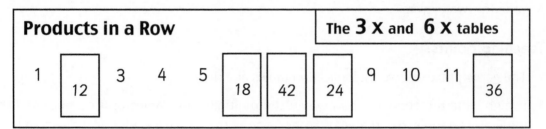

Products in a Row   The **3 X** and **6 X** tables

1   12   3   4   5   18   42   24   9   10   11   36

Game

Factors

A game for two or three players.

Teaching points:

▶ The game gives division practice but without mentioning the word *division*.

▶ It provides a way of learning and remembering the meaning of the word *factor*.

▶ It encourages pupils to notice that some numbers appear in more than one multiplication table.

▶ It shows that although some numbers have more factors than others, this has nothing to do with the magnitude of the number.

▶ It teaches pupils that factors always come in pairs: *two* numbers are multiplied together to create a product.

Equipment needed:

▶ A playing board featuring some multiples of various times tables (two boards are provided on the CW for different levels of difficulty).

▶ A die.

▶ A token for each player.

▶ Paper and pencil.

▶ Rods (or coins) for collecting and scoring.

Rules:

Take turns to throw the die and move around the board. When your token lands on a number, write down all the possible factors except 1 and the number itself. For example, all the factors of 10 are 1, 2, 5 and 10 but for this game only 2 and 5 will count. Read out your list, using the word 'factor' each time. For example, if you land on 10 say: *2 and 5 are factors of 10*. Players accumulate rods (or coins) to match each of the factors they identify. The winner has the most rods (or coins) after all the players have been around the board twice.

Tips:

Do not allow pupils to add up their winnings as they go along, since all scoring is based on addition, whereas the game itself focuses on multiplication and division. If possible, judge the winner by eye without adding to find exact scores.

The game should be played with the teacher as one of the players (but one whose score does not count), to check the pupils' answers and to model for the pupils how to find as many factors as possible for each number.

To avoid muddling pupils, never use the word *multiple* when referring to the numbers on the board. If you must give them a name, call them *products* in this game. The main focus should be on *factors*.

Insist that factors must always come in pairs. For example, pupils recognising an even number may offer 2 as a factor, and could then be prompted: *Yes, 2 and what else?*

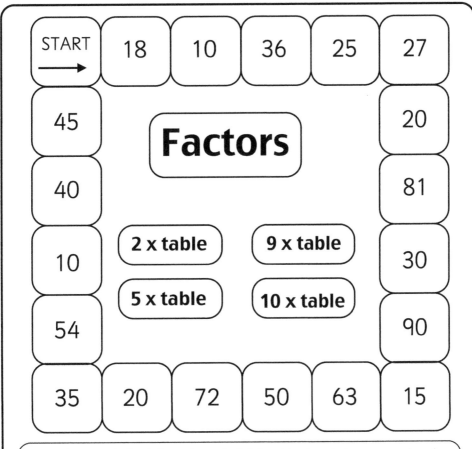

RULES This game is for 2 or 3 players. You need a 1–6 die, a token for each player, paper and pencils and Cuisenaire rods [or coins] for scoring.

Take turns to throw the die and move around the board. When you land on a number, write down all the factors except one and the number itself. For example, all the factors of 10 are 1, 2, 5 and 10, but for this game only 2 and 5 will count.

Read out your list, using the word 'factor' each time, e.g. if you land on 10 say: '2 and 5 are **factors** of 10.' If your opponents agree with your list, take rods [or coins] to match the value of each factor.

Notice that in this game all the numbers come from the four multiplication tables named in the middle.

The game ends when all the players have been round the board twice. Sort your rods into lengths of 10 [or coins into stacks of 10] to find who has won the most.

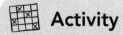 **Activity**

Use rectangle sketches to help derive new multiplication facts

This activity encourages pupils to practise reasoning from known facts that are beyond the times tables facts. For example, given the fact that 15 × 6 is 90, how can we use that knowledge to find 7 × 15? Most pupils at this stage would understand that something must be added to 90, but many would be unsure whether to add a group of 15 or a group of 6.

Putting the information on a sketch is a quick way to clarify our thinking. The rectangle shows 15 times 6, and as soon as the rectangle is altered to show 7 times 15, we can see that one 'slice' 15 long, or one group of 15, must be added.

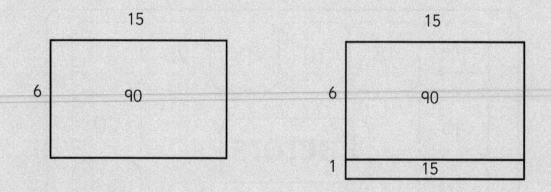

Give pupils practice, as in the example below. Encourage pupils to sketch a rectangle for each written problem, and then to turn their paper over and visualise the sketch in their mind. Once pupils are familiar enough with the technique, they should try to answer these types of questions mentally.

Here are four sample questions:

6 × 10 = 60,   *so 6 × 12 =*

10 × 14 = 140,   *so 11 × 14 =*

12 × 5 = 60,   *so 13 × 5 =*

9 × 15 = 135,   *so 9 × 16 =*

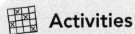 **Activities**

Change the shape of the multiplication rectangle

Use large cubes to start off these activities: 1 cm cubes are too fiddly, but cubes of about three times the size are ideal. (Mine are made of foam and called 'DIME Cubes'.)

1. Take 12 cubes and have pupils arrange them into a rectangle representing a multiplication fact of their choice. The possibilities are: 3 × 4, 2 × 6 or 1 × 12. Show pupils how they can change the shape of their rectangle by halving one side and moving half the rectangle so as to double the other side. For example, a 2 × 6 rectangle can become a 4 × 3 rectangle, and vice versa. Similarly, for a 1 × 12 shape, the rectangle can be halved along the 12-unit side and regrouped to create a new rectangle measuring 2 × 6.

   Have pupils practise transforming one shape of rectangle into another, while explaining aloud exactly what is happening. Pupils should read each newly formed rectangle as a multiplication, just as they learned to do during earlier activities with Cuisenaire rods.

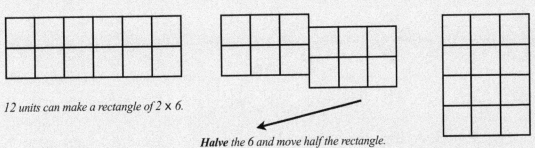

12 units can make a rectangle of 2 × 6.

__Halve__ the 6 and move half the rectangle.

The new rectangle is 4 × 3: __half__ as wide and __twice__ as high.

2. Have pupils explore other small rectangles, made of an even number of cubes, in the same way. Ask pupils why there are three possible shapes for 12 (see above) but only two possible shapes for 4 or 14. Use the word *factor* and also encourage pupils to use the term.

3. Extend the above activity to numbers with factors other than 2. For example, ask pupils how many different shapes of rectangles can be made out of 9 cubes? [Answer: two.] Can we transform one rectangle into the other by halving and doubling, as before? [Answer: no, but we can use the same principle, with 3 as our factor. This time, one side is split into thirds and the other side is tripled.] How many shapes of rectangle will 18 produce? [Answer: three.] Have pupils practise transforming each rectangle into another and encourage them to explain what is happening, in their own words.

4. Ask pupils how many possible shapes there are for 5 or 7. [Answer: one.] This is a good opportunity to talk about prime numbers and to explore other small primes. In terms of the rectangular array that models multiplication, a prime number is a number that can only be formed into a long thin rectangle, 1 unit high (and more than 1 unit wide).

(Continued)

(Continued)

5. Use diagrammatic sketches to illustrate all the same rectangles as in the steps above, this time without the concrete materials being present. For example, sketch a rough square, labelling the two sides 4 and the central area 16. Sketch a second rectangle, longer and thinner than the square (but there is no need to try to keep to scale), and label the centre 16. Ask pupils what the dimensions of the sides will now be if one side is doubled and the other side is halved. Let pupils practise more of these kinds of manipulations on paper.

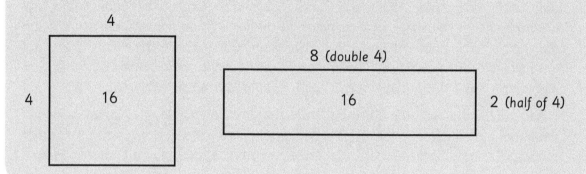

Game

Areas on a Grid

This is a game for two players. You can find a short demonstration video of this game on the CW.

Teaching points:

▶ This is a game of strategy.

▶ The game relates multiplication and division through the area model.

▶ It draws players' attention to the fact that multiplication is commutative.

▶ It draws players' attention to the fact that some multiples appear in more than one times table.

Equipment needed:

▶ Squared paper (see CW) and pencils.

▶ A die on which the following numbers are shown: 6, 8, 12, 16, 18 and 24 (write on a blank die or use stickers over the faces of an ordinary die).

Rules:

Each player marks out for themselves a 10 × 10 grid on squared paper. Take turns to throw the die and shade in a rectangle of the same area as the number thrown, on your own grid. You may choose any shape of rectangle with the required area, the aim being to fit as many rectangles as possible into the grid. For example, a throw of 6 can be represented by a rectangle measuring either 1 × 6 or 2 × 3. The area must be created by a single rectangle, i.e. six individual squares are not a valid substitute for a rectangle measuring 6 × 1 or 2 × 3.

The first player to run out of space loses the game. (Players should take turns to be the first player to start.)

Variation 1:

Children who are still working at the concrete stage can draw their grid on 1 cm squared paper and use Cuisenaire rods to create the area to match the throw. After playing the game with rods several times, you can help children to progress to the basic – and more abstract – version of the game by allowing them to use rods to try out the possible sizes and placement of various rectangles, before marking the position on the grid, removing the rods and shading in the area.

Variation 2:

Both players use the same grid, which measures 12 × 12 squares, and take turns to be the first to start a game. As you play, take turns to throw the die and shade a rectangle to match, anywhere on the shared grid. The first player who cannot find space on the grid to shade a new rectangle loses the game.

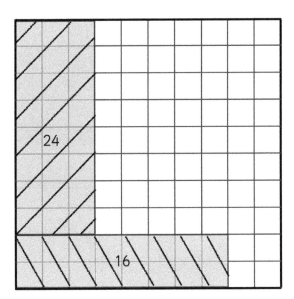

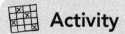 **Activity**

Boxes for long multiplication

This activity is about beginning to work towards long multiplication.

Pupils who have been taught the area model of multiplication and division, and are confident about using sketches of rectangles for supporting their thinking about tables facts, will be in a very strong position when it comes to multiplication and division problems that lie beyond the times tables. In this activity, pupils are introduced to the idea of using sketches to try out a method that is closely related to the area model of multiplication and division, called the 'boxes' method. The method is very versatile and can be used for any problem that involves multiplication, including advanced problems such as opening bracket in algebra or multiplying fractions and decimals. For much more detailed information about the 'boxes' method, and how it can be applied to division, and how it relates to written methods for long multiplication and division, you can find three whole chapters devoted to topics such as these in Part III of *Overcoming Difficulties with Number*.

Start with a sketch to represent a familiar tables fact, for example 4×3. Next, add a ten to one of the numbers, and present the new problem: 14×3 or 4×13. After sketching a single rectangle for the new multiplication problem, direct the child to split the rectangle into two boxes, so that the 2-digit number is partitioned into tens and units. There is no need to make any attempt to keep to scale. After finding the areas of the two boxes, combine the two products.

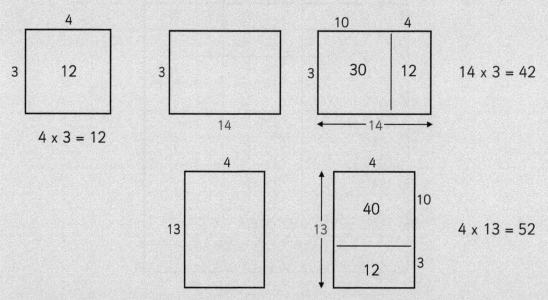

At a later stage, try problems in which two 2-digit numbers are multiplied together, for example 44×13. Since both numbers are beyond the times tables, both sides of the rectangle will be partitioned, creating four boxes and therefore four products to add together. The principle is exactly the same as before and the resulting calculation is a great deal easier for most pupils than the standard written algorithm for long multiplication.

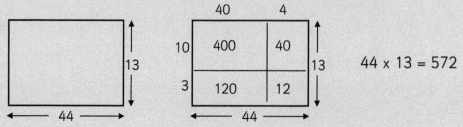

Recommended Books and Resources

The following suggestions are not intended to be a comprehensive list of all the available books and resources that might be of interest to a parent or teacher of a dyscalculic learner. After all, most of us these days have access to search engines that can provide exhaustive and up-to-date lists in a matter of moments. Instead, the list below includes only books and resources that I am thoroughly familiar with – from having read or used them on countless occasions – and that I can genuinely recommend from personal experience.

Suggestions for further reading

Ronit Bird (2009) *Overcoming Difficulties with Number: Supporting Dyscalculia and Students who Struggle with Maths*, Sage.

Ronit Bird (2011) *The Dyscalculia Resource Book*, Sage.

Ronit Bird (2013) *Exploring Numbers Through Dot Patterns*, iBooks (via iTunes).

Ronit Bird (2013) *Exploring Numbers Through Cuisenaire Rods*, iBooks (via iTunes).

Ronit Bird (2014) *Understanding Times Tables*, iBooks (via iTunes).

Brian Butterworth (1999) *The Mathematical Brain*, Macmillan.

Eva Grauberg (1998) *Elementary Mathematics and Language Difficulties*, Whurr.

Derek Haylock (2010) *Mathematics Explained for Primary Teachers*, Sage.

Derek Haylock (2012) *Understanding Mathematics for Young Children*, Sage.

Martin Hughes (1986) *Children and Number: Difficulties in Learning Mathematics*, Basil Blackwell.

Tim Miles and Elaine Miles (eds) (2004) *Dyslexia and Mathematics*, Routledge.

Mahesh Sharma (1980–1993) *Math Notebook*, Center for Teaching/Learning of Mathematics, Framingham, MA. (Professor Sharma's publications, videos and DVDs are available in the UK from Berkshire Mathematics.)

Ian Thompson (ed.) (1997) *Teaching and Learning Early Number*, Open University Press.

Ian Thompson (ed.) (1999) *Issues in Teaching Numeracy in Primary Schools*, Open University Press.

Ian Thompson (ed.) (2003) *Enhancing Primary Mathematics Teaching*, Open University Press.

Dorian Yeo (2003) *Dyslexia, Dyspraxia & Mathematics*, Whurr.

Assessments

Note that only an Educational Psychologist can provide a formal diagnosis of a specific learning difficulty such as dyscalculia.

GL Assessment's *Dyscalculia Screener* [www.gl-assessment.co.uk/products/dyscalculia-screener]: an online computer assessment that can be administered to individuals or groups.

Nadia Nosworthy's *Numeracy Screener* [www.numeracyscreener.org/]: a 2-minute paper and pencil test that can be administered to individuals or groups.

Emerson & Babtie's *Dyscalculia Assessment* [Bloomsbury Education, ISBN 9781408193716]: a book that provides a comprehensive guide to conducting an assessment interview with an individual child.

Some suppliers of concrete resources

Cuisenaire rods: The Cuisenaire Company, UK (www.cuisenaire.co.uk); ETA Hand2Mind, USA (www.hand2mind.com/brands/cuisenaire-rods)

Dice in many sizes, materials and colours: The Dice Shop Online (www.thediceshoponline.com)

Dot pattern cards and digit cards: free downloads from my own website: www.ronitbird.com/teaching-resources-for-dyscalculia/

Slavonic abacus: Learning Resources; Xavier Education

Various mathematical teaching resources: Tarquin (www.tarquingroup.com)

Recommended online resources

British Dyslexia Association: www.bdadyslexia.org.uk

Cuisenaire Environment (virtual Cuisenaire rods): https://nrich.maths.org/4348

Daniel Ansari interviews and lectures on video: www.numericalcognition.org/media.html

Dyslexia Action: www.dyslexiaaction.org.uk

Help for Dyscalculia and Maths Difficulties Facebook page: www.facebook.com/HelpforDyscalculia/

Various free resources, games and information from my own website: www.ronitbird.com

Videos on YouTube: www.youtube.com/channel/UCohFUmEat0UxOnNmRh92P_Q

APPENDIX

Introduction to concrete manipulative materials

Manipulative materials are any materials that allow pupils to physically touch, move and rearrange them. In mathematics, they can model operations on numbers as well as the numbers themselves, and so allow learners to explore ideas, patterns and relationships in a concrete, rather than an abstract, way. Concrete materials are multisensory in that they can be appreciated by sight and by touch. They promote learning by visual, spatial and kinaesthetic routes. Teachers who ensure that all work with concrete materials is accompanied by lots of talk and discussion also cater for the auditory route to learning.

There is a variety of concrete material available to maths teachers these days, but too much variety can create problems. Presenting new models to illustrate new procedures can leave pupils with an incoherent view of maths as a series of isolated topics. For example, using a spike abacus for demonstrations of place value but for nothing else encourages pupils to compartmentalise place value thinking quite separately from thinking about mental calculations. Another common example is teaching division as repeated subtraction, but later explaining fractions through shading pictures of pizza slices, which does nothing to help pupils see the interconnection between the two concepts. This kind of fragmentation is particularly detrimental to learners with dyscalculia or those with little number sense or natural 'feel' for numbers. Pupils with difficulties benefit from having the kind of coherent model that highlights the patterns and connections within the field of mathematics.

In my view, by far the best and most versatile apparatus to use with pupils who experience difficulties with maths are continuous base-10 materials such as Cuisenaire rods and Dienes blocks. They are the most robust materials, in the sense of being capable of modelling many different situations and procedures at many different levels. Naturally, for very young children discrete materials such as counters, nuggets or cubes will precede work with rods or blocks, but overuse of discrete material tends to encourage pupils to cling to inefficient counting-in-ones strategies. Many of the activities in this book are designed to take pupils beyond such immature strategies. Working with the right concrete materials and explicitly building connections between topics helps to foster a cohesive view of mathematics as a rational subject whose components are interrelated and interdependent.

Counters

Counters do not have to be small round plastic objects. Other examples of discrete objects that can be used as counters include cubes, wooden bricks, lolly sticks, plastic shapes, games tokens, beans, beads, pebbles, buttons, paper clips, shells, straws, Smarties, toothpicks, dried pasta shapes, bolts, washers, strips of paper, lengths of ribbon, cards, pencils, and many more. I particularly like the nuggets made of coloured or iridescent glass that Dorian Yeo introduced me to, and that are sold as flower vase fillers and table decorations.

Changing the size and shape of counters from one activity to the next can be both valuable and fun for children, larger items being more suitable for younger children and for those with dyspraxia. However, it is best to avoid too much variety of size or colour. For example, counters with solid colours are easier to distinguish and count than rainbow-coloured or patterned ones, regular shapes like discs and cubes are easier to distinguish than irregular shapes like handprints or alphabet letters, and it is easier to see the pattern of five if each of the five counters are the same size and shape as each other. Counters are very useful for work with smaller numbers but are not suitable for numbers much above 20.

Counters are particularly useful for arranging and rearranging into dot patterns. In my own teaching, I use the dice patterns for the numbers 1 to 6 and doubles or near-double patterns for the numbers 7 to 10. These kinds of distinctive visual patterns allow the learner to recognise and comprehend each number as a whole, so that, say, the familiar dice pattern for 5 can be instantly read as 5 without any need to count the items. By extension, a pattern showing two 5s side by side can be easily read as 10, again without any need to count. Being able to visualise, and therefore know for sure, one fact about each number provides pupils with a secure starting point from which to derive new facts through logic and reasoning.

Numicon

Numicon is a system in which flat plastic rectangular shapes contain circular holes into which round pegs can be fitted, the number of holes corresponding to the number that is being represented. It is a popular system in many schools, partly because it is supported by so many ready-made resources.

Numicon provides separate boards for each of the numbers up to 10 with the holes regularly spaced and arranged in two parallel rows, such that all the even numbers are rectangles, while all the all odd numbers have a protrusion creating an L-shape at one end. The problem with this organisation of numbers into pairs is that the larger numbers are difficult to distinguish without counting the holes. For example, 7 must be read as $2 + 2 + 2 + 1$, and is therefore easily confused with 9 which is presented as $2 + 2 + 2 + 2 + 1$. Similarly, the numbers 6, 8 and 10 are easily confused. A more significant problem is that I find the static shapes of the Numicon materials unhelpful for exploring number bonds: although they are perfect for showing the difference between odd and even numbers, they are much less successful at revealing the various ways in which numbers can be built out of, and split back into, number components.

The Numicon board-and-peg system is no substitute for base-10 materials such as Cuisenaire rods or Dienes. Unlike base-10 equipment, Numicon numbers are made of discrete items (i.e. the number 5, for example, is presented as five ones), discrete materials being far more limited in scope than continuous materials (in which the number 5, for example, is presented as one five). However, Numicon does offer a possible substitute for dot patterns: both are systems for organising quantities from 1 to 10 into a particular, fixed arrangement. Like dot patterns, Numicon pegs become cumbersome and impractical for numbers much beyond 20, and in both systems there is a danger of promoting counting strategies because the nature of the equipment emphasises the fact that all numbers can be seen as a collection of ones. The limitation of discrete materials has obviously been recognised by Numicon, who now include Cuisenaire rods (which they call number rods) amongst their recommended apparatus.

Cuisenaire Rods

Cuisenaire rods were invented by the Belgian educator Georges Cuisenaire in the 1940s to teach arithmetic to primary school children. They consist of a set of rods, made of wood or plastic, each with a cross-section measuring 1 centimetre square. The 10 different lengths of rods start at 1 cm long and increase by increments of 1 cm. Although the largest rod is the orange 10-rod, Cuisenaire rods are compatible with Dienes blocks which provide for larger denominations. Each size of Cuisenaire rod has its own distinctive and unvarying colour, which makes its length easy to identify without the need for measuring it against unit cubes and counting the units. This is a compellingly significant characteristic and is, indeed, the main advantage of using continuous materials, rather than discrete objects. Because the rods do not carry labels or unit markings, they encourage quantities to be seen as a whole, rather than a collection of single units. This, in turn, encourages the development of efficient calculation methods that do not depend on counting in ones.

Cuisenaire rods became very popular in the 1950s and 1960s, and were considered at the time to be a turning point in the teaching of elementary mathematics. Their unfortunate lapse into disuse had more to do with the logistical difficulties of classroom management than to any uncertainty about their intrinsic educational value, when used correctly.

I have used Cuisenaire rods in my own teaching for many years. As an aid to parents who want to support their children at home, I have produced a small leaflet of ideas that you can download from the CW for this book. I can warmly recommend Professor Mahesh Sharma's various publications as well as his teacher training videos (available in the UK from Berkshire Mathematics, and in the USA from the Center for Teaching/Learning of Mathematics, in Framingham, Massachusetts.). Other information on using the Cuisenaire rods can be obtained from the Cuisenaire Rod Company in the UK, or hand2mind (previously ETA) in the USA.

Dienes Blocks

Zoltan Dienes produced his 'attribute blocks' not long after Cuisenaire produced his rods. The idea has been copied many times since then and the blocks are now often known generically as 'base-10 materials'. They consist of wooden or plastic blocks, all of the same colour, and are based on 1 cm cubes formed into single cubes (1), longs (10) and square flats (100). Base-10 sets nowadays also offer large cubes to represent 1000. Unlike Cuisenaire rods, base-10 materials have scored surfaces to highlight the 1 cm cube units from which they are built. Unlike the rods, there are no blocks to represent the numbers between 1 and 10, which means that the numbers below 10 have to be represented by discrete cubes and counted out one by one. For this reason, I prefer to use Cuisenaire rods, supplemented by the larger Dienes blocks.

Stern materials

Stern materials were developed by Dr Catherine Stern at roughly the same time as Cuisenaire rods and are very similar in structure and purpose. Stern blocks are based on 2 cm cubes, rather than Cuisenaire's 1 cm cross-section, which makes them satisfyingly chunky for small hands and for those with dyspraxia who may find the 1 cm rods too fiddly. Stern blocks are deliberately notched, so that they look like a series of cubes stuck together, which inevitably means that many children will count the cubes in order to find the length of the longer blocks. In order to minimise counting, each length has a fixed colour. Unfortunately, the same colours do not represent the same numbers on Stern blocks as on Cuisenaire rods, making the two systems incompatible despite their conceptual similarities.

There are some very useful and beautifully-made pieces of equipment designed to go with the Stern blocks. This partly explains why Stern is so much more expensive than either Cuisenaire or Dienes. I particularly like the number boxes, especially the 10-box, the 20-tray, the number track and the dual board. Less successful in my view are the pattern boards, which were the inspiration for Numicon, in which quantities up to 10 are arranged in pairs.

Every suggestion that I make in this book that involves Cuisenaire rods can be performed just as well, and in exactly the same way, with Stern blocks. The Stern blocks' only disadvantage – apart from the notched surfaces showing all numbers as a collection of ones, as already mentioned – is that their scale does not allow them to be combined with base-10 blocks. This limits their use to early numeracy work and to numbers below 100.

Hybrid materials

Bead strings, Unifix cubes and various types of abacus all attempt to bridge the divide between discrete and continuous materials. They are all useful in their own way, though none are as versatile as the combination of Cuisenaire rods and Dienes blocks.

Of the various lengths and types of bead strings, I have found the most useful to be a string of ten beads, with a colour change after five beads, because it models the all-important complement pairs that add up to 10. See Section 1 of this book for more details and for instructions for making bead strings.

Of the different kinds of abacus, I much prefer the Slavonic abacus, which is arranged as a field of 100 beads with a colour change after five beads and after five rows of beads. The colour change allows pupils to read quantities with a minimum of counting in ones. Ideas for using a Slavonic abacus with pupils who have difficulties with maths can be found in Eva Grauberg's work.

How to use concrete materials

Concrete materials should be carefully introduced and demonstrated by the teacher, who should explain to pupils what they are for: to make a connection between numerical magnitude and the abstract symbols we use to record numerical quantities, to make maths principles visible, and to help learners develop insight and intuition. Appropriate concrete materials allow learners to make meaning for themselves and to create a model for understanding maths that they can internalise. This cognitive model supports pupils' progression to abstract high-level thinking.

Concrete materials are not intended to be a primitive alternative to calculating machines and should never be used in a mechanical way, simply to find an answer.

Whenever using concrete materials, it pays to be sensitive to the danger of the counting trap and to be aware of the potential for unintentionally reinforcing bad habits or inefficient calculations strategies. It is, for example, extremely important to use concrete materials in a way that discourages pupils from persistently counting in ones. For this reason, in my own teaching I always prefer: counters arranged in predictable dice or domino patterns rather than random patterns or fixed patterns that are insufficiently visually distinctive; the smooth surfaces of the coloured Cuisenaire rods as opposed to the notched or scored blocks belonging to the Stern and Dienes materials; whole rods to represent the numbers up to 10 rather than rows or collections of single cubes each representing the number 1; the Slavonic abacus in preference to either a spike abacus or an abacus with a different colour for each row of beads; bead strings that mimic the Slavonic abacus' layout by a change in colour after every group of five in preference to bead strings constructed of many different colours of beads or with ten consecutive beads all of the same colour; number tracks that mimic the Slavonic abacus' layout by a change in colour after every group of five spaces in preference to numbered tracks.

Concrete materials should not be used only for demonstration purposes, nor should they be used only for very basic work. They are for pupils to handle and explore, and they are most useful when the same materials are used at different stages, for different topics and at different levels of difficulty. As teachers, we must keep reminding our pupils that the actual mathematics is not what happens to numerals on paper, but what happens to numbers that are subjected to mathematical operations. Paper and pencil are just useful ways to record what happens, or to support our memory while we engage in mental calculation and abstract thinking.

In *The Dyscalculia Toolkit* you will find more than 100 ideas for activities that propose the use of concrete materials as a route to learning and understanding maths. A small proportion of these – perhaps a tenth – are based on discrete materials, such as counters, while the rest all require continuous materials such as Cuisenaire rods and/or base-10 blocks. A further 100 activities and many of the games in the book are designed to help pupils' progress by leading them to make the important transition from concrete to abstract mathematical thinking.

Index